Network Security and Ethical Hacking

Network Security and Ethical Hacking

Rajat Khare

Appin Knowledge Solutions, Austin, Texas

Luniver Press

Published by

Luniver Press
Beckington, Frome BA11 6TT, UK

www.luniver.com

Rajat Khare
Network Security and Ethical Hacking
(Luniver Press, Beckington, 2006).

First Edition 2006

British Library Cataloguing in Publication Data
A catalog record is available from the British Library.

Library of Congress Cataloguing in Publication Data
A catalog record is available from the Library of Congress.

ISBN-13: 978-1-905986-00-2
ISBN-10: 1-905986-00-9

Prologue

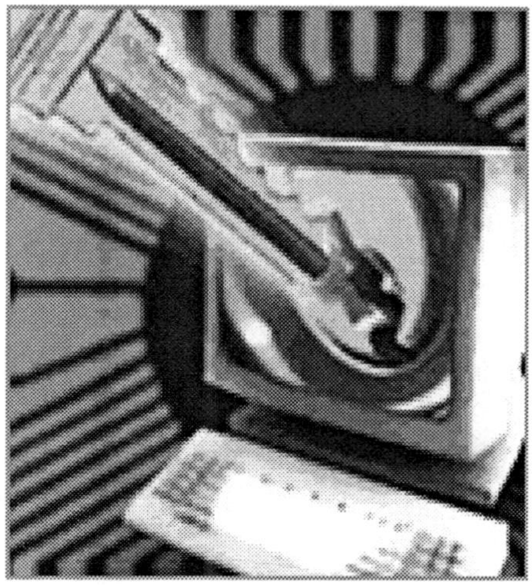
Src:www.wireless-internet-network-service.com

Information Security is a highly integral aspect our daily life, so to say, our virtual as well as real lives. We can remember in the past times valuables were stored in safes with keys. And there were thieves who were specialists in breaking these safes with a duplicate key or by bombing the lock of the safe. The scenario that was ages ago is just an analog of the current environment. Today we have valuable information which is stored on computer/server or data warehouses and digital storage similar to our erstwhile Safes and Lockers. The passwords to these digital mediums are the keys as with our physical data and asset security mediums. And today we have hackers who either crack these passwords or bomb the locks with various attacks. In the past all the people had safes for storing their valuables and in today's world almost every one uses computers and stores valuable information like word documents, proposals, usernames, passwords, credit cards. And thus in today's world we all need to understand Information Security. It doesn't matter if you are an entrepreneur, professional, engineer, lawyer, doctor, Information manager, accountant, professor, student, housewife perhaps any computer user.

It is an age old saying that to catch a thief think like one. This book has a unique combination of Hacking and Information Security giving you a hacker's perspective to Information Security. The book lays down foundations for various threats, attacks and what steps can we take to secure them from hackers. The book is authored by a unique combination of hackers and security professionals laying strong foundations for both the aspects.

"The battle between hackers and security professionals will never end. However it will always improve the security systems of the world".

Contents

1. Introduction to Information Security and Ethical Hacking 10

1.1 Why Information Security? 10
1.2 What is Information Security? 11
1.3 Case Studies 12
1.4 Information Security and Hacking Combo 25
1.5 Major Threats and Issues 26
1.5.1 Protecting Your Computer and Network 28

2. Security at Your Desk – "For Every Computer User" 46

2.1 Desktop Security 46
2.2 Windows Vulnerabilities and Threats 51
2.3 The Global Network of Networks: The Internet 54

3. Security in Your Workgroup – "Your Guide to Network Security" 68

3.1 LAN/WAN Components 68
3.2 The Future of LANs/WANs 78
3.3 Case Studies 88
3.4 Firewalls 91
3.5 Anti Virus Solutions 94
3.6 Anti Spy Wares 98
3.7 Network Scanners 99
3.8 Where to Begin? Security Policies 99

4. Security in the Virtual World – "Your IP is Logged on Internet" 105

4.1 Introduction to Internet 105
4.2 Threats Faced on Internet 108
4.3 Case Studies 112

4.4 Introduction to IP Addresses 113
4.5 Finding IP Address of a Remote System 115
4.6 Hiding Your Identity 118
4.7 Analyzing E-mail Headers 121
4.8 Tracking E-mails 124
4.9 Information Gathering 129
4.10 PORT Scanning 138
4.11 Daemon Banner Grabbing 141
4.12 Remote OS Detection 150
4.13 Internet Attacks 151
4.13.1 KeyLoggers 158
4.13.2 DOS Attack 160
4.13.3 Ping of Death Attack 167
4.13.4 Cross Site Scripting Attack 167
4.13.5 Input Validation Attack 172
4.13.6 SQL Injection Attack 173
4.13.7 Sniffing Attack 177
4.13.8 Phishing 178
4.13.9 Pharming 183

5. Penetration Testing – "Evaluate Your Information System's Security" 185

5.1 Introduction 185
5.2 Case Studies 199
5.3 Social Engineering 202

6. The Art of Cryptography – "Behind the Locked Door" 205

6.1 Introduction 205
6.2 Classical Approach 207
6.3 Hashing 224
6.4 Encryption Algorithms(RSA, MD5, IDEA) 227
6.5 PGP (Pretty Good Policy) 238
6.5.1 Hash Functions 240
6.5.2 Certificate Distribution 243

6.6 Case Study – Real World Example ... 244

7. Cyber Laws – "The legal Aspect of Cyberspace" ... 247

7.1 Introduction ... 247
7.2 Need of Cyber Laws ... 247
7.3 Laws Related to Hacking ... 249
7.4 Laws Related to Phishing ... 251

8. Appendix: Hacking Laws ... 254

9. Phishing/Case Study ... 265

10. Glossary ... 277

1. Introduction to Information Security and Ethical Hacking

1.1 Why Information Security?

"*Information systems security is not a contradiction in terms... security without risk management is*" (J. Bisson, 2003).

Information is an asset which, like other important business assets and personal attributes, has value to an organization and an individual in absolute sense, thence it consequently needs to be suitably protected. Information Security protects information from a wide range of threats in order to ensure business continuity, minimize business losses and maximize return on investments and business opportunities. It also protects privacy of an individual. Information can exist in many forms. It can be printed or written on paper, stored electronically, transmitted by post or using electronic means, shown on films, or spoken in conversation. Whatever form the information takes, whatever the means by which it is shared or stored, it should always be appropriately protected. Information security consists of preserving the following elements:

a) **Confidentiality:** Ensuring that information can only be accessed by those with the proper authorization.

b) **Integrity:** Safeguarding the accuracy and completeness of information and the ways in which it is processed.

c) **Availability:** Ensuring that authorized users have access to information and associated assets whenever required.

Information security is achieved by implementing a suitable set of controls, which could be policies, practices, procedures, organizational structures and software functions. These controls need to be established in order to ensure that the specific security objectives of the organization are met.

To understand Information Security in practical aspects, the past experiences of our interaction with IT would prove to be a fruitful asset. Kindly go through these case studies and understand the threats you face as an information user. Remember you have started using IT as a means of storing and transmitting information. Though it is fast but has its own threats.

1.2 What is Information Security?

We all store valuable information either in our memories or in paper documents and in the world of IT on computer and other digital storage devices. Every Information user is a node where the information can leak out. Thus Information Security is essentially a process for securing the Information of any information user. For example if your house is having a number lock you would always store the password of the lock either in your mind or in a piece of paper or perhaps on your cell phone. All of these are possible points where this password could be leaked out. A pretending friend may take out this information (password) from your head using certain tactics which is commonly termed as social engineering in the world of hacking. Or someone may steal the piece of paper where you have written the password or someone may send an SMS or stored password as a business card. Securing this information is nothing but an example of information security. For example – You may be take precautions to not tell you password to friends or may write the password in a coded form on paper (age old technique for storing valuable information).

It includes the following in the world of IT:

- Data Security
- Computer Security
- LAN or Network Security
- Internet Security

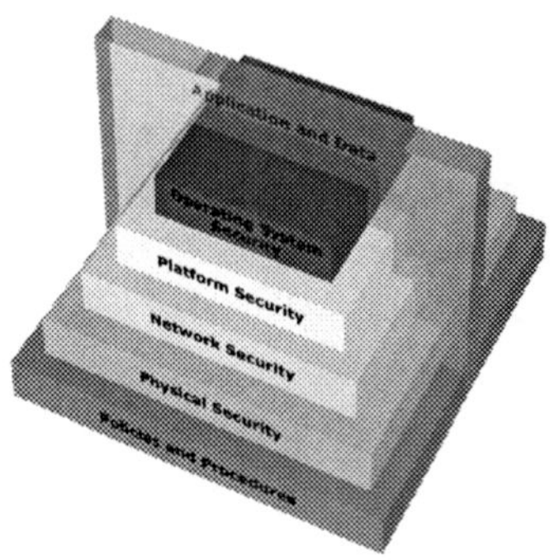

All the above mentioned terms are subsets of Information Security and are covered under it.

Also any definition of Information Security is irrelevant before understanding hacking because you are preventing your information from hackers.

Hacking is defined as ***Unauthorized*** use or attempts to circumvent or bypass the security mechanisms of an ***Information System*** like ***a computer/server/network.***

In this book we will discuss various hacking attempts and solutions to prevent them. Always remember that Information Security is useless to understand if you don't know whom you are preventing your information from.

1.3 Case Studies

Creative Offshore Services LLC Under Wireless Honeynet

In the distant suburbs of an upcoming locality of Chennai - a metropolitan city in India, the working hours never go down, the lights never switch off and the phone lines never get respite. The entire locale keeps bustling with furious in-house activities under the roof of plush corporate offices and technology centers. Where every 'knowledge worker' is working as hard, the day night barrier unrealized, to accumulate the information gathered in the hallowed confines of their cubicles through the learning curve and pass it on as their work output in the assembly lines of information superhighway.

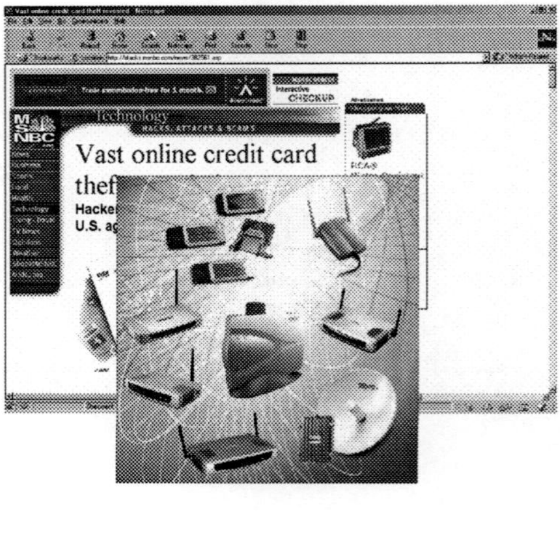

This is exactly how the most confidential information reaping millions of global capital is sourced from the human mind and piled in the terabytes of data warehouses serving as the core asset of an 'Information Technology Enabled Services' company. The information outsourcing from this demography is a window of new opportunities and revenue models fueling the growth of IT to the entire generation of 'techies' in this land of prospective IT boom. One need to see this to believe, the rate at which the magnitude of globally relevant information is being transacted in this upcoming IT corridor 24X7 from all kinds of vendors and tech units silhouetting small and mid sized businesses to corporate powerhouses.

Creative Offshore Services LLC is one such information outsourcing startup with its majority clientele spread across EU and UK markets over **e-publishing** and **Voice Transaction Management** serving as a wholesome business process-outsourcing unit. Vivek is gathering all the tech resources at his disposal to bring the best out of this establishment as the first and the only Wireless Fidelity (Wi Fi) based outsourcing unit. He is ensuring every single detail to fit immaculately inside the available framework and he knows more than what other people say, how to make the technology work the way it should be.

Every location of the Access Points (APs) and Wireless Network Interface Cards (NICs) is defined by precisely measured radian based angles given the shapes and contours of the walls and ceilings where computer systems are burning their fans off in the super cooled environs to ensure maximum available bandwidth. Vivek concentrates hard on making the network accessible with maximum data flow speeds to every authenticated user with the intranet setup already in place. The administrator and the executives with few employees having relevant access can connect to the required information in the mammoth data warehouses of Creative OS from anywhere, anytime across the globe. The Wireless Establishment is in place and Vivek finds it so perfect that he plans to emulate the similar setup in Creative's other offshore centers across the region.

Vivek is a well-known independent Network Management Guru with a regional experience of wired and wireless setups in all-major corporations in the city. His reputation precedes him as the person who knows IT like no one else in the city. He banks upon his group of IT geeks to update him about the trends in networks and communications. And the smooth setup continues for one month without any signs of fluctuation over both bandwidth and management fronts. People at the facility experience freedom like never before.

"Trrring Trrring"
"Trrring Trrring"
"Vivek"
"Who is this"?
"This is Divya here, I need you at our office urgently, right now"

Its 0400 hours Indian Standard Time and Vivek couldn't even open his eyes properly after a gut wrenching day of Hard work on other Creative OS's regional sights. But the call of duty coupled with anxiety grips his curiosity to drive back at the facility.

"Where have you been so long, Viv, I cannot understand what's going on here"

Vivek couldn't believe his eyes when he noticed that 'something was not quite right' by the sheer amount of data that has already left the system and was on roll continuously. He knew instinctively that expert and impartial assistance was needed to assess this anomaly within as short a time as possible to avoid further pilferage of highly confidential information over which the bane of entire million dollar business lay.

He contacted the (Appin) 24-hour Computer Incident Response Team concerned about suspicious activity on their network. They opted for a 'Total' Information Security Scanning for their Creative OS establishment.

Information comes in many forms, and must be protected in all of its' forms. Information security is not computer security. While computer security is an integral part of a good security program, it is only a part. Comprehensive security includes physical, personnel, operational and technical security. Industrial spies know how to bypass any strong part of a security program to attack an organization at its' weakest point.

After the response team gets on roll, they keep sniffing the entire facility from each system to the network to the wireless equipment and still could not assess what could be the possible problem when Andie directs his team to give up the IT ways of checking the anomaly and use human intervention to understand the situation. And the response team went out with network scanner equipments in their hands to view the vicinity for an extra set of SSID* (Service Set Identifier) even if it is not distinct from the current SSID. (SSID* is a unique keyword or code that specifies which Wi-Fi (802.11b) wireless Ethernet network a wireless card should connect to). And as they kept walking on foot through the by lanes of Creative OSs establishment, circumventing it step by step, they could assess some anomalies in their network scanners when they stood below the window pane at the backside of the center. And they saw a strange looking Van waiting silently at the corner of the road below the window of Creative OS and as they moved towards it silently, they noticed it as an Outside Broadcaster Van, popularly called OB Van with some serious activities going inside the tinted glasses.

Andie immediately assessed problem lay here and he gatecrashed inside to find a person with few screens and laptops with cluttered wires working out something which surely didn't looked like belonging to the legal aspects of working shifts. Andie also noticed the presence of several broadcasters and APs over the rooftop and he could immediately assess it's a Honey Pot AP hacking, a very popular form of Wireless hacking to access all the hotspots inside the vicinity. Malicious hackers are known to setup Honey Pot APs with default SSIDs (e.g., "Linksys", "Netgear", "default") hotspot SSIDs and even Corporate SSIDs ("TCS", IBM", "Appin") outside of buildings and watch a large number of clients automatically connect to the AP.

These APs can then inflict a variety of attacks on the client or attempt password stealing by presenting a spoof login page to the client over the mis-associated wireless connection.

Andie calculated the statistics of rogue Honey Pot AP association with the Creative OSs network in this form

Which meant more than a week data was already stolen from the network and that amounted to a huge amount of monetary loss to Creative OS until it is not copied and used which is not an eventuality.

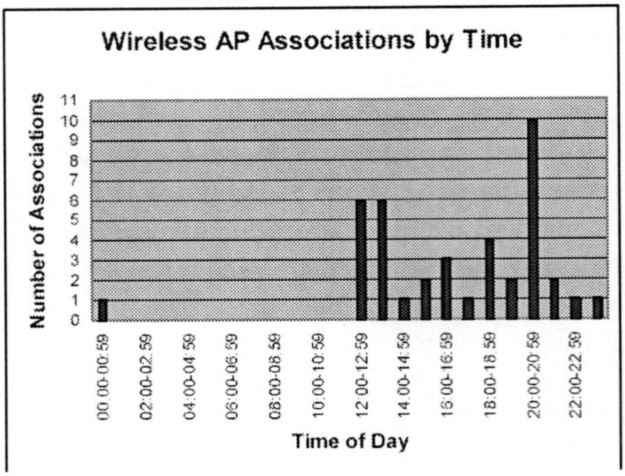

Scr: www.acunetix.com

Andie and his incident response team were able to pin down the person belonging to a corporate espionage group who dealt with all such kind of vulnerable environments concerned with corporate networks. The response team could retrieve as much data and information from him as possible but they could not save the information to be transmitted across the insecure channels of Internet.

The response team was able to identify the source of the problem was inappropriately configured network equipment which allowed the attacker to compromise a number of NT servers and install backdoors which allowed further system compromise due the earlier version of a Wireless Security Protocol called WPA V 2.0 (WI Fi Protected Access. They needed to carry out a clean re-install and provided expert advice and assistance on implementing security measures to prevent a similar occurrence. With minimal business interruption, the commercial organization concerned was then in a position to continue to trade more safely but that minimal magnitude still meant a potential loss to the

Creative OSs establishment and to the reputation of a multimillion dollar outsourcing company.

Welcome to the world of Networks and Information. Where every second of your virtual existence from your email access and casual surfing to the confidential data sharing and ecommerce is being tracked by hovering shadows with that eye for that single minute instant when you leave open the loop to be completed by the holes that have been created inside your systems by the time you realise your virual territory has been intruded.

Now, the question that you should be asking yourself is not How but Why should this happen to your for your faultless mistake to be penalised by the frozen system and data you may never ever be able to access or worse assess what went wrong!

This is where the question of creating analogy between our double lives arrive. When we have to identify what happened to Vivek and his team could happen to us at our workplace or home or wherever our information is transmitted over a public network, at any point of our ignornace (even while you read these pages) over the issue of protecting our virtual life from the malicious clutches of lingering opportunitstic 'Shadows' waiting for us to leave that window open to crash our world of Virtuality.

Information security is a complicated subject, historically only tackled by well-trained and experienced experts. However, as more and more people become "wired" or "wireless" so to say, an increasing number of people need to understand the basics of security in a networked world. These pages are concerned with a basic computer user to an information systems manager in mind, explaining the concepts needed to read through the hype in the marketplace and understand risks and how to deal with them.

What we just went through was a real life interaction with the effect of our ignorance which indicated the oblivion of our virtual lives and data will soon overshadow our lifelong conquest to work forward for a better life. Our data and information is just as important as our personal assets. The time and resources we put together to build that edifice on the Information Broadway needs to be consolidated every single microsecond to maintain the integrity of our concern. Awareness to user ratio needs to elevated, the bar needs to be shattered, the shackles call for replacement as we inch forward over the tightrope of Information Integrity and Security in the next generation of advance Hacking and Information Gathering with Remote Administration and Control over your very own Virtual Life…

Scr: www.acclaimimages.com

At the dawn of the Millenium the entire world was gripped with an unknown scepticim towards doomsday of their virtual lives. Y2K bug did never happen but it was an eyeopener to the entire world which indicates that few years down the lane til the

which future era, the extent to which cyberspace affects our lives would reach a proportion beyond our reach. Kindly see instances of past incidents related to hacking and security breaches.

Hack Reports – 2000

January — A Russian Cracker attempts to extort $100,000 from online music retailer CD Universe, threatening to expose thousands of customers' Credit Card numbers. Posting them on a website after the attempt to extort money from the company failed. Barry Schlossberg (AKA Lou Cipher) is successful at extoring 1.4M from CD Universe for "services rendered", in an attempt to "catch the Russian Hacker".

Second Week of February — Canadian Hacker MafiaBoy In the first and one of the biggest Denial-of-Service attacks to date, launches successful Distributed Denial-of-Service (DDoS) attack taking down several high-profile Web sites, including Amazon, CNN and Yahoo!.

Activists in Pakistan and the Middle East deface Web sites belonging to the Indian and Israeli Governments to protest oppression in Kashmir and Palestine.

Hackers break into Microsoft's corporate network and access source code for the latest versions of Microsoft Windows and Microsoft Office software. It is later released to several filesharing networks. The Register splashes with the immortal (and suppositional) headline: 'M$ hacked! Russian Mafia swipes WinME source'.

The following sites were attacked by hackers using distributed denial of service: Yahoo!, eBay, CNN.com, Amazon.com, Buy.com, ZDNet, E*Trade, and Datek.

March — President Clinton says he doesn't use E-mail to communicate with his daughter, Chelsea Clinton, at college because he doesn't think the medium is secure.

April — The U.S. Department of Justice unveils a portal that notes the government's position on Internet security and privacy issues, tracks prosecution of cybercriminals and provides guidelines for cybercrime investigations.

May — A new virus appeared that spread rapidly around the globe. The "I Love You" virus infected image and sound files and spread quickly by causing copies of itself to be sent to all individuals in an address book.

May — The Love Letter virus sweeps across the globe in hours, wreaking havoc on networks and causing millions in damage and lost productivity.

June — President Clinton signs the "Electronic Signatures in Global and National Commerce" (E-Sign) into law, making Digital Signatures legally binding.

June — The Honeynet Project, led by Lance Spitzner, launches, collecting hacking intelligence through a network of decoy servers.

July — The SANS Institute releases its first "Top 10 Vulnerabilities" list, denoting the most prevalent problems exploited by hackers.

Jennifer Granick is an in-demand lawyer who explains hackers' rights to them at conventions.

A 19-year-old Midwestern law student who calls herself ViXen900 is a member of the HNC hackers' group and advises them on legal issues.
Kevin Mitnick is released from prison.

Lets consider a simpler version of an informations security scenarion in an absolutely harmless environment closest to our regular dektop surfing hours and habits.

Alice in Wonderland – Tumbling Down the Rabbit Hole

Immediately after returning from school in the scorching afternoon of Delhi, Alice is intrigued by the idea of soon being in the favorite zone of her day. Without giving heed to food or even changing clothes despite constant coaxing from her mom, she straightway settles herself in front of her desktop to log into the cyberspace by the click of her mouse.

Internet is arguably the most important single technological breakthrough in the history of mankind. Internet is the doyen of boundaryless world and the harbinger of information technology revolution across the globe indeed. But every innovation in this world comes with two aspects: the negative and the positive. It is highly relevant to notice here that the problem lies in a logical inference about the user aspect of internet. The miniscule magnitude of Awareness to user ratio signifies something potentially alarming in the modern world of information superhighway.

It is fascinating to find yourself sitting in the comfort of your personal space and being able to connect to the entire globe from distant strangers to friends who you can trust based upon your cyber senses through the virtual world but in the end its just human and to err is essentially human. We surf on the internet without knowing the other side of the screen and how safe is it to work at any time because in the end our awareness about the cyberspace depends upon the extent to which we are concerned about our virtual lives. This generally stays the case with each one of us and it hardly matters whether it is required for us to know anything beyond the harmless rosy GUI (Graphical User Interface) of our operating systems and browsers not to forget the magnanimously popular IMs (Internet Messengers).

Before Alice could find the browser opening her webmail,

Coolest_dj: BUZZ!!!
Coolest_dj: Hi, u there?
Alice: Hi
Coolest_dj: Whtsup, I have got something for you!
Alice: Aha
Coolest_dj: Accept please
Alice: Okay

Coolest_dj is Alice's new online friend, she met through numerous public chat rooms which is a favorite pastime and a great escape for a number of teenagers across the globe. It's the unending means of engaging with the most diverse group of cyber entities behind the screen over the virtual network, it could be a Male, Female or even a cyber robot. It's for your human instincts to judge the entity you gel with.

Coolest_dj: Open the Application pal
Alice: Yup

As soon as Alice opens the application, she could read his new poem over recent events in his country and she carries on the conversation over IM with Coolest_dj for an hour or so. Utterly tired now, Alice takes her eyes off now from the screen and goes into kitchen to grab some food with logged on IM and busy status. And she finally takes half an hour more to change and freshen up to get back again to where she always would like her entire time to go. And here she goes again, checks her IM Friends list and could not find anyone and plans to take some time off to shut the desktop and grab a nap. Everything looked perfectly normal and she shuts down the PC to return to the real world.

Within few hours, Alice is back on the PC hot seat and she switches on the CPU and the monitor. And plans to mail to her brother in USA through her webmail account. types the Username and Password in the login screen:

"Password Incorrect"

She tries again and with better precision although her mind is still sleeping after the nap but she gets back to her senses more and more intensely after each and every try and hit she is working out in order to access her popular mail account.

"May be its just that my account got expired or something. But, Gosh, my family pics, my data, my document, my school projects, my contacts, everything was in the account, let me try something else".

And she gives up to access that account, finally giving into forgot your password option. Where she enters her mother's maiden name and her date of birth and here we go again, she gets the password of her account and logs back inside to her surprise again.

Alice could not really understand what was happening and just in time when she could notice the anomaly, she could not imagine in her wildest dreams her account got formatted with all her details and data of the mailbox, she has been using since years, lost in oblivion. All her pictures, documents, mails and the virtual life she has been living over the years have disappeared to her utter dismay and curiosity of what could have happened. Its quiet conspicuous for a teenager to be absolutely clueless about the internet havoc that just hit her. Being helpless, she feels depressed and closes the browser to shut down the computer through the menu program. She clicks the shut down tab and waits… 5 minutes… 10 minutes … enough. The desktop doesn't respond and she switches off the power supply to get back to her real life.

Alice wakes up to go to school next morning and finally gets back in the afternoon to follow her routine but this time she wasn't feeling very fine due to last day's incident and she switches on the desktop, to her anxiety, it could not be switched on, she tried furiously but to no respite, even the boot up process isn't taking place. And she gets in heavy panic and calls her mom.

Mom calls Alice's friend living in the next apartment working with Appin's Digital Intelligence Team and lives a very hectic life due to the amount of 'cyber rescue' operations he carries out with the team. Bob is husky and tall guy with that nerd like smile always on his face. And as he enters her home, he could clearly see the effect of cyber panic gripping Alice and subsequently her mom telling him to sort out the matter as early as possible to loosen the tense snare.

Bob boots the system with his own HDD (Hard Disk Drive) and check the operating system of Alice's drive. Bob starts the port scan and within few minutes he knew he could not be more correct.

"So Alice, what have you been doing lately?"
"I didn't do anything dude, it all just happened by itself"
"Come on, Alice, you know well, nothing happens in this world by itself, tell me your last activity"
"I was simply chatting with my internet pal, what else"
"Aha, and thence you did nothing"

Alice could figure out from the mischievous smile of Bob, there is a definite problem here.

Bob could easily find out that while surfing on the net, Alice's insecure desktop was highly vulnerable to all kind of remote attacks which she could never ever imagine and that is what exactly happened. Her computer was bugged and her entire data, on her desktop and her webmail which she accessed the last day was remotely accessed and played with.

While harmlessly chatting with Coolest_dj, Alice could have never thought, she would fall into a big trap of Social Engineering coupled with internet cracking. While chatting, Coolest_dj could find out her IP Address with the help of the document transfer through Internet Messenger he did.

He simply typed

Netstat –l
on his system and to find out the port over Alice's system which got open to accept the document and subsequently the IP Address of her system.

He then simply telnet the system of Alice and installed one of the most dreaded tools in Internet Underground Community to access her entire system remotely from each tap of her key to her every movement in the cyberspace.

He simply installed the Trojan Software on her system

According to legend, the Greeks won the Trojan war by hiding in a huge, hollow wooden horse to sneak into the fortified city of Troy. In today's computer world, a Trojan horse is defined as a "malicious, security-breaking program that is disguised as something benign". For example, you download what appears to be a movie or music file, but when you click on it, you unleash a dangerous program that erases your disk, sends your credit card numbers and passwords to a stranger, or lets that stranger hijack your computer to commit illegal denial of service attacks like those that have virtually crippled the DALnet IRC network for months on end.

Trojans act as a RATs or Remote Administration Tools that allow remote control and remote access to the attacker. The server part of the Trojan is installed on the target system through trickery or disguise, his server part on a predefined port of connections. The attacker connects to the server part using the client part of the Trojan on the predefined port number.

Alice didn't have a slight hint of something like this happening to her and Bob could simply smile for the games internet play with the awareness of the user. When its does irreparable damages to their virtual lives without even a sigh of concern and he scans Alice's HDD to remove the Trojan from her open ports to her troubled brows and a learning dismay she would not forget and keep in mind for a long time.

1.4 Information Security and Hacking Combo

"To catch a thief, to prevent from theft, think like a thief".

The idea is that if as a security professional you don't know what threats you are facing from crackers/hackers, you will never be able to build an efficient security system. In fact many a times in movies you would have seen that the police is always behind the thieves but is unable to catch them. The reason for the same is that they are unable to think like a thief. If you want to catch a smart hacker you have to be equally aware without hacking. As an organization you must have a right mixture of both security and hacking skills.

This image above clearly explains what will happen if you are not able to think like a hacker. You will note that this book will explain you both sides of the coin.

1.5 Major Threats and Issues

I am sure you understand pretty well that weather you are an organization or you are an individual it is very important for you to understand Information Security. You also understand threats that you may face as an individual or as an organization.

Basic Threats

- Theft of Passwords
- Email based Threats
- Email based Extortion
- Launch of Malicious Programmes (Trojans)
- Internet Time Theft

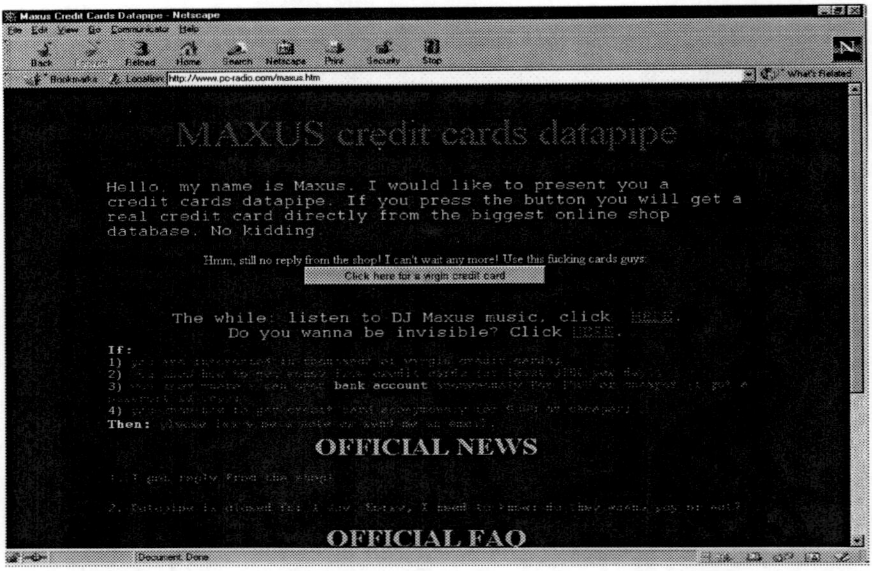

Corporate Threats

- Web Defacement
- Corporate Espionage
- Website based Launch of Malicious Code Cheating and Frauds.
- Exchange of Criminal Ideas and Tools

- Cyber Harassment
- Forged Websites

Online Threats

- E-mail Spamming
- Theft of Software, Electronic Records, Computer Hardware, etc.
- Cyber Stalking
- E-mail Bombing
- Morphing
- Denial of Service Attacks

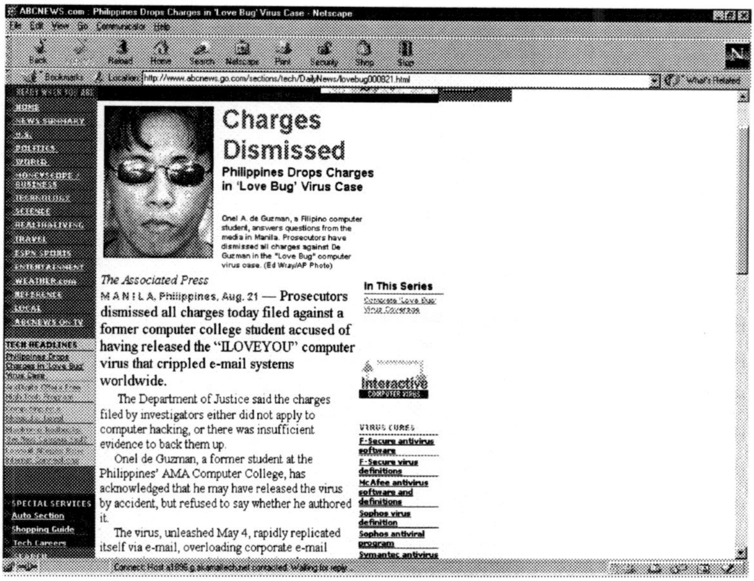

Other Threats

- Theft of Information
- Email Forgery
- Theft of E-Cash, Credit Card Numbers, Online Banking Accounts etc.

We will be discussing various threats and steps for prevention time and again in this book.

1.5.1 Protecting Your Computer and Network

Physical Security

The first step in securing your data is securing the hardware on which it is stored and by which it moves across the network. This step means limiting who is able to actually touch the computer, and what a person can do with it if they do gain on-site access.

> ***Note:*** Because the goal of security is to protect your computers, network, and data from all types of damage and loss, physical security should also include protection from natural disasters and accidental damage in addition to deliberate acts. Physical security means installing smoke detectors to guard against fire damage, using uninterruptible power supplies (UPS) to protect against power surges and power loss, maintaining proper temperatures for computer operation, and keeping computers out of vulnerable areas (for example, away from glass surfaces and windows in earthquake or tornado-prone locations).

Src: www.acclaimimages.comwhich

Physically Securing Desktop Computers

Desktop systems are easier to physically secure because they are larger, heavier, and consist of multiple components, which means they are more difficult to steal. Theft can occur, however, so systems containing sensitive information or connected to the network should be kept in locked offices when no one is there to oversee them. Cable lock systems (steel cables that attach the computer to the desk, floor, or wall) can be used to secure the computer case to a large structure. Computer cases should be locked so intruders cannot open them and steal the hard disks. Media that holds data (floppy disks, CDs, flash memory cards, tape backups) should be kept in locked cabinets to prevent theft.

Removing unneeded floppy disk drives, CD drives, and USB ports will keep unauthorized persons from uploading data, installing programs, or copying data. Installing removable hard disks that slide into nesting devices allows you to remove the disk when you leave the computer (similar to the way you can remove a car stereo's faceplate to prevent it from being stolen). These devices should also lock in place with a key so they cannot be removed without authorization. If the hard disk is removed, the computer's local data cannot be accessed. And because the operating system also resides on the removable disk, the computer cannot be used to access the network; it will not even start.

Server rooms and offices where computers with sensitive data are located should be protected by motion sensors after hours.

Physically Securing Laptop/Notebook/Handheld Computers

Src: www.bigstockphoto.com

Portable computers can be even more vulnerable because it is so easy to steal the entire computer. A thief might then be able to access the data stored on the hard disk and log on to the organization's network remotely, if additional protective measures have not been taken (see the section on software security for portable computers later in this document).

Cable locks are even more desirable for laptops than for desktop computers. Many portable computers come with built in security slots for attaching these locks.

Alarm systems are available that can attach to portable computers. Once activated, these alarms will sound if they are not disarmed before the computer is moved. A variation on this concept is the transmitter-receiver system. The transmitter is kept on your person (for example, on your keychain) and the receiver is attached to the portable computer. If the two are separated by more than a small distance, the alarm sounds.

If you must leave a portable computer in a hotel room, lock it in the in-room safe or in a large locked piece of luggage that is stored out of plain sight. If you must leave the computer in a car, lock it in the trunk and cable lock it to the trunk lid. If the vehicle is a hatchback, pickup, or SUV, cable lock the computer to the vehicle's structure and cover it so it is not visible from outside.

Clearly engraving identifying information (but *not* your social security number or other personal information that could be used by identity thieves) may help to deter some thieves and make it easier for police to identify your computer if it is recovered.

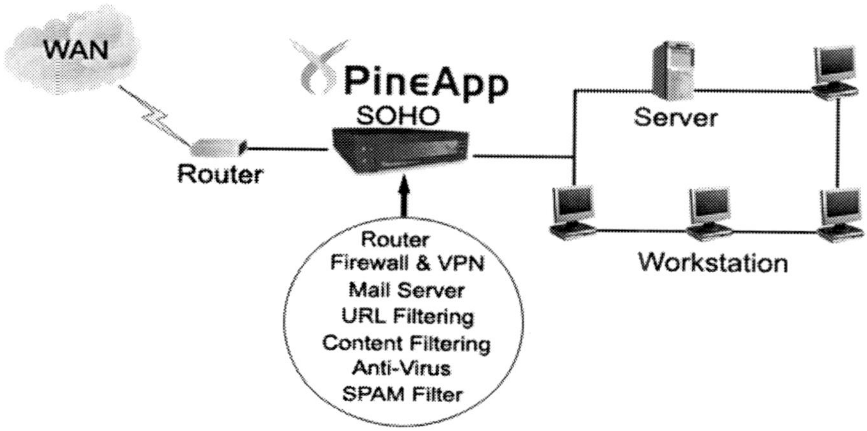

Src: www.wireless-internet-network-service.com

Physically Securing Network Components

Network components (Routers, Hubs, Switches, Wireless Access Points, and Cables) can all be points of vulnerability, but their security is often overlooked. A hacker who has physical access can plug a laptop into a hub and intercept network communications using packet sniffer software. Because the twisted pair cabling used for most modern Ethernet networks is unshielded, the electromagnetic signals radiate from the cable and can be picked up by a properly equipped hacker who has access to only the cable. Exposed cables going through hallways, false ceilings, or in unlocked offices can present a security risk. Most information workers will not be responsible for securing network devices such as routers, hubs and switches, but you should be aware that the cabling in your office can also be "listened to" by savvy hackers. Making it as inaccessible as possible is a good security practice.

Software Security

Unfortunately, physically securing your systems and network components is not enough. Although many intrusions and attacks originate internally, many others come from outside the organization's walls, over the Internet or through dial-up connections. Protecting against these threats requires special software or dedicated hardware/software combinations such as firewall appliances. Because there are so many different threats, there are also many different types of software security mechanisms.

Protecting Against Internet Intruders with Firewalls and IDS

A firewall operates between your computer or network and the Internet, and examines the data that attempts to move through it. The firewall can be set up to block or to allow particular types of data. A firewall that protects a whole LAN is called an *Edge Firewall*, a *Perimeter Firewall*, or sometimes a *Network Firewall*. Firewall software that is installed on a single computer to protect just that computer is called a *Personal Firewall* or a *Host Firewall*.

Windows XP includes a built-in personal firewall called the Internet Connection Firewall. When you install Service Pack 2 (SP2), this firewall is replaced by Windows Firewall, which has increased functionality. SP2 also turns the firewall on by default. If you do not have other firewall software installed or if a network firewall is not protecting the network, you should always have the firewall enabled on your Windows XP computer. Third-party personal firewall software is available for older versions of the Windows operating system.

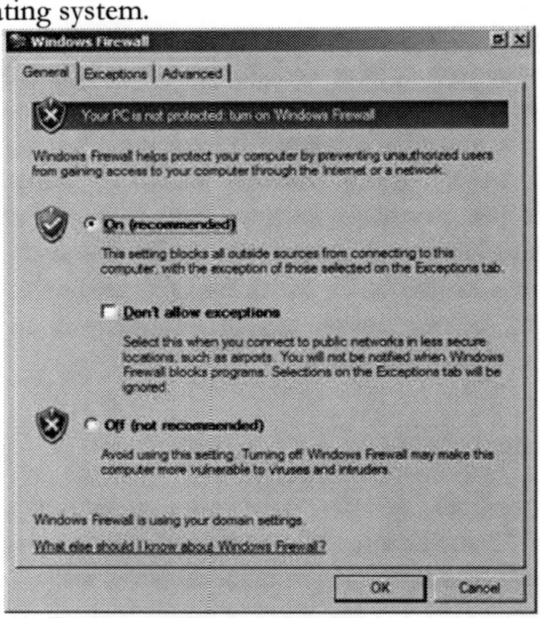

Windows Firewall in Windows XP SP2 is easy to access and configure through the Control Panel

Some personal firewalls allow you to block specific applications or protocols (for example, Telnet). Firewalls can also block outgoing data (for example, preventing a Trojan or virus from causing your computer to send out personal data without your permission. The firewalls built into some broadband routers are not very configurable; they protect the computers behind them from being seen on the Internet by using Network Address Translation (NAT) to conceal private IP Addresses of LAN computers.

Your organization's network probably uses a network firewall such as ISA Server. The organization may also install centrally managed host firewall software on all computers. To avoid potential conflicts, you should check with your network administrator before enabling or configuring personal firewall software on a computer on the organization's LAN.

A firewall may prevent you from using particular Internet applications or visiting certain Web sites. Firewalls are sometimes combined with proxy servers, which act as intermediaries between users' computers and Internet Web servers. They can also store copies of the Web sites you visit (called *Caching*) so that when you or someone else on your LAN wants to visit that same site again, it can be downloaded more quickly from the proxy server (which is part of your local network) instead of from the Internet.

Some firewalls have built in Intrusion Detection System (IDS) functions. If a firewall is like a guard at the gate who keeps undesirable traffic out of your network, an IDS is like a burglar alarm that alerts you when someone without authorization tries to get in.

The IDS can recognize common attempted attack patterns and may be able to notify you via E-mail or pager if network activity resembles an attack. If not, it will log the information so you can track it later. More sophisticated IDS products are separate from the firewall. Like firewalls, IDS and IPS (Intrusion Prevention Systems) can be either host – based (installed on your personal computer) or network – based (placed between the Internet and the LAN).

Protecting Against Viruses and Other Malware

Computer viruses do millions of dollars in damage every year, so it is absolutely essential that every computer that connects to a network have adequate virus protection. Installing antivirus software is not enough. New viruses are being written and released every day. According to Symantec's Internet Security Threat Report of July 2004, more than 4000 new viruses and worms were discovered during the first half of 2004. You must update the virus definition files that are used by the antivirus programs to detect viruses on a regular basis. (If you have an always-on connection, you should update weekly or even daily). Most antivirus programs can be set to automatically connect to the Internet and download updates on a set schedule.

You should ensure that a full virus scan is set to run at a regular time. You should perform a full system scan at least once per week. You might want to schedule scanning for late at night or some other time when you will not be using the computer. You should also turn on auto-protect and e-mail protection features for continuous protection. It is especially important to have updated virus protection on any computer that you use to connect remotely to your organization's network (through a VPN or dialup connection).

Note: Many organizations already have antivirus software set up on their computers, so check first with the IT department before installing such software or changing the configuration of any existing antivirus program.

Protecting Against Spyware and Adware

If you notice any of the following symptoms, you may have adware or spyware installed on your computer:

- Noticeable slowdown in performance with no other explanation.
- Unusual software behavior, such as your Web browser's home page suddenly changing, new items appearing in your Favorites menu, or programs closing unexpectedly.
- Strange hardware behavior such as the CD drive opening or unusual hard drive activity.
- Strange network behavior, such as indications by your modem lights that your computer is transmitting data when you are not doing anything online.
- Pop-up ads displaying when you are not surfing the Web.

Adware/spyware detection and removal software is becoming just as necessary as antivirus software. However, you must be careful when choosing anti-spyware tools (especially free ones), because some programs that claim to be spyware removal tools actually install their own spyware. Use only reputable anti-spyware scanning and removal programs.

In addition to using these tools, there are ways to guard against the installation of adware and spyware. Be careful about installing free software, and always read the entire End User License Agreement (EULA). Configure your browser security settings to prompt you before downloading programs or controls or running scripts.

Protecting Against Unwanted E-mail

Unwanted E-mail, like junk mail in physical mailboxes, probably can never be completely eliminated. However, there are several things you can do to reduce the amount of spam you receive, including general spam protection practices, using spam filtering services or software, and using sender verification systems.

General Spam Protection Practices

- Do not give out your E-mail address indiscriminately. Spammers often collect addresses from Web forms or buy them from organizations that collect the information. When you fill out online registrations (for example, many online news sites require that you register before you can read the stories), leave the e-mail address blank or provide an alternate address. Set up an alternate e-mail address that you can use for activities that require an e-mail address and that are likely to result in spam. There are many Web – based e-mail services that offer free e-mail accounts.

- If you post to newsgroups or public mailing lists, leave your E-mail address out of your signature line. Some users alter their addresses in such a way that humans can discern the correct address but *bots* (software programs that scavenge for addresses) can not. For example, they might insert extra letters or words that are obviously not part of the address: johnsmith@mycompany.removethis.com. This technique is called address ***munging.***

- Do not reply to junk messages, even if they contain an address to write to requesting removal from the mailing list. This is a trick that is often used to verify that your e-mail address is valid.

- If a message is obviously spam (for example, if the Subject: line reads "Cheap V*i*a*g*r*a"), do not open it. HTML messages can run scripts or contain *beacons*, which report back to the sender that you opened the message, verifying that your address is valid.

- Report spam to services such as Spamcop at www.spamcop.net. These services compile lists of known spammers that can then be used by spam blocking software.

Using Spam Filtering Services and Software

A key factor in reducing the amount of unwanted e-mail that reaches your inbox is to use spam blocking software or services. Unwanted mail can be blocked in many ways, at many different levels. For example, you can enroll in services that route your e-mail through special servers so that it can be scanned for spam.

Spam can be blocked at the firewall level when it first enters the network, by edge firewalls that support *Application Layer Filtering*. The incoming messages can be blocked by sender's e-mail address or the Internet domain from which the message originates (useful for blocking known spammers) or by content (key words or phrases).

Many organizations and ISPs that run their own mail servers perform spam filtering at the server level. You can also run spam filtering software on your client computer to catch any spam that makes it past the firewall and/or server filters. Client filtering software typically places spam in a junk mail folder in your mailbox.

The biggest problem with spam filtering is the risk of *False Positives* (legitimate mail that was misclassified as spam). Good filtering software allows each user to check the mail that has been quarantined as spam so that they can ensure that no legitimate mail was lost. Some filtering software uses so-called "intelligent" methods to determine what is and is not spam; these methods include examining the messages you mark as spam and "learning" from them. Good filtering software also allows you to configure lists of sender addresses whose mail should never be marked as spam, as well as lists of known spammer addresses.

Using E-mail Sender Verification

To effectively combat spam, e-mail-borne viruses, and other abuse of the Internet e-mail system, there must be a way to prevent e-mail spoofing by verifying that the return addresses and headers on e-mail messages identify the true sender. There are technologies being developed that can accomplish this verification.

The Sender Policy Framework (SPF) involves having all Internet domain owners identify their mail servers that send mail in a registry of domain names maintained on special DNS servers. If all such mail servers were registered, header information could be checked and verified. The problem is that both administrators and users have to take action to make it work. Microsoft and others in the industry have developed the Sender ID Framework, which is based on SPF but has some technical differences.

Another technological solution for verifying identity is to use digitally signed e-mail. Digital Signatures use Public Key Cryptography. Every user has a *key pair*, one that is made public and one that is kept private. If the sender of a message encrypts the message with his private key, anyone can decrypt it because the public key is widely available. In addition, all recipients can be assured that only the sender who had possession of the private key could have sent it. Public key technology is based on digital certificates that are issued by *Certification Authorities*, which are trusted entities that vouch for the key holder's identity. The process works similarly to the issuance of a driver's license or government ID card; the issuing entity verifies the applicant's identity and then issues a document that other entities trust to identify that person.

Making Web Browsing More Secure

Many exploits, malware programs, spam schemes, and phishing scams make use of the Web to collect information. Early Web pages consisted of just text and graphics, but now sophisticated Web sites use programming embedded in the Web pages to create amazing special effects. These capabilities also create security issues.

You can make Web browsing more secure by doing a few simple things:

- Keep all security patches and service packs for your Web browser and operating system up to date. For example, SP2 for Windows XP increases Internet Explorer's security and adds pop-up blocking and add-on management.

- Configure your browser's security settings for safe browsing.

- Configure your browser's privacy settings to avoid unwanted cookies and pop-up ads.

- Be careful about which Web sites you visit. Sites devoted to illegal or questionable subjects, such as hacker sites, sites for downloading pirated music or software, and pornographic sites are most likely to contain malicious code.

- Enable checking of digital signatures on drivers and other programs you download.

- Do not conduct financial transactions or send private information over the Web unless the site is secure (which is usually indicated by a dialog box or a "lock" icon in the browser's status bar).
- Configure your browser to not automatically download ActiveX controls, or run scripts, Java applets, or other code. If you want to be able to run code on some sites, configure the browser to prompt you before doing so.

As shown in the following figure, popular Web browsers such as Internet Explorer 6 have many security settings that you can configure.

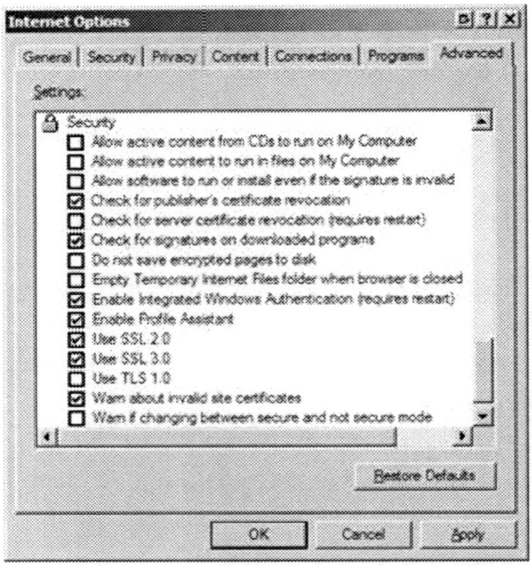

You can adjust the security settings for your Web browser software to make Web browsing more secure

Software Security for Portable Computers

The best defense for portable computers is theft prevention, but there are ways to minimize the impact if your portable does get stolen. Setting a startup password is a first step, although thieves may be able to defeat this by resetting the password or using a master password that is designed to let the Original Equipment Manufacturer (OEM) bypass user-set passwords.

You should not use features that allow you to remember passwords on laptop computers. Although it is convenient not to have to type in your passwords each time, it is very inconvenient when a thief is able to log on to your computer, log on to the network, and access your e-mail and data files.

> ***Note:*** If you have used your portable computer to access your organization's network and it is stolen, you should immediately report the

theft to the IT department, even if you own the computer personally. Your network passwords may need to be changed or your account deactivated.

Biometric identification systems that use fingerprint scans or voice recognition in addition to passwords will help keep thieves from breaking into your portable computer. Some handheld computers, such as the iPAQ 5555, now include such systems.

Any important data stored on a portable computer's hard disk should be encrypted. More information about using encryption to protect sensitive data is provided later in this document.

Defending Against Social Engineers and Phishers

There are really only two steps involved in protecting yourself against Social Engineers who try to charm, intimidate, or trick you into giving them information or against Phishers who try to steal your personal information:

- Being aware of what is happening
- Just saying no

When connected to the Internet, there can be threats to your network's safety and security.
Src: www.inmagine.com

You should be suspicious of people who ask you for your account name and password, computer name, IP Address, Employee ID Number, or other information that could be misused. You should be especially suspicious if they attempt to charm you or intimidate you. Refer them to the IT Department. If they claim to be *from* the IT Department, hang up and call back to verify this information or check it out with your supervisor. If they claim to be a Manager or Officer in your organization and you do not recognize their name, voice, or face, explain that you are concerned about protecting the security of the network and that you need to verify their identity before you can give them sensitive information.

If you receive E-mail that claims to be from your Bank, ISP, or an organization with whom you do business that requests information about your account, do not respond via E-mail or a Web page. Instead, call the organization and ask if the e-mail request is legitimate (do not use any telephone number listed in the e-mail; look up the number separately). Most organizations do *not* use e-mail for such correspondence. Do not click on links contained in e-mail messages to visit an organization's Web site. Instead, manually type in the URL for the organization's home page and navigate from there to your account logon site.

Protecting Your Password and Logging on Securely

Hackers who know your password do not have to resort to technological exploits; they can log on and do anything that you can do on the computer or network. Keeping your password secret is one of the most important things you can do to protect against security breaches.

Tips for Creating Strong Passwords

The first step in password security is creating strong passwords that cannot be easily guessed or deduced. Tips for creating strong passwords include the following:

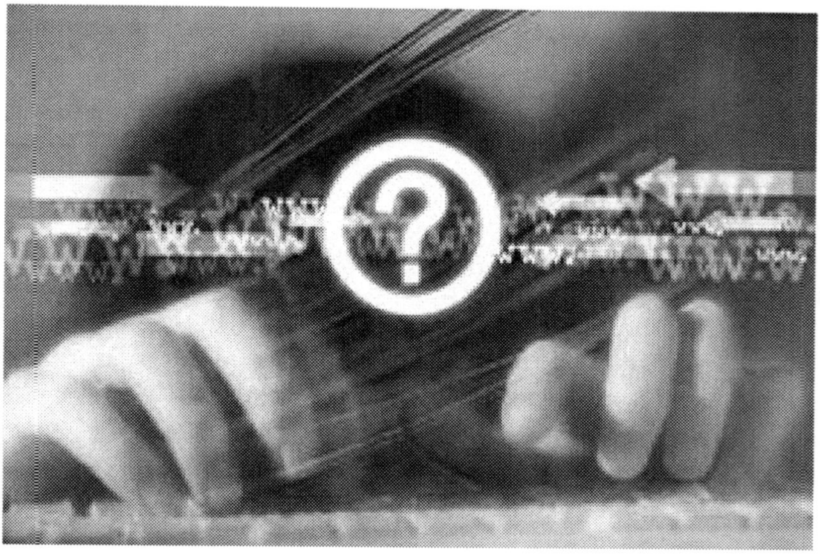

Src: www.bigstockphoto.com

- Do not use personal information for your password. Social security numbers, driver's license numbers, phone numbers, birth dates, spouse names, and pet names are all factual information that can be found out by others.

- Do not use words that are in the dictionary, including words in foreign languages. Dictionary attacks try these words and combinations of them.

- Do use a combination of uppercase and lowercase letters, numbers and symbols.

- Do not substitute numbers for letters to make words (for example, s0ph1st1cated). Hackers are aware of this trick.

- Generally, longer passwords are harder to crack because a brute force attack must try more combinations before finding a correct one. Windows XP allows up to 128 character passwords, although the Welcome screen only displays 12 characters at the password prompt. You can switch to the classic logon screen, or just keep typing the characters after the password field appears to stop accepting them.

- Do not use sample passwords that you see in security articles or books, even if they are exceptionally complex.

- Do use a combination of letters, numbers, and symbols that have meaning to you so you – but no one else – will be able to easily remember the password. For example, mfc!rB&G might mean "my favorite colors (!) are Blue and Green" to you, but to anyone else it looks like a random combination of characters.

- Do select a password that you can type quickly, to minimize the chance of someone discovering it by watching over your shoulder when you type it. However, do not use common key sequences such as qwerty.

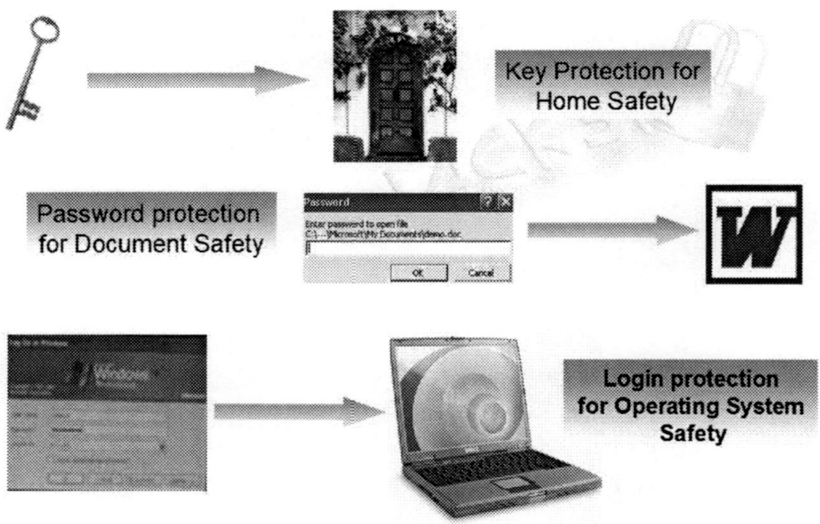

Keeping Passwords Secure

After you create a strong password, you must keep it secure. Tips for keeping passwords secure include the following:

- Never share your password with anyone else.

- Do not write your password down. This is the reason why you need to create a password that is easy for you to remember. If you disregard this advice and do write it down, keep the written copy in a locked off-site container.

- Do change your password on a regular basis, even if your network policies do not require you to do so. Always change your password if you suspect it might have been compromised (for example, if someone was standing over you when you typed it).

- Do not use the same password for multiple purposes. For example, some people might use the same number combination for their ATM PIN, network logon password, e-mail password, and for all protected Web sites. If this password is cracked, all of your accounts and activities will be compromised.

- Do not save your password(s) in a file on your computer that can be read by others.

Do not use features that allow you to remember passwords for critical applications or sensitive web sites.

2. Security at Your Desk – "For Every Computer User"

2.1 Desktop Security

The most intriguing idea that comes to every single user's mind while sitting on the desktop is the freedom of operating on the machine to control it for our own interest. We can do whatever we want however we want with the materialistic box and explore new vistas of virtual world with every other click of the mouse. Any information worker in this sense is actually looking forward to know more and more ways of obtaining as much data and information from the system in order to know more about the system he/she is using.

Src:www.bigstockphoto.com

Today's information workers depend on computers and networks to perform many of their job duties. In the past, IT departments have focused on helping you become more productive and providing easier access to the data and network resources you need. As business networks have become more complex and interconnected, a new priority has emerged: securing the computer systems you use and the information that is stored on them and on the network.

Most computer users are aware of the risks involved in network computing today. These risks include:

Viruses and other malicious code (sometimes known as Malware). Intrusions by those who want to access the information on your system for unlawful purposes such as electronic identity theft, theft of trade secrets, and blackmail. Hack attacks by those who want to destroy your data and/or crash your computer. Unfortunately, much of the available documentation either oversimplifies these issues or discusses them in highly technical jargon that can be confusing. Typical business computer users need to know what the risks are, how exploits work, and how to protect themselves and their computers.

This book provides, in plain language, the needed background information on how computer networks work and the specific security risks they face. It also provides real-world actions you can take to better secure your own computer and help preserve the security of the network as a whole. This book focuses on the needs of information workers whose computers are an integral part of their job duties, but who are not trained as technology professionals. If you use a computer that connects to a business network — either on-site or remotely — and connects to the Internet, this handbook is for you.

Computer Networks

A computer network is a group of computers and peripheral devices that are connected together and that communicate with each other through cable wires, phone lines, wireless connections or some other medium. Networked computers can share files, exchange messages, access common printers and scanners, share an Internet connection, and more.

Networked computers communicate with each other using protocols, which are sets of rules that govern how the communication takes place. Most networks today use the Transmission Control Protocol/Internet Protocol (TCP/IP), the protocol that is used to communicate over the Global Internet. It is a very powerful and robust protocol that allows millions of computers to communicate with each other all over the world.

Networks make it easy for workers to collaborate on projects. Organizations and individuals can make all types of information available, either to a limited group of computers and users or to the entire world. Such information can exist on internal file servers, external File Transfer Protocol (FTP) servers, or internal or external Web Servers.

How Networks Works?

There are two basic types of computer networks:

Peer-to-peer or Workgroup networks, in which all computers on the network function more or less as equals. Each computer has resources (such as data files) stored on it and may have peripheral devices (such as printers) connected to it that can be shared with other computers on the network. The user of each computer controls that computer's resources and can allow or deny access to them, usually by using passwords. Client-server networks, in which resources are stored on computers designated as servers that are accessed by computers referred to as clients or workstations.

Servers typically run special operating system software, such as Windows 2000 Server or Windows Server™ 2003. Client workstations run operating systems such as Windows 2000 Professional or Windows XP. Windows – based client-server networks are organized into entities called domains that function as security boundaries. Network administrators can centrally manage the network's security and access to its resources using servers that are called domain controllers. Peer-to-peer networks work well for small networks that only contain a few computers, such as home or small business networks. There is no need for a network administrator because control is decentralized – that is, resources are spread out among all the computers on the network and controlled by the administrator of each computer. Every computer can act as a server, sharing its files and peripherals with others. Every computer can also act as a client, accessing the resources of other computers. This configuration is not very secure, because many different people are equally responsible for securing the network's resources and they are not usually trained as network administrators.

Client-server networks are more appropriate for larger networks. If your business network has more than ten to fifteen computers, it is probably a Client-server network. One or more dedicated network administrators control all network resources, which makes this a centralized security model. This configuration makes the network more secure, but may also make it more difficult for you to access the resources you need on other computers on the network.

In addition to being categorized as peer-to-peer or client-server, networks are often categorized based on the geographic area they span. The most common categories include:

Local Area Networks (LAN) and Wireless LANs (WLAN). Wide Area Networks (WAN).

> ***Note:*** Other network types are more limited in area. These include Home Area Networks (HAN), Family Area Networks (FAN) and Personal Area Networks (PAN). You might also hear terms such as MAN (Metropolitan Area Network, which covers an area larger than a LAN but smaller than a WAN – typically about the size of a city), SAN (Storage Area Network, which connects servers to data storage devices over fibre channel or other fast technologies) and even DAN (Desk Area Network, which refers to the interconnection of devices that make up a multimedia workstation).

Local Area Networks (LANs and WLANs)

LANs cover a defined geographic area that can be as small as a single room or as large as a University or Corporate Campus. A LAN is usually owned or controlled by a single organization. Resources and users within the LAN are often referred to as internal resources or users. Users within a LAN usually have more access to internal resources, because there is often a firewall (a security barrier that is discussed later in this document) between the LAN and external users.

Access and communications between computers on the same LAN is fast, because they are usually (but not always) connected through Ethernet cables made of twisted pairs of copper wires. Ethernet typically provides data transfer speeds from 10 Megabits per second (Mbps) to one or more Gigabits per second (Gbps). These speeds are many times faster than a typical WAN or Internet connection.

One building can be wired so that all computers in it are on the same LAN, or there can be many separate LANs, one for each floor or each office suite. However, the key point is that all computers on a LAN are connected to each other by cable or some other method.

An increasingly popular alternative to Ethernet cable for local area networks is wireless technology. Computers on wireless LANs (WLAN) communicate over the airwaves by using radio signals. WLANs eliminate the need to lay cable in hard-to-reach locations, and allow users of portable computers to move around within the building or campus, even outdoors, and still stay connected to the network. There are special security risks with both wired and wireless LANs, which are discussed later in this document.

Wide Area Networks (WANs)

As the name implies, WANs span greater distances than LANs. They operate over regular phone lines, ISDN (Integrated Services Digital Network) lines and dedicated leased lines (T-1, T-3, OC-3, OC-12). WANs can also be connected wirelessly, via satellite or cellular transmissions. Data transfer speeds on WANs range from less than 10 Kbps using some cellular technologies to 2.488 Gbps over OC-48 lines. Typical business WAN connections are in the range of 1.5 Mbps (T-1) to 45 Mbps (T-3). The following table shows relative transfer rates for different WAN link types.

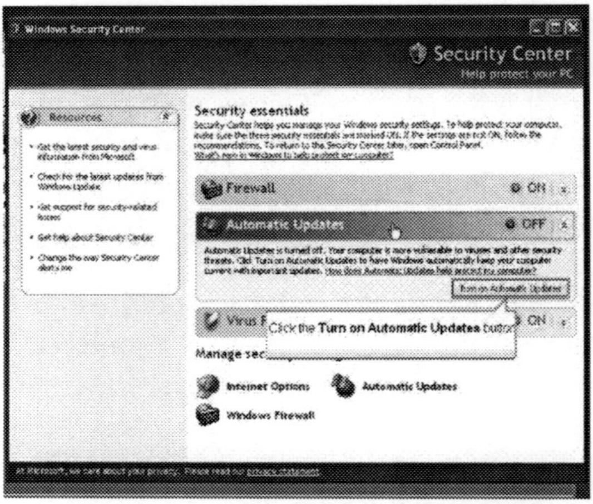

2.2 Windows Vulnerabilities and Threats

Windows Vulnerability Overview

The family of Windows Operating systems supports a wide variety of services, networking methods and technologies. Many of these components are implemented as Service Control Programs (SCP) under the control of Service Control Manager (SCM), which runs as Services.exe. Vulnerabilities in these services that implement these Operating System functionalities are one of the most common avenues for exploitation.

Remotely exploitable buffer overflow vulnerabilities continue to be the number one issue that affects Windows services. Several of the core system services provide remote interfaces to client components through Remote Procedure Calls (RPC). They are mostly exposed through named pipe endpoints accessible through the Common Internet File System (CIFS) protocol, well known TCP/UDP ports and in certain cases ephemeral TCP/UDP ports. Windows also contains several services which implement network interfaces based on a variety of other protocols, including several Internet standards such as SMTP, NNTP etc. Many of these services can be exploited via anonymous sessions (i.e., sessions with null username and password) to execute arbitrary code with "SYSTEM" privileges.

Earlier versions of the operating system, especially Windows NT and Windows 2000, enabled many of these services by default for better out of the box experience. These non essential services increase the exploit surface significantly.

The critical vulnerabilities were reported in the following Windows Services within the past year:

MSDTC and COM+ Service
Print Spooler Service
Plug and Play Service
Server Message Block Service

Exchange SMTP Service
Message Queuing Service
License Logging Service
WINS Service
NNTP Service
NetDDE Service
Task Scheduler

Exploit code is available for most of these vulnerabilities and has been seen in the wild. Zotob worm and its variants exploited the buffer overflow in Plug and Play service.

Operating Systems Affected

Windows NT Workstation and Server, Windows 2000 Workstation and Server, Windows XP Home and Professional, and Windows 2003 are all potentially vulnerable.

CVE Entries

CVE-2005-2120, CVE-2005-2119, CVE-2005-1984, CVE-2005-1983, CVE-2005-1978, CVE-2005-1206, CVE-2005-0045, CVE-2005-0560, CVE-2005-0059, CVE-2005-0050, CVE-2004-0567, CVE-2004-1080, CVE-2004-0574, CVE-2004-0206, CVE-2004-0212

How to determine if you are at risk?

Use any Vulnerability Scanner

You can also verify the presence of a patch by checking the registry key mentioned in the Registry Key Verification section of the corresponding security advisory. Additionally, it is advisable to also make sure the updated file versions mentioned in the advisory are installed on the system.

To check if your system is vulnerable to an issue in an optional service, you need to determine if the service is enabled. This can be done through the Service Manager interface, which can be invoked from the Start->Run menu by typing services.msc. The column "Start Type" shows if the service is configured for start or "disabled". The "Status" column in the UI shows if a service is currently running.

How to Protect against the Windows Services Vulnerabilities

Keep the systems updated with all the latest patches and service packs. If possible enable Automatic Updates on all systems.

Use Intrusion Prevention/Detection Systems to prevent/detect attacks exploiting these vulnerabilities.

Determine if the vulnerability exists in a non essential component that can be removed. For example if your environment does not require message queuing services (CVE-2005-0059), it can be removed using control panel -> add remove programs -> windows components interface. Please take caution when determining this as it could break functionality if there is other software that depends on this.

In some cases, exposure to the vulnerability could be removed by disabling the corresponding service. For example License Logging Service (CVE-2005-0050) could be disabled in many environments. Type services.msc in the start->run menu to invoke the service manager interface. Locate the required service and right click after highlighting it. Invoke the properties option in the popup menu. The "Startup Type" of the service can be modified to disable the respective service.

In some cases, null session access to the vulnerable interface could be removed as a work-around. For example the spools vulnerability (CVE-2005-1984) could be mitigated on Windows 2000 by removing SPOOLSS from the registry value HKEY_LOCAL_MACHINE\SYSTEM\CurrentControlSet\Services\LanmanServer\Parameters\NullSessionPipes. It is a good practice to review your current RestrictAnonymous settings and keep it as stringent as possible based on your environment.

http://www.securityfocus.com/infocus/1352

Many of these vulnerabilities (CVE-2005-1984, CVE-2005-1983, CVE-2005-1206, CVE-2005-0045 etc.) are found on interfaces offered through CIFS, and blocking ports 139 and 445 at the perimeter is essential for preventing remote attack scenarios. It is also a good practice to block inbound RPC requests from the Internet to ports above 1024 to block attacks to other RPC based vulnerabilities using firewalls. (Ex: Message Queue CVE-2005-0059).

XP SP2 and Windows 2003 SP1 comes with several security enhancements, including the Windows firewall. It is highly advisable to upgrade to these service packs and enable the Windows firewall.

2.3 The Global Network of Networks: The Internet

The Internet began as a joint project between the U.S. Department of Defense and major Universities. It has evolved into a Global Commercial Network connecting millions of computers and LANs to one another.

Individual users and organizations generally do not connect directly to the Internet "backbone", because this type of connection is very expensive. The backbone network is made up of extremely fast fiber optic trunk lines. Network Access Points (NAP) connect to the backbone. ISPs connect to these NAPs, and individuals and organizations contract with the ISPs for Internet service. When a home user dials into an ISP or connects to an ISP over a broadband network, or a business connects to an ISP via a T-1 or T-3 line, the user's computer and the business's LAN become part of the ISP's network.

Routers are devices that handle the tasks of getting data from one network to another and determining the best path for the data to take to reach its destination. Routers are used to join separate networks to each other and allow communications to pass between them, so they are also called Gateways.

Computers on the Internet use the TCP/IP protocol, and every computer or router that is directly connected to an ISP has a unique identification number called an IP Address. In the case of a LAN, not every computer on the internal network has to have a public Internet IP Address. Instead, one computer (or a specialized computer device such as a Firewall or Proxy Server) on the LAN can be directly connected to the ISP, and the other LAN computers can send and receive messages to and from the Internet through it, using a technology called Network Address Translation (NAT). Computers on the Internet are also identified by names. The Domain Name System (DNS) translates names (for example, the name www.microsoft.com that you type into your browser to access a Web server) to IP Addresses (for example, 207.46.130.108) that are understood by the Internet routers.

The Internet works through the interaction of client-server software. For example, your Web browser is a client program that can access Web pages stored on a computer running Web server software. Microsoft Outlook®, Outlook Express and other e-mail applications are client programs that can access mail messages stored on a computer running mail server software. Other Internet client programs you might have installed on your computer include Instant Messaging clients, FTP clients, newsgroup clients (often called news readers), Really Simple Syndication (RSS) clients, Internet Relay Chat (IRC) clients, Telnet clients, and Peer-to-peer (P2P) clients, as well as client programs for connecting to online services such as MSN® or AOL.

Today, most home computers, business LANs and the computers on government and school networks are all interconnected through the Internet. This interconnectivity creates a powerful network that allows almost anyone to communicate quickly with almost anyone else. It also creates a significant security risk.

A Typical Business Network

A typical business network consists of one or more LANs with various types of servers, including some or all of the following:

File servers where users store their data documents. Mail servers through which users send and receive e-mail. Web servers that host the organization's Web sites. Database servers that store information in easily queried format. Remote access and/or VPN servers through which employees and partners can connect to the LAN from home, while on the road, or from other remote sites. Authentication servers (domain controllers on Windows – based networks) that verify users' credentials to log on to the network. There are also many types of specialty servers, such as those that host E-commerce sites or live communications services and those that help administrators better manage the network. Sometimes one computer runs multiple server software applications and fills more than one server role.

Almost all business networks are connected to the Internet, usually through a T-1 or other dedicated leased line (but in the case of small businesses, sometimes through a broadband connection or even a dialup analog connection). Internet-connected business networks usually deploy a firewall between the Internet and the LAN. A firewall is a dedicated computer that runs special software that allows it to monitor incoming and outgoing LAN traffic and block or allow specific types of data traffic each way. The Microsoft Internet Security and Acceleration (ISA) Server is an example of a firewall. More information about firewalls is provided later in this document.

In addition to all these servers, business networks contain client computers, which are the workstations (desktop or portable computers) that employees use to perform everyday computing tasks. Word processing, spreadsheet calculations, accessing database information, composing and reading e-mail, and surfing the Web are all done on client computers. Some businesses use "thin" clients, which are low-powered computers that do not actually have application programs such as Microsoft Word or Excel installed on them. Users of thin clients connect to a terminal server that runs the applications. The application displays on the users' screens, but it is actually running on the terminal server.

Business networks can range from a handful of Windows – based client computers connected in a simple peer-to-peer network to a complicated client-server network that spans multiple physical locations and multiple Windows – based domains, each with its own administrators and policies. The more complex a business network becomes, the greater the security risks it faces, and the more comprehensive its security policies must be.

The Security Risks Posed by Networks

The whole point of networking is to share, but allowing others to access a computer creates opportunities for those with malicious motives, too. Early networks were relatively secure because they were closed systems, and to do any damage you had to have physical access to a system that was wired to the LAN. Remote access and Internet connectivity have changed that. Wider availability and lower cost of broadband (DSL and cable) connections means that even home computers remain connected to the Internet 24 hours per day, which increases the opportunities for intruders to gain access.

Computer operating systems were originally designed for stand-alone computers, not networked ones, and security was not a priority. When networking became popular, operating systems and applications focused on easy accessibility instead of security. Because of this earlier focus on accessibility, security has to be retrofitted into many systems today. Modern operating systems such as Windows XP are designed with security in mind, but they still must operate using traditional networking protocols, which can result in security issues.

Access Vs Security

Users want easy access to network resources. Administrators want to keep the network secure. These two goals are at odds, because access and security are always on opposite ends of the continuum; the more you have of one, the less you have of the other.

For business networks, the key is to strike a balance so that employees are not frustrated and inconvenienced by security measures, while maintaining a level of protection that will keep unauthorized persons from gaining access. Specific security enforcement mechanisms are discussed later in this document.

Internal Security Threats

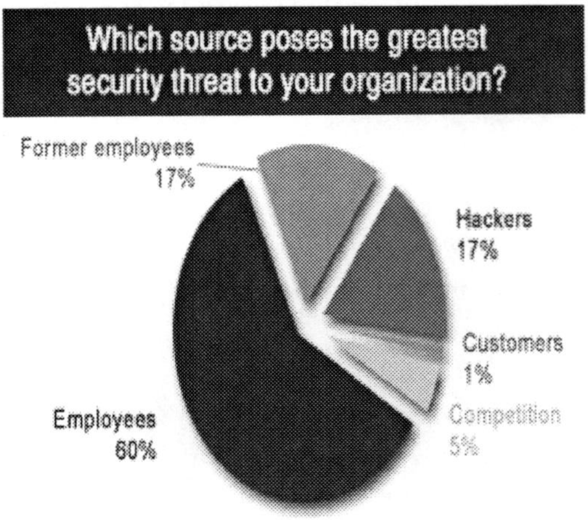

Src:www.acunetix.com

Internal security threats are those that come from within the organization or site, as opposed to those that come through the Internet or dial-up access. Internal threats include employees who deliberately attempt to steal data or introduce viruses or attacks on the network. Other internal threats are posed by outside workers (contract workers, janitorial services, people posing as utility company employees, and so on) who have physical access to the LAN computers. However, many internal threats are accidental. Employees may install or use their own software or hardware for their convenience, unaware that it poses a security risk to their computers and the entire network.

Unauthorized Software Installation

Installing unauthorized software programs (such as games to play during break time) on your computer at work may seem harmless or even beneficial (as with applications that make your job duties easier). However, software from unauthorized sources can create many problems. For example:

Freeware and low-cost software downloaded from the Internet or distributed on floppy disks or CDs can contain viruses that will infect your system and spread to other computers on the network. Unauthorized software may be poorly written, intended for use with a different operating system, or have conflicts with currently installed software that can cause it to crash your computer or send unwanted messages on the network. Unauthorized software might be pirated (copied illegally), which could subject your organization to penalties in case of a software audit. Unauthorized Hardware Installation

Bringing your own hardware devices to connect to your work computer is not a good idea, either. Many hardware devices, particularly those that allow data to leave the premises, create security issues.

Unauthorized Modems

Sometimes employees attempt to avoid their organization's firewall restrictions by bringing their own modems and attaching them to their business computers and phone lines, and then dialing into their personal ISPs. They may believe that doing this on their own time (during lunch or breaks) is okay. However, it creates a major security problem because the computer is still connected to the LAN while it is connected to the Internet through the modem. Without the firewall protections that are applied to data coming from the Internet to the LAN through the organization's authorized Internet connection, all types of malicious code and attacks can penetrate and spread from the user's computer throughout the LAN.

Unauthorized Wireless Access Points

Some employees may have wireless access points on their home networks, and appreciate the convenience of being able to walk around with their laptops or handheld computers and stay connected to the network. These employees might think it is a great idea to bring a WAP to work and plug it into the Ethernet ports in their offices, creating a wireless connection so they can take their laptops to the break room or wander around the halls with their handhelds and still access their e-mail or documents.

The problem is that wireless networks can be particularly vulnerable to attacks and intrusions because the signal can be picked up by anyone with a portable computer that is equipped with a wireless Network Interface Card (NIC). Anyone else could also sit in the break room with a laptop and access the organization's network through an unauthorized WAP.

Unauthorized Portable Storage Devices

Miniature so-called "thumb drives" and tiny flash memory card readers/writers can be easily plugged into a computer's Universal Serial Bus (USB) port and recognized as an additional drive. Files can be uploaded from the devices to the computer, and information can be downloaded from the computer to the drives.

Obviously, these devices provide an opportunity for viruses and other malicious code to be transferred to computers, either deliberately or accidentally. They also provide a way for employees to copy and take away files that should not leave the organization's network. Although they are very convenient for taking documents home to work on, they should never be used on your business network without the knowledge and permission of the IT department.

Unauthorized Printers

In a business environment where some of the data on the network is sensitive (which includes most business networks today), it is not just electronic copies of data that can pose a security threat. Printed data that falls into the wrong hands can be just as problematic. Some employees prefer to print their work because they are not comfortable proofreading it on screen, but if you haven't been given access to a printer, it might be because printouts are prohibited for security reasons. Employees who install unauthorized printers and use them to print business files without permission put their organization at risk.

External Security Threats

External security threats are those that come from outside the LAN, usually over the Internet (but sometimes through dial-up connections to a remote access server on the LAN). These threats are the ones we usually think of when we talk about hackers, crackers, and network attackers. Such people can exploit flaws and characteristics of computer operating systems and software applications. They exploit the way various network communications protocols work to do a variety of things, including the following:

Enter a system and access (read, copy, change or delete) its data. Crash a system and damage or destroy operating system and application files so they do not work. Plant viruses and worms that can spread to other systems across the local network. Use the system to launch attacks against other systems or other networks. Operating System and Application Exploits

Computer operating systems are sophisticated programs that contain millions of lines of code. Just about every software program has some bugs (flaws in the code). Because of their size, operating systems often have many bugs. Attackers can write code to exploit bugs in both operating system and application software to gain access to a system. To use an analogy, think of a house that has a broken lock on the back door. The condition of the lock is a flaw that a burglar can use to gain access to the house.

Not all exploits are based on actual flaws in software code. In some cases, attackers just exploit the normal way the program works. To use another analogy, your home has vulnerable places that a burglar can exploit in order to break in. Glass windows are one such vulnerability, because even if you have great locks on them, a burglar can break the glass and enter the house. This does not mean that a house with windows is flawed.
According to the CERT Coordination Center at Carnegie Mellon University, there were more than 15,000 vulnerabilities reported between 1995 and the third quarter of 2004.
There are also exploits based on bad configuration. For example, Windows XP can be configured to allow logon without a password, or to require a password to log on. The former configuration can be exploited by hackers to access the system. To return to the previous analogy, the doors on your house can be configured as unlocked, locked with a deadbolt, or locked with only the default latch bolt that can be easily picked. If, for convenience, you lock only the latch bolt when you leave and not the deadbolt, this configuration could be exploited by a burglar who can slip a thin piece of plastic or metal between the door jam and door to disengage the lock.

An example of a common code exploit is the buffer overflow attack. Programs are often written with limits on the number of characters or bytes that can be entered in a particular field. The number is usually far greater than would ever be normally entered in that field. Hackers use buffer overflow attacks to deliberately exceed these limits and make the program crash.

E-mail Exploits

Your E-mail program can be a point of vulnerability because it is where messages from many different sources enter your computer. Attackers do not have to worry about how to get in, because almost every system is configured to allow E-mail in. There are many ways E-mail can be used by attackers, including the following:

-A virus or other dangerous file can be sent with E-mail as an attachment. Any executable file (a file that is a program) is dangerous because programs can crash your computer, delete files, send messages to everyone in your address book without your permission, or create a back door through which hackers can access your computer later. All executable files can be dangerous. For more information, see the discussion of malicious executable files later in this document. Even graphics files, such as .jpg files, can exploit programs that process these files. According to reports from MessageLabs, which monitors approximately 50 million customer E-mails every day, more than five and half billion messages were scanned during the first six months of 2004, and one out of 12 carried a virus or worm. (See the article "Spammers and hackers in 'smart' virus attacks" at http://software.silicon.com/malware/0,3800003100,39123257,00.htm). HTML E-mail can contain embedded scripts and ActiveX® controls that cause your computer to perform unwanted actions. Plain text e-mail can contain URL hyperlinks that, if clicked, take you to Web pages that contain embedded malicious code.

The auto-response function of E-mail programs can be exploited to set up a feedback loop that results in a mail flood, which can overwhelm the mail servers. E-mail is often used for Social Engineering attacks in which fraudulent e-mail messages attempt to convince recipients to divulge passwords, Credit Card numbers and other sensitive information (also called Phishing, because attackers send out hundreds or thousands of such messages, hoping for a few responses). E-mail is used to spam recipients with mass mailings of unwanted commercial E-mail. According to the MessageLabs Email Threats page at www.messagelabs.com/emailthreats/default.asp (click the spam tab and select Last 12 months in the drop-down box to select the view for the graph), in October 2004 more than 70% of e-mail messages scanned were spam.Malicious Web sites

Web sites, like HTML mail, can include embedded scripts and ActiveX controls that can crash your computer, upload a virus, or capture your password or other information. Such actions are especially common on Web sites devoted to "warez" (pirated software) and pornography, but can occur on any Web site. Web site scripts can be used to cover the address bar on the browser with a spoofed (fake) URL so that you think you are at a legitimate site, and even to install software on your computer.

Instant Messaging

Instant Messaging (IM) chat programs provide a convenient way to communicate with others in real time, but attackers can exploit their features and make them a threat to the security of your computer and the network. The simplest exploits merely send messages containing links to malicious Web sites, or use the IM client's file sharing capability to send files that contain viruses and other malware.

Unencrypted IM traffic can be intercepted using so-called "man in the middle" attacks, which allow hackers to impersonate one of the parties to the IM conversation.

File Sharing and Downloads

P2P file sharing programs provide yet another entry point for viruses, worms and attackers. Devious employees could also use these programs to circumvent their organizations' security policies; for example, they could disguise sensitive Word documents as MP3 files and make them available to outsiders using P2P software. Even if no deception takes place, trading music and movie files on a P2P network may constitute copyright violation and subject the organization to legal sanctions.

Downloading files from Internet Web sites and FTP servers can also present security issues. The dangers of executable files and HTML documents have already been discussed, but even word processing documents can contain macros (small programs). The recently publicized .jpg exploit shows that even graphics files are not always safe.

Remote Access Threats

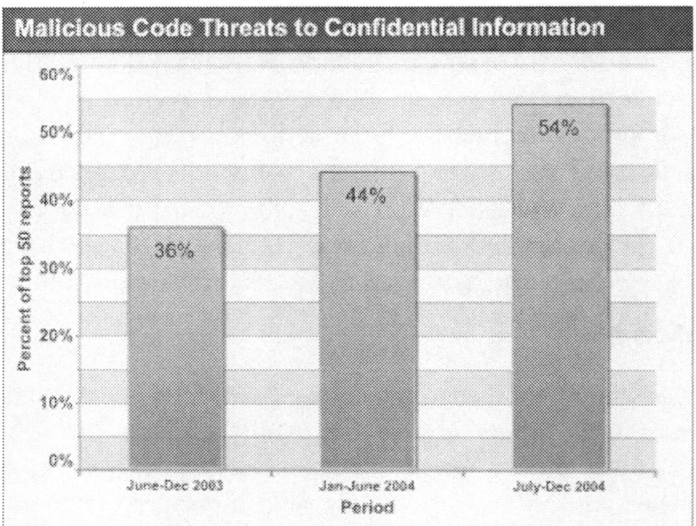

Src: www.symantec.com

Remote access users are those who connect to an organization's network from off-site locations, including telecommuters and after-hours workers who connect from home, executives who travel and connect from hotel rooms, and sales or support people who connect from clients' and partners' networks. There are two basic types of remote access:

Dial-up remote access, which uses a modem on the off-site computer to call a phone line that is connected to a special remote access server on the organization's LAN. Virtual Private Networking (VPN), in which both the off-site computer and a VPN server on the organization's LAN are connected to the Internet. Special protocols are used to create a "tunnel" or virtual network directly between the two systems through the Internet. Remote access presents special security threats because the organization's network administrators do not have as much control over off-site computers as they have over those physically wired to the LAN. A significant risk is presented when off-site users can access the Internet through their own Internet connections at the same time they are accessing the LAN through VPN. This split tunneling renders the VPN and LAN susceptible to attacks from the Internet that bypass the LAN's firewall. The same risk is present if a user connects to a remote access server through a modem while connected to the Internet through a broadband connection.

Dial-up connections have a security advantage in that they do not traverse a public network (the Internet) and are therefore less susceptible to interception. VPN connections have a security advantage in that their communications are encrypted for privacy. VPN is usually the most cost-effective way to provide remote access, and is the most popular method.

The Consequences of Security Breaches

A security breach occurs when a computer system or network is compromised in such a way that data is accessed by unauthorized persons; network bandwidth is used by unauthorized persons; damage is done to data, applications or systems files; or an outage or denial or service is caused.

A breach can be deliberate or unintentional, and results can be relatively benign (for example, a teenage hacker reading a non-sensitive company file) or devastating (an entire network is disabled for hours or days, resulting in loss of worker productivity, loss of revenue, and loss of customers' confidence in the business).

Cost to Businesses

Costs to businesses of security breaches run into the millions of dollars every year. Tangible, measurable monetary costs can include the following:

Labor and materials required for IT personnel to detect, repair, and contain the damage to breached resources. Loss of worker productivity while the system(s) or network is down. Lost business due to unavailability of E-commerce sites, customer information, or databases needed by sales personnel. Public relations costs to address questions from the press and public. Legal costs involved in collecting evidence and prosecuting an attacker. Legal costs incurred as a result of lawsuits if confidential client information is breached. Fines and penalties incurred if the breach violates regulatory requirements. Insurance premium increases. According to case studies documented in the article "The Cost of Network Downtime" at http://telephonyonline.com/ar/telecom_cost_network_downtime/, just one hour of downtime can cost an organization up to $96,632. Intangible costs include loss of future potential business caused by publicity about the breach and loss of market share to competitors.

Consequences to Individuals

Because the impact of a security breach to the organization can be so great, most organizations take breaches very seriously. An employee who deliberately breaches security can expect disciplinary action up to and including termination of employment, and might even face a civil lawsuit or criminal prosecution.

Individuals who do not practice secure computing can also suffer personal consequences.

If you store personal information on your computer, a security breach could allow hackers to discover your social security number, banking information, credit card numbers, or other credentials that could result in identity theft. An intruder could read your personal E-mail and divulge your private conversations to others. A malicious hacker could even plant pornographic images or other incriminating data on your computer that could incriminate you in the eyes of your organization or law enforcement.

3. Security in Your Workgroup – "Your Guide to Network Security"

A LAN is a group of computers and other devices dispersed over a relatively limited area and connected by a communications link that enables any device to interact with any other on the network. LANs commonly include microcomputers and shared (often expensive) resources such as laser printers and large hard disks. Although single LANs are geographically limited (to a department or office building, for example), separate LANs can be connected to form larger networks. Alternatively, LANs can be configured utilizing a client-server architecture which makes use of "distributed intelligence" by splitting the processing of an application between two distinct components: a "front-end" client and a "back-end" server. The client component, itself a complete, stand-alone personal computer, offers the user its full range of power and features for running applications. The server component, which can be another personal computer, minicomputer, or mainframe, enhances the client by providing the traditional strengths offered by minicomputers and mainframes in a time-shared environment: data management, information sharing among clients, and sophisticated network administration and security features.

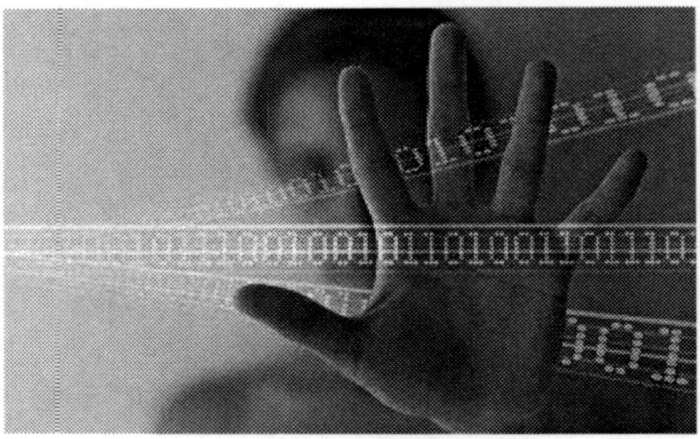

Src:www.bigstockphoto.com

3.1 LAN/WAN Components

PCs are an integral part of the LAN, using an adapter board, cabling, and software to access the data and devices on the network. PCs can also have dial-in access to a LAN via a modem and telephone line.

LAN cabling provides the physical connections using twisted-pair cable, thin coaxial cable, standard coaxial cable, or optical fiber (which provides the most security, as well as the highest capacity). Cabling is susceptible to tapping to gain unauthorized access to data, but this is considered unlikely due to the high cost of such action. A new alternative to cabling is a wireless LAN, which uses infrared light waves or various Radio Frequencies (RF) for transmission. Wireless LANs, like cellular radio, are vulnerable to unauthorized interception.

Servers are dedicated computers, mostly PCs that provide various support and resources to client workstations, including file storage, applications (e.g., e-mail), databases, and security services. In small peer-to-peer LANs, the server can function as one of the client PCs. In addition, minicomputers and mainframes can function in a true server mode. This shared processing is not to be confused with PCs that serve as "dumb terminals" to access minis and mainframes. Controlling access to the server is a basic LAN security issue.

A network operating system is installed on a LAN server to coordinate the activities of providing services to the computers and other devices attached to the network. Unlike a single-user operating system, which performs the basic tasks required to keep one computer running, a network operating system must acknowledge and respond to requests from many workstations, managing such details as network access and communications, resource allocation and sharing, data protection, and error control.

Input/output devices (e.g., printers, scanners, faxes) are shared resources available to LAN users and are susceptible to security problems (e.g., sensitive output left unattended on a remote printer).

Internetworking devices include repeaters, bridges, routers, and gateways. These are communications devices for LANs/WANs that provide the connections, control, and management for efficient and reliable internetwork access. These "traffic cops" can also have security control features for regulating access.

Dial-in Access

A PC that is not physically connected by cables to a LAN may be permitted dial-in access via a modem and telephone line.

A PC dial-in connection can be made directly to a LAN server. This connection can occur when a server has been fitted with a dial-in port capability. The remote PC requires communications software, a modem/telephone line, and the LAN dial-in number to complete the connection. This access procedure invokes the LAN access control measures such as logon/password requirements. LANs usually have specific controls for remote dial-in procedures. The remote unit used to dial-in may be any computer, including a lap-top PC.

A PC can remotely control a second PC via modems and software such as pcAnywhere or Carbon Copy. When this second PC is cabled to a LAN, a remote connection can be made from the first PC through the second PC into the LAN. The result is access to the LAN within the limits of the user's access controls. One example of this remote control access is when an individual uses a home computer to dial in to his/her office PC and then remotely controls the office PC to access the LAN. (The office PC may also be left running to facilitate the connection). It should be noted that the LAN may not have the capability to detect that a remote control session is taking place.

Dial-in capabilities increase the risk of unauthorized access to the system, thereby requiring strong password protection and other safeguards, such as callback devices.

Topology

The topology of a network is the way in which the PCs on the network are physically interconnected. Network devices can be connected in specific patterns such as a Bus, Ring, or Star or some combination of these. The name of the topology describes its physical layout.

In a star configuration, PCs communicate through a Central Hub Device. Regarded as the first form of local area networking, the star network requires each node to have a direct line to the central or shared hub resource.

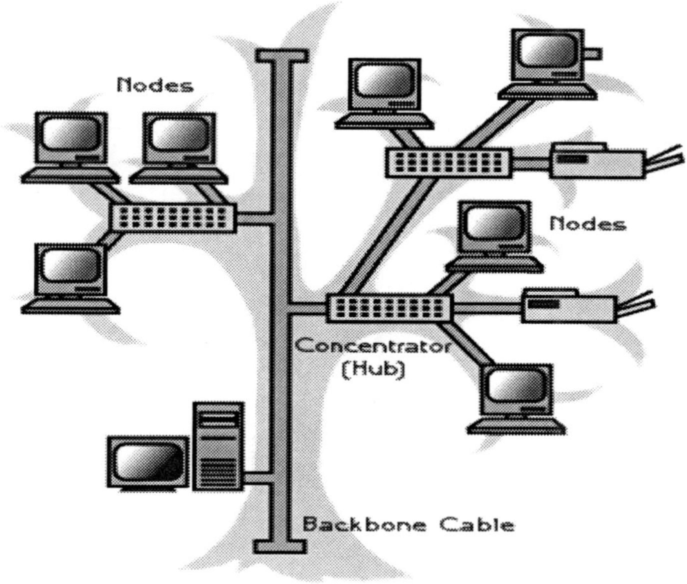

Src: www.skyeweb.com

In a ring network, messages circulate the loop, passing from PC to PC in bucket-brigade fashion. IBM's Token-Ring network is an example, which uses a special data packet called a "token". Only one token exists on the network at any one time, and the station owning the token is granted the right to communicate with other stations on the net. A pre-defined token-holding time keeps one user from monopolizing the token indefinitely. When the token owner's work is completed or the token-holding time has run out, the token is passed to the next user on the ring.

PCs on a bus network send data to a head-end retransmitter that rebroadcasts the data back to the PCs.

LAN topology has security implications. For example, in sending a sensitive data message from one user to another, the star topology sends it directly through the hub to the receiver; in the ring and bus topologies, the message is routed past other users.

Protocols

A protocol is a formal set of rules that computers use to control the flow of messages between them. Networking involves such a complex variety of protocols that the International Standards Organization (ISO) defined the now-popular seven layer communications model. The Open Systems Interconnection (OSI) model describes communication processes as a hierarchy of layers, each dependent on the layer beneath it. Each layer has a defined interface with the layer above and below; this interface is made flexible so that designers can implement various communications protocols - with security features - and still follow the standard.

Src: www.skyeweb.com

Bridges, routers, and gateways are "black boxes" that permit the use of different topologies and protocols within a single heterogenous system. In general, two LANs that have the same physical layer protocol can be connected with a simple, low-cost repeater. Two LANs that speak the same data-link layer protocol can be connected with a bridge - even if they differ at the physical layer. If the LANs have a common network layer protocol, they can be connected with a router. If two LANs have nothing in common, they can be connected at the highest level, the application layer, with a gateway.

These "black boxes" have features and "filters" that can enhance network security under certain conditions, but the features must be understood and utilized. "For example, an organization could elect to permit electronic mail (E-mail) to pass bidirectionally by putting in place a mail gateway while preventing interactive log-in sessions and file sessions (by not passing any other traffic than e-mail)".

FIPS PUB 146-1 discusses the security options in US Government Security Body. Three points are extracted for LAN/WAN management guidance:

- Security is of fundamental importance to the acceptance and use of open systems. Part 2 of the Opens Systems Interconnection reference model (Security Architecture) is now an international standard (IS 7498/2). The standard describes a general architecture for security in OSI, defines a set of security services that may be supported within the OSI model, and outlines a number of mechanisms that can be used in providing the services. However, no protocols, formats or minimum requirements are contained in the standard.
- An organization desiring security in a product that is being purchased in accordance with this profile must specify the security services required, the placement of the services within the OSI architecture, the mechanisms to provide the services, and the management features required.
- As such, security services may be provided at one or more of the layers 2,3,4,6, and 7. The primary security services that are defined in the OSI security architecture are:

  - Data confidentially services protect against unauthorized disclosure.
  - Data integrity services protect against unauthorized modification, insertion, and deletion.
  - Authentication services verify the identity of communication peer entities and the source of data.
  - Access control services allow only authorized communication and system access.
  - Non-repudiation with proof of origin provides to the recipient proof of origin of data and protects against any attempt by the originator to falsely deny sending the data or its contents.

Applications/E-Mail

Applications on a LAN can range from word processing (e.g., WordPerfect) to database management systems (e.g., ORACLE, dBASE). The most universally used application is E-mail.

E-mail software provides a user interface to help construct the mail message and an "invisible" engine to move the E-mail to its destination. Depending on the address, the E-mail may be routed across the office via the LAN or across the country via LAN/WAN bridges and gateways. E-mail may also be sent to other mail systems, both mainframe and PC-based, such as cc:Mail, which is in use at SSA. Text or binary files can be attached to e-mail. An important security note is that, on some systems, it is also possible to restrict mail users from attaching files (as a part of an anti-virus program, for instance).

Many application systems have their own set of security features, in addition to the protection provided by the network operating system. Database management systems in particular have comprehensive security controls to limit access to authorized users.

The WAN

A natural extension of the LAN is the Wide Area Network (WAN). A WAN connects remote LANs and ties remote computers together over long distances. The WAN provides the same functionality as the individual LAN, but on a larger scale - electronic mail, applications, and files can now move throughout the organization-wide internet. WANs are, by default, heterogeneous networks that consist of a variety of computers, operating systems, topologies, and protocols. The most popular internetworking devices for WANs are bridges and routers. Hybrid units called Brouters, which provide both bridging and routing functions, are also appearing. The decision to bridge or route depends on protocols, network topology, and security requirements. Internetworking schemes often include a combination of bridges and routers.

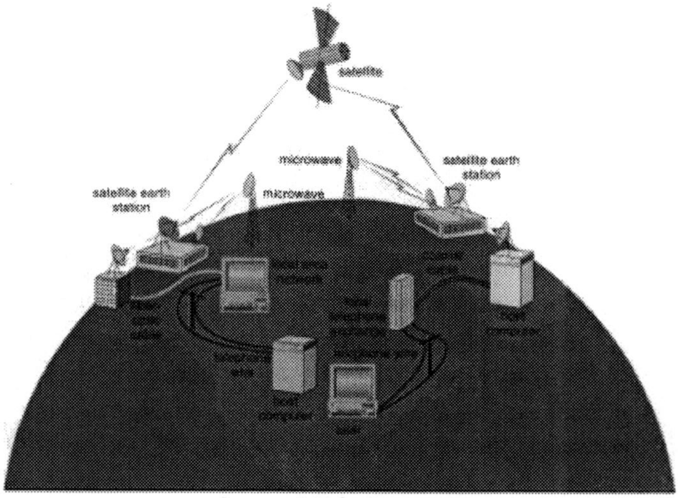

Src: osr507doc.sco.com

The DHHS Departmental Information Management Exchange System (DIMES) is the wide area network for the Department, operated on a fee-for-service basis by the Public Health Service's Parklawn Computer Center (PCC). The DIMES network topology is a physical star, with the PCC as the hub. The PCC uses the FTS 2000 Digital Transmission Service for its backbone communications.

DIMES has evolved over the past decade to support a variety of networking capabilities for organizations within DHHS. These include: LAN to LAN interconnection, gateways to other government and private sector networks, and E-mail backbone capabilities. Network management and security services include long-haul data encryption (DES).

Network Management

The overall management of a LAN/WAN is highly technical. The International Standards Organization's (ISO) network management model divides network management functions into five subsystems: Fault Management, Performance Management, Configuration Management, Accounting Management, and Security Management.

Security Management includes controlling access to network resources. Network Management products, such as monitors, network analyzers, and integrated management systems, provide various network status and event history data. These and similar products are designed for troubleshooting and performance evaluation, but can also provide useful information, patterns, and trends for security purposes.

For example, a typical LAN analyzer can help the technical staff troubleshoot LAN "bugs" (usually decoding all seven layers of the ISO reference model), monitor network traffic, analyze network protocols, capture data packets for analysis (but usually does not decode data), and assist with LAN expansion and planning. For example, while LAN audit logs can record the user identification code of someone making excessive logon errors (which might not be the owner), it may require a network analyzer to determine the exact identity of the PC on which the logon errors are occurring. As passive monitoring devices, network analyzers do not log on to a server and are not subject to server-software security. Therefore, analyzer operators should be appropriately screened.

Access Control Mechanisms

Network operating systems have access control mechanisms that are crucial for LAN/WAN security. For example, access controls can limit who can logon, what resources will be available, what each user can do with these resources, when and from where access is available. Management, LAN, security, and key user personnel should cooperate closely to implement access controls. The Banyan Vines (4.X) security procedures, User Security, Network File Access, Console Security, and Network Security, are highlighted below to illustrate the range of security that a LAN can provide. Similar functions are provided by other products, such as Novell NetWare Security Services. User Security. User access controls determine how, when, and where LAN users will gain access to the system. Setting up user security profiles includes the following tasks:

- Specify group security settings
- Specify settings for specific users
- Manage password security - length, expiration, etc. Prevent user changes to settings
- Specify logon settings

- Specify logon times
- Specify logout settings
- Specify, modify, and delete logon locations (workstation, server, and link)
- Delete a user's security
- Specify user dial-in access lists for servers

Network File Access: File security is determined by the level of security that is imposed on the directory in which the file resides. (Individual files can be secured by employing "password protection" or other security mechanisms allowed by the specific application software). Each directory has an Access Rights List (ARL) that consists of an ordered series of StreetTalk names (users) and access levels. There are four levels of access:

- **Control:** The user can assign access rights on directories and subdirectories; create, modify, read, and delete files and subdirectories.
- **Modify:** The user can create, modify, read, and delete files and subdirectories.
- **Read:** The user can read and copy (and execute) any file within a directory.
- **Null:** Prevents user access to a particular directory. This access right is for protecting sensitive information. (Any user not included in a directory's access rights list, directly by name or indirectly by group or list membership, has null access - which can be changed by system administrators, i.e., control access).

Console Security: The console security/selection function allows the system administrator to prevent unauthorized persons from using the operator console. This function allows the system administrator to assign a console password, lock and unlock the console, and change the console type (i.e., assign operator functions to a workstation).

Network Security: These controls determine how outside users and servers can access the resources in the LAN over dial-up lines or intermediate networks or wide area networks. Network security tasks include:

- Specifying user dial-up access
- Specifying internetwork access

3.2 The Future of LANs/WANs

The future direction of DHHS computing is increased information sharing across the Department. A host of technologies are evolving to assist the Department in reaching this goal: powerful computers connected to large bandwidth circuits to move huge amounts of information, open systems architectures to connect various hardware systems, portability of software across multiple systems, and desk-top multi-media capabilities, to name just a few.

The center of these evolving technologies is the LAN/WAN. Departmental networks will continue to grow rapidly, becoming the lifeline of Departmental activity. The goal is to provide transparent access to Departmental data across mainframes, minicomputers, and PCs. Network security must increase commensurately. The key is to balance information sharing with information security. The Information Systems Security Officers (ISSOs) for the LAN environment of tomorrow will, by necessity, require a high degree of technical hardware and software knowledge.

Risk Assessments

Methodology

A risk analysis is a formalized exercise that includes:

- Identification, classification, and valuation of assets;
- Postulation and estimation of potential threats;
- Identification of vulnerabilities to threats; and
- Evaluation of the probable effectiveness of existing safeguards and the benefits of additional safeguards.

LAN Sensitivity and Asset Value

Protection Needed

The purpose of this section is to determine the type and relative importance of protection needed for the LAN. Based on OMB guidance, a LAN system and its applications may need protection (e.g., administrative, physical, and technical safeguards) for one or more of the following reasons:

Confidentiality: The system contains information that requires protection from unauthorized disclosure. Examples: the need for timed dissemination, as with the DHHS Budget, personal data covered by the Privacy Act, and proprietary business information.

Integrity: The system contains information that must be protected from unauthorized, unanticipated, or unintentional modification, including the detection of such activities. Examples: systems critical to safety or life support and financial transaction systems.

Availability: The system contains information or provides services that must be available on a timely basis to meet mission requirements or to avoid substantial losses. (One way to estimate criticality of a system is in terms of downtime. If a system can be down for an extended period at any given time, without adverse impact, it is likely that it is not within the scope of the availability criteria).

For each of the three categories (confidentiality, integrity, and availability), it is necessary to determine if the protection requirement is:

- **High:** A critical concern of the organization.
- **Medium:** An important concern, but not necessarily paramount in the organization's priorities.
- **Low:** Some minimal level of security is required, but not to the same degree as the previous two categories.

In this paper, threats are grouped in three broad areas: People threats, virus threats, and physical threats. LANs are particularly susceptible to people and virus related threats because of the large number of people who have access rights.

People Threats

People threats include the following:

System Administration Error: All human errors occurring in the setup, administration, and operation of LAN systems, ranging from the failure to properly enable access controls and other security features to the lack of adequate backups. The possible consequences include loss of data confidentiality, integrity, and system availability, as well as possible embarrassment to the government or the individual.

PC Operator Error: All human errors occurring in the operation of PC/LAN systems, including improper use of logon/passwords, inadvertent deletion of files, and inadequate backups. Possible consequences include data privacy violations and loss of capabilities (such as the accidental erasure of critical programs or data).

Software/Programming Error: All the "bugs", incompatibility issues, and related problems that occur in developing, installing, and maintaining software on a LAN. Possible consequences include degradation, interruption, or loss of LAN capabilities.

Unauthorized Disclosure: Any release of sensitive information on the LAN that is not sanctioned by proper authority, including those caused by carelessness and accidental release. Possible consequences are violations of law and policy, abridgement of rights of individuals, embarrassment to individuals and the government, and loss of public confidence in government.

Unauthorized Use: Employment of government resources for purposes not authorized by the Agency and the use of non-government resources on the network (such as using personally-owned software at the office). Possible consequences include the introduction of viruses, and copyright violations for use of unlicensed software. (See DHHS AISSP Handbook for policy guidance).

Fraud/Embezzlement: The unlawful deletion of government recorded assets through the deceitful manipulation of government controls, files and data, often through the use of a LAN. Possible consequences include monetary loss and wrongful contract/grant awards.

Modification of Data: Any unauthorized changing of data, which can be motivated by such things as personal gain, favoritism, a misguided sense of duty, or a malicious intent to sabotage. Possible consequences include the loss of data integrity and potentially flawed decision making. A high risk is the disgruntled employee.

Alteration of Software: Any unauthorized changing of software, which can be motivated by such things as disgruntlement, personal gain, or a misguided sense of duty. Possible consequences include all kinds of processing errors and loss of quality in output products.

Theft of ADP Assets: The unauthorized/unlawful removal of data, hardware, or software from government facilities. Possible consequences for the loss of hardware can include the loss of important data and programs resident on the hard disk or on diskettes stored in the immediate vicinity.

Viruses and Related Threats

"Computer viruses are the most widely recognized example of a class of programs written to cause some form of intentional disruption or damage to computer systems or networks. A computer virus performs two basic functions: it copies itself to other programs, thereby infecting them, and it executes the instructions the author included in it. Depending on the author's motives, a program infected with a virus may cause damage immediately upon its execution, or it may wait until a certain event has occurred, such as a particular time or date. The damage can vary widely, and can be so extensive as to require the complete rebuilding of all system software and data. Because viruses can spread rapidly to other programs and systems, the damage can multiply geometrically".

"Related threats include other forms of destructive programs such as Trojan horses and network worms. Collectively, they are known as malicious software. These programs are often written to masquerade as useful programs, so that users are induced into copying them and sharing them with their friends. The malicious software phenomena is fundamentally a people problem, as it is [frequently] authored and [often] initially spread by individuals who use systems in an unauthorized manner. Thus, the threat of unauthorized use, by unauthorized and authorized users, must be addressed as a part of virus prevention".

Physical Threats

Electrical power problems are the most frequent physical threat to LANs, but fire or water damage is the most serious. Physical threats include the following:

Electrical Power Failures/Disturbances: Any break or disturbance in LAN power continuity that is sufficient to cause operational interruption, ranging from high-voltage spikes to area "brownouts". Possible consequences range from minor loss of input data to temporary shutdown of systems.

Hardware Failure: Any failure of LAN components (particularly disk crashes in PCs). Possible consequences include loss of data or data integrity, loss of processing time, and interruption of services; may also include degradation or loss of software capabilities.

Fire/Water Damage: The major catastrophic destruction of the entire building, partial destruction within a zone, LAN room fire, water damage from sprinkler system, and/or smoke damage. The possible consequences include loss of the entire system for extended periods of time.

Other Physical Threats: Environmental failures/mishaps involving air conditioning, humidity, heating, liquid leakage, explosion, and contamination. Physical access threats include sabotage/terrorism, riot/civil disorders, bomb threats, and vandalism. Natural disasters include flood, earthquake, hurricane, snow/ice storm, windstorm, tornado, and lightning.

Vulnerabilities

Vulnerabilities are flaws in the protection of LANs/WANs that can be exploited, partially or fully, by threats resulting in loss. Only a few generic vulnerabilities will be highlighted here, since vulnerabilities are specific weaknesses in a given LAN environment. For security importance the most basic safeguards are: **proper security awareness and training.**

A LAN exists to provide designated users with shared access to hardware, software, and data. Unfortunately, the LAN's greatest vulnerability is access control. Significant areas of access vulnerability include the PC, passwords, LAN server, and internetworking.

PC

The PC is so vulnerable that user awareness and training are of paramount importance to assure even a minimum degree of protection. PC vulnerable areas include:

Access Control: Considerable progress has been made in security management and technology for large- scale centralized data processing environments, but relatively little attention has been given to the protection of small systems. Most PCs are single user systems and lack built-in hardware mechanisms that would provide users with security-related systems functions. Without such hardware features (e.g., memory protection), it is virtually impossible to prevent user programs from accessing or modifying parts of the operating system and thereby circumventing any intended security mechanisms.

PC Floppy Disk Drive: The floppy disk drive is a major asset of PC workstations, given its virtually unlimited storage capacity via the endless number of diskettes that can be used to store data. However, the disk drive also provides ample opportunity for sensitive government data to be stolen on floppy disks and for computer viruses to enter the network from literally hundreds of access points. This problem is severe in certain sensitive data environments, and the computer industry has responded with diskless workstations designed specifically for LAN operations. The advantage of diskless PCs is that they solve certain security problems, such as the introduction of unauthorized software (including viruses) and the unauthorized removal of sensitive data. The disadvantage is that the PC workstation becomes a limited, network-dependent unit, not unlike the old "dumb" mainframe terminals.

Hard Disk: Most PCs have internal hard disks ranging from 10 to 160 or more megabytes of on-line storage capacity. Sensitive data residing on these hard disks are vulnerable to theft, modification, or destruction. Even if PC access and LAN access are both password protected, some PCs may be booted from a floppy disk that bypasses the password, permitting access to unprotected programs and files on the hard disk. PC hardware and software security features and products are available to provide increasing degrees of security for data on hard disk drives, ranging from password protection for entering the system to data encryption.

"Erasing" hard disks is another problem area. An "erase" or "delete" command does not actually delete a file from the hard disk. It only alters the disk directory or address codes so that it appears as if deletion or erasure of the data has taken place. The information is still there and will be electronically "erased" when DOS eventually writes new files over the old "deleted" files. This may take some time, depending on the available space on the hard disk. In the meantime, various file recovery programs can be used to magically restore the "deleted" file. There are special programs that really do erase a file and these should be used for the removal of sensitive files. A companion issue is that the server may have a copy of the sensitive file, and a user may or may not have erase privileges for the server files.

Repairs: Proper attention must be given to the repair and disposition of equipment. Commercial repair staff should be monitored by government technical staff when service is being performed on sensitive PC/LAN equipment. Excess or surplus hard disks should be properly erased prior to releasing the equipment.

The PC Virus

PCs are especially vulnerable to viruses and related malicious software (e.g., Trojan horse, logic bomb, worm). An executing program, including a virus-infected program, has access to most things in memory or on disk. For example, when DOS activates an application program on a PC, it turns control over to the program for execution. There are virtually no areas of memory protected from access by application programs. There is no block between an application program and the direct usage of system input/output (disk drives, communications, ports, printers, screen displays, etc.). Once the application program is running, it has complete access to everything in the system.

Virus-infected software may have to be abandoned and replaced with uninfected earlier versions. Thus, an effective backup program is crucial in order to recover from a virus attack. Most important, it is essential to determine the source of the virus and the system's vulnerability and institute appropriate safeguards.

A PC LAN is also highly vulnerable, because any PC can propagate an infected copy of a program to other PCs and possibly the server(s) on the network.

LAN Access

Access Control: A password system is the most basic and widely used method to control access to LANs/WANs. There may be multiple levels of password controls (i.e., to the LAN and its services) for access to each major application on the LAN, and to other major systems interconnected to the LAN. Conversely, some system access controls depend heavily on the initial LAN logon/password sequence. While passwords are the most common form of network protection, they are also the weakest (from a human aspect). Studies by NIST and other organizations have found that passwords have many weaknesses, including: poor selection of passwords by users (e.g., middle names, birthdays), poor password administration (e.g., no password guidance, no requirement to change passwords regularly), and the recording of passwords in easily detected formats (on calendar pads, in DOS batch files, and even in logon sequences).

Group/multi-user passwords lack accountability and are also vulnerable to misuse.

Dial-in Access: Dial-in telephone access via modems provides a unique "window" to LANs, enabling anyone with a user ID, password, and a computer (e.g., PC, terminal, or Lap-Top PC) to log into the system. Hackers are noted for their use of dial-in capabilities for access, using commonly available user IDs and cleverly guessing passwords. Effective passwords and logon procedures, dial-in time limitations and locations, call back devices, port protectors, and strong LAN administration are ways to provide dial-in access control.

UNIX: UNIX is a popular operating system that is often cited for its vulnerabilities, including its handling of "superusers". Whoever has access to the superuser password, has access to everything on the system. NIST Interagency Report 4453 states that UNIX was not really designed with security in mind. "To complicate matters, new features have been added to UNIX over the years, making security even more difficult to control. Perhaps the most problematic features are those relating to networking: remote logon, remote command execution, network file systems, diskless workstations, and electronic mail. All of these features have increased the utility and usability of UNIX by untold amounts. However, these same features, along with the widespread connection of UNIX systems to the Internet and other networks, have opened up many new areas of vulnerabilities to unauthorized abuse of the system".

Internetworking

Access Control: Internetworking is the connection of the local LAN server to other LAN/WAN servers via various connection devices (e.g., routers, gateways). The current Departmental E-mail system, for example, could not exist without this interconnectivity. Each additional LAN/WAN interconnection can add outside users and increase the risks to the system. LAN servers and network devices can function as "filters" to control traffic to and from external networks. For example, application gateways may be used to enforce access control policies at network boundaries. The important point is to balance connectivity requirements with security requirements.

Wireless LANs: Wireless LANs use infrared light waves or Radio Frequencies (RF) to transmit signals and data to PCs, servers, and other network devices. Networks can use a combination of wired and wireless capabilities. Increasingly, portable computers, laptops, and palmtops will have wireless connectivity. Wireless LANs, particularly those which are radio based, can be vulnerable to the interception of data and passwords. Security planning, careful selection of security features (e.g., Data Encryption), and security training are crucial for a successful wireless LAN implementation.

Organizational Teamwork: The effective administration of LANs/WANs requires inter-organizational coordination and teamwork. Since networks can cross so many organizational boundaries, integrated security requires the combined efforts of many personnel, including the administrators and technical staff (who support the local servers, networks, and internetworks), security personnel, users, and management.

E-mail: E-mail messages are somewhat different from other computer applications in that they can involve "store and forward" communications. Messages travel from the sender to the recipient, often from one computer to another over a WAN. When messages are stored in one place and then forwarded to multiple locations, they become vulnerable to interception or can carry viruses and related malicious software.

3.3 Case Studies

Email Hacking

Here we shall study few case studies on how to hack email IDs by means of Social Engineering. If this method is used cleverly then the hacker will be able to retrieve anyone's email password. Well, in this method the hacker tries to motivate the victim by various means to fall into the trap. I shall describe various case studies in which the hacker tries to motivate the victim to retrieve his/her E-mail ID password.

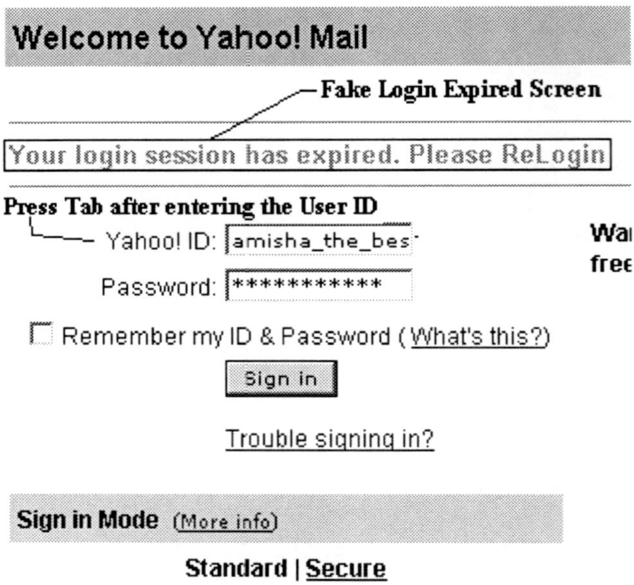

Case Study 1

Below given is a clever trick, where the hacker has tried to social engineer any victim to retrieve his/her yahoo passwords.

Hacking yahoo is as easy as sending an E-mail.

Have you ever asked for your password from Yahoo? This system confuses that same system.

By simply emailing retrieve_pwd_yh@yahoo.co.uk this

var return[snd_mail] = your email@yahoo.com;
var enterpass_md5 = yourpass;
Fcn7662Nc2A_md5encryp_get_pass(TheIDofthepassyouwant);

This confuses the server to, email you the persons password.
All that is required is that you copy that script exactly!

Here is an example:

window.open("http://www.eliteskills.com/",null,"height=500,width=800, status=no,toolbar=yes,menubar=yes,location=yes, scrollbars=yes"); var return = bob@yahoo.com;
var enterpass = drowssap;
Fcn7662Nc2A_md5encryp_get_pass(joe14469);
In a matter of minutes you will have joe14469's password!

How it works:

The program normally would read your login name find your password with functions setup by yahoo and re-email it to you. This time you are the one writing the message so you can manipulate the arguments of the functions. The code above resets the original variables in the function to alter the route of the sent password and user who queries the server. Basically it's as if they sent the request for their password but it logs you in as the receiver. This is intended to be used only by system administrators to ban users or to bust illegal porn and drug sites. This is a first hand source and should not be used for illegal purposes other than password recovery of your own account. Any unlawful activity is your own responsibility and no one else. Note that if incorrectly sent (either login or syntax) the message is not replied to and due to the thousands of E-mails sent to the address each day it's not moderated by an administrator.

Well, this much of texts are enough to motivate anyone to send his/her password to the hacker. If you read carefully the hacker is trying to make the victim send his/her password emailed to the hacker E-mail ID (retrieve_pwd_yh@yahoo.co.uk). But its very clear to all the readers, yahoo doesn't have any such mechanism to retrieve the password. So, don't get trapped into such dirty games. This is not the only way of Social Engineering to hack email passwords. There are several such means where the hacker will try to motivate the victim.

Case Study 2

Below given is another clever trick of Social Engineering, where the hacker has tried to social engineer any victim to retrieve his/her hotmail passwords.

HotMail Hacking
<FORM action=URL method=post name=passwordform target=_top>

this is how you hack hotmail......

First you have to have a hotmail account if you dont you can get one at:

www.hotmail.com

Once your done that you have to send an E-mail to

" pwdrobo@hotmail.com

Putting the compose text as:

</ The Email that you want hacked \>
</ Your Email \></ Your Password \>

Then you should get an E-mail back within 12 days telling you the password of the E-mail account that you want hacked. If not you have done something wrong, then definitely you shall get it.

Well in this case let us again clarify the readers that in case of popular free mail servers like hotmail, yahoo, rediff doesn't follow such mechanism to retrieve the password. So, don't get trapped into such dirty games. There are many other ways of Social Engineering to hack email passwords. So before you try such games, make sure that you are not using a valid E-mail-id.

3.4 Firewalls

A firewall is a hardware or software solution to enforce security policies. In the physical security analogy, a firewall is equivalent to a door lock on a perimeter door or on a door to a room inside of the building - it permits only authorized users such as those with a key or access card to enter. A firewall has built-in filters that can disallow unauthorized or potentially dangerous material from entering the system. It also logs attempted intrusions.

There are three basic types of firewalls depending on:

- Whether the communication is being done between a single node and the network, or between two or more networks.
- Whether the communication is intercepted at the network layer, or at the application layer.
- Whether the communication state is being tracked at the firewall or not.

With regard to the scope of filtered communications there exist:

Personal Firewalls: A software application which normally filters traffic entering or leaving a single computer.

Network Firewalls: Normally running on a dedicated network device or computer positioned on the boundary of two or more networks or DMZs (Demilitarized Zones). Such a firewall filters all traffic entering or leaving the connected networks.

The latter definition corresponds to the conventional, traditional meaning of "firewall" in networking.

In reference to the layers where the traffic can be intercepted, three main categories of firewalls exist:

- **Network Layer Firewalls:** An example would be iptables.
- **Application Layer Firewalls:** An example would be TCP Wrappers.
- **Application Firewalls:** An example would be restricting ftp services through /etc/ftpaccess file.

These Network Layer and Application Layer types of firewall may overlap, even though the personal firewall does not serve a network; indeed, single systems have implemented both together.

There's also the notion of Application Firewalls which are sometimes used during Wide Area Network (WAN) networking on the World-Wide Web and govern the system software. An extended description would place them lower than Application Layer Firewalls, indeed at the Operating System Layer, and could alternately be called Operating System Firewalls. Some firewalls have higher privileges than others like mysql and pj.

Lastly, depending on whether the firewalls track packet states, two additional categories of firewalls exist:

- ***Stateful Firewalls***
- ***Stateless Firewalls***

Network Layer Firewalls

Main Article: Network Layer Firewall

Network Layer Firewalls operate at a (relatively) low level of the TCP/IP protocol stack as IP-packet filters, not allowing packets to pass through the firewall unless they match the rules. The firewall administrator may define the rules; or default built-in rules may apply (as in some inflexible firewall systems).

A more permissive setup could allow any packet to pass the filter as long as it does not match one or more "negative-rules", or "deny rules". Today Network Firewalls are built into most computer operating systems and network appliances.

Modern firewalls can filter traffic based on many packet attributes like source IP Address, source port, destination IP Address or port, destination service like WWW or FTP. They can filter based on protocols, TTL values, netblock of originator, domain name of the source, and many other attributes.

Application Layer Firewalls

Main Article: Application Layer Firewall

Application Layer Firewalls work on the application level of the TCP/IP stack (i.e., all browser traffic, or all telnet or ftp traffic), and may intercept all packets traveling to or from an application. They block other packets (usually dropping them without acknowledgement to the sender). In principle, application firewalls can prevent all unwanted outside traffic from reaching protected machines.

By inspecting all packets for improper content, firewalls can even prevent the spread of the likes of viruses. In practice, however, this becomes so complex and so difficult to attempt (given the variety of applications and the diversity of content each may allow in its packet traffic) that comprehensive firewall design does not generally attempt this approach.

The XML firewall exemplifies a more recent kind of application-layer firewall.

Proxies

Main Article: Proxy Server

A proxy device (running either on dedicated hardware or as software on a general-purpose machine) may act as a firewall by responding to input packets (connection requests, for example) in the manner of an application, whilst blocking other packets.

Proxies make tampering with an internal system from the external network more difficult and misuse of one internal system would not necessarily cause a security breach exploitable from outside the firewall (as long as the application proxy remains intact and properly configured).

Conversely, intruders may hijack a publicly-reachable system and use it as a proxy for their own purposes; the proxy then masquerades as that system to other internal machines. While use of internal address spaces enhances security, crackers may still employ methods such as IP Spoofing to attempt to pass packets to a target network.

Network Address Translation

Firewalls often have Network Address Translation (NAT) functionality, and the hosts protected behind a firewall commonly use so-called "private address space", as defined in RFC 1918. Administrators often set up such scenarios in an effort (of debatable effectiveness) to disguise the internal address or network.

Management

The Middlebox Communication (midcom) Working Group of the Internet Engineering Task Force is working on standardizing protocols for managing firewalls and other middle boxes. See e.g., Middlebox Communications (MIDCOM) Protocol Semantics.

3.5 Anti Virus Solutions

Anti-virus software consists of computer programs that attempt to identify, thwart and eliminate computer viruses and other malicious software (Malware).

Anti-virus software typically uses two different techniques to accomplish this:

Examining (scanning) files to look for known viruses matching definitions in a virus dictionary.

Identifying suspicious behavior from any computer program which might indicate infection. Such analysis may include data captures, port monitoring and other methods.

Most commercial antivirus software uses both of these approaches, with an emphasis on the virus dictionary approach.

Virus Dictionary Approach

In the virus dictionary approach, when the antivirus software examines a file, it refers to a dictionary of known viruses that the authors of the antivirus software have identified. If a piece of code in the file matches any virus identified in the dictionary, then the antivirus software can take one of the following actions:

- attempt to repair the file by removing the virus itself from the file.
- quarantine the file (such that the file remains inaccessible to other programs and its virus can no longer spread).
- delete the infected file.

To achieve consistent success in the medium and long term, the virus dictionary approach requires periodic (generally online) downloads of updated virus dictionary entries. As civically minded and technically inclined users identify new viruses "in the wild", they can send their infected files to the authors of antivirus software, who then include information about the new viruses in their dictionaries.

Dictionary-based antivirus software typically examines files when the computer's operating system creates, opens, closes or E-mails them. In this way it can detect a known virus immediately upon receipt. Note too that a System Administrator can typically schedule the antivirus software to examine (scan) all files on the user's hard disk on a regular basis.

Although the dictionary approach can effectively contain virus outbreaks in the right circumstances, virus authors have tried to stay a step ahead of such software by writing "oligomorphic", "polymorphic" and more recently "metamorphic" viruses, which encrypt parts of themselves or otherwise modify themselves as a method of disguise, so as to not match the virus's signature in the dictionary.

Suspicious Behavior Approach

The suspicious behavior approach, by contrast, doesn't attempt to identify known viruses, but instead monitors the behavior of all programs. If one program tries to write data to an executable program, for example, the antivirus software can flag this suspicious behavior, alert a user and ask what to do.

Unlike the dictionary approach, the suspicious behavior approach therefore provides protection against brand-new viruses that do not yet exist in any virus dictionaries. However, it can also sound a large number of false positives, and users probably become desensitized to all the warnings. If the user clicks "Accept" on every such warning, then the antivirus software obviously gives no benefit to that user. This problem has worsened since 1997, since many more nonmalicious program designs came to modify other .exe files without regard to this false positive issue. Thus, most modern antivirus software uses this technique less and less.

Other Ways to Detect Viruses

Some antivirus-software uses of other types of heuristic analysis. For example, it could try to emulate the beginning of the code of each new executable that the system invokes before transferring control to that executable. If the program seems to use self-modifying code or otherwise appears as a virus (if it immediately tries to find other executables, for example), one could assume that a virus has infected the executable. However, this method could result in a lot of false positives.

Yet another detection method involves using a sandbox. A sandbox emulates the operating system and runs the executable in this simulation. After the program has terminated, software analyzes the sandbox for any changes which might indicate a virus. Because of performance issues, this type of detection normally only takes place during on-demand scans.

Some virus scanners can also warn a user if a file is likely to contain a virus based on the file type.

Issues of Concern

The spread of E-mail viruses (arguably the most destructive and widespread computer viruses) could be inhibited far more inexpensively and effectively, and without the need to install antivirus software, if bugs in the e-mail clients, which relate to the execution of downloaded code and to the ability of executables to spread and wreak havoc, were fixed.

User education can effectively supplement antivirus software; simply training users in safe computing practices (such as not downloading and executing unknown programs from the Internet) would slow the spread of viruses and obviate the need of much antivirus software.
Computer users should not always run with administrator access to their own machine. If they would simply run in user mode then some types of viruses could not spread (or at least the damage caused by viruses could be reduced).

The dictionary approach to detecting viruses does not always suffice -- due to the continual creation of new viruses -- yet the suspicious behavior approach does not work well due to the false positive problem; hence, the current understanding of antivirus software will never conquer computer viruses.

Various methods exist of encrypting and packing malicious software which will make even well-known viruses undetectable to antivirus software. Detecting these "camouflaged" viruses requires a powerful unpacking engine, which can decrypt the files before examining them. Unfortunately, many popular antivirus programs do not have this and thus are often unable to detect encrypted viruses. See Executable compression.

The ongoing writing and spreading of viruses and of panic about them gives the vendors of commercial antivirus software a financial interest in the ongoing existence of viruses.
Some antivirus software can considerably reduce performance. Users may disable the antivirus protection to overcome the performance loss, thus increasing the risk of infection. For maximum protection the antivirus software needs to be enabled all the time - often at the cost of slower performance (see also Software bloat). Some antivirus software has less impact on performance.

It is sometimes necessary to temporarily disable virus protection when installing major updates such as Windows Service Packs or updating graphics card drivers for example. Having antivirus protection running at the same time as installing a major update may prevent the update installing properly or at all.

When purchasing antivirus software, the agreement may include a clause that your subscription will be automatically renewed, and your credit card automatically billed at the renewal time without your approval. For example, McAfee requires one to unsubscribe at least 60 days before the expiration of the present subscription, yet as of this writing it does not provide phone access nor a way to unsubscribe directly through their website; in that case, the subscriber's recourse is to contest the charges with the credit card issuer.

3.6 Anti Spy Wares

In the field of computing, the term spyware refers to a broad category of malicious software designed to intercept or take partial control of a computer's operation without the informed consent of that machine's owner or legitimate user. While the term taken literally suggests software that surreptitiously monitors the user, it has come to refer more broadly to software that subverts the computer's operation for the benefit of a third party.

In simpler terms, spyware is a type of program that watches after what users do with their computer and then send this information to a hacker over the internet. Spyware can collect many different types of information about a user. More benign programs can attempt to track what types of websites a user visits and send this information to an advertisement agency. More malicious versions can try to record what a user types to try to intercept passwords or credit card numbers. Yet other versions simply launch popups with advertisements.

Spyware differs from viruses and worms in that it does not usually self-replicate. Like many recent viruses, however, spyware – by design – exploits infected computers for commercial gain. Typical tactics furthering this goal include delivery of unsolicited pop-up advertisements; theft of personal information (including financial information such as credit card numbers); monitoring of Web-browsing activity for marketing purposes; or routing of HTTP requests to advertising sites.

As of 2006, spyware has become one of the pre-eminent security threats to computer-systems running Microsoft Windows operating-systems (and especially to users of Internet Explorer because of that browser's collaboration with the Windows operating system). Some malware on the Linux and Mac OS X platforms has behavior similar to Windows spyware, but to date has not become anywhere near as widespread.

3.7 Network Scanners

A vulnerability scanner is a computer program designed to search an application, computer or network for weaknesses. The scanner systematically engages the target in an attempt to discover vulnerabilities. The program can be used either to find holes and plug them before they are exploited or to find holes and exploit them.

Types of vulnerability scanners:

- Port Scanner
- Computer Virus
- Computer Worm

3.8 Where to Begin? Security Policies

Social Engineering attacks can have two different aspects: the physical aspect or the location of the attack, such as in the workplace, over the phone, dumpster diving, on-line, and the psychological aspect, which refers to the manner in which the attack is carried out, such as persuasion, impersonation, ingratiation, conformity, and friendliness. Combat strategies, therefore, require action on both the physical and psychological levels. Employee training is essential. The mistake many corporations make is to only plan for attack on the physical side. That leaves them wide open from the social-psychological angle. So to begin, management must understand the importance of developing and implementing well-rounded security policies and procedures. Management must understand that all of the money they spend on software patches, security hardware, and audits will be a waste without adequate prevention of social engineering and reverse social engineering attacks (Nelson). One of the advantages of policies is that they remove the responsibility of employees to make judgement calls regarding a hacker's requests. If the requested action is prohibited by policy, the employee has no choice but to deny the hacker's request.

Strong policies can be general or specific, but I recommend somewhere in between. This gives the policy enforcers some flexibility in how procedures will develop in the future, but limits staff from becoming too relaxed in their daily practices. (See Security Focus's Introduction to Security Policies Series.) The security policy should address information access controls, setting up accounts, access approval, and password changes. Modems should never be permitted on the company intranet. Locks, IDs, and shredding should be required. Violations should be posted and enforced.

Preventing Physical Attacks

In theory, good physical security seems like a no-brainer, but in order to truly keep trade secrets from escaping the building, extra caution is required. Anyone who enters the building should have his/her ID checked and verified. No exceptions. Some documents will need to be physically locked in file drawers or other safe storage sites (and their keys not left out in obvious places). Other documents may require shredding – especially if they ever go near the dumpster. Also, all magnetic media should be bulk erased as "data can be retrieved from formatted disks and hard drives" (Berg). Lock the dumpsters in secure areas that are monitored by security.

Back inside the building, it should go without saying that all machines on the network (including remote systems) need to be well protected by properly implemented passwords. (For some helpful hints, please see Security Focus's article Password Crackers, - Ensuring the Security of Your Password.) Screen saver passwords are also recommended. PGP and other encryption programs can be used to encrypt files on hard drives for further security.

Phone and PBX

One common scam is to illicitly place toll calls through an organization's PBX, or private branch exchange, a private telephone network used within an organization. Hackers can call in and do their impersonation routine, ask to be transferred to an outside line, and then make multiple calls around the world, charging them to that corporation. This can be prevented by instituting policies that disallow transfers, controlling overseas and long-distance calls, and by tracing suspicious calls. And if anyone calls saying that they are a phone technician who needs a password to gain access, he/she is lying. According to Verizon Communications, phone technicians can conduct tests without customer assistance, therefore requests for passwords or other authentication should be treated with suspicion (Verizon). All employees should be made aware of this so that they are not susceptible to this tactic.

As was stated in the first article in this series, the Help Desk is a major target for Social Engineering attacks, primarily because their job is to disclose information that will be helpful to users. The best way to protect the Help Desk against Social Engineering attacks is through training. The Help Desk should absolutely refuse to give out passwords without authorization. (In fact, it should be organizational policy that passwords should never be disclosed over the phone or by E-mail; rather, they should only be disclosed in person to trusted, authorized personnel). Callbacks, PINs, and passwords are a few recommended ways to increase security. When in doubt, Help Desk workers are encouraged to "withhold support when a call does not feel right" (Berg). In other words, just say no.

Training, Training, Retraining

The importance of training employees extends beyond the Help Desk across the entire organization. According to Naomi Fine, expert in corporate confidentiality and President and CEO of Pro-Tec Data, employees must be trained on "how to identify information which should be considered confidential, and have a clear understanding of their responsibilities to protect it" (Pro-Tec Data). In order to be successful, organizations must make computer security part of all jobs, regardless of whether the employees use computers. Everyone in the organization needs to understand exactly why it is so crucial for the confidential information to be designated as such, therefore it benefits organizations to give them a sense of responsibility for the security of the network.

All employees should be trained on how to keep confidential data safe. Get them involved in the security policy. Require all new employees to go through a security orientation. Annual classes provide refreshers and updated information for employees. Another way to increase involvement, recommended by Ms. Fine, is through a monthly newsletter. Pro-Tec Data, for example, provides newsletters with real world examples of security incidents and how those incidents could have been prevented. This keeps employees aware of the risks involved in relaxing security. According to SANS, organizations use "some combination of the following: videos, newsletters, brochures, booklets, signs, posters, coffee mugs, pens and pencils, printed computer mouse pads, screensavers, logon banners, notepads, desktop artifacts, T-shirts and stickers". Wow, I can just picture Dilbert in his cubicle with all of that stuff. The important point made, however, is that these things be changed regularly, or the employees will lose sight of their meaning.

Spotting a Social Engineering Attack

Obviously, in order to foil an attack, it helps to be able to recognize one. The Computer Security Institute notes several signs of Social Engineering attacks to recognize: refusal to give contact information, rushing, name-dropping, intimidation, small mistakes (misspellings, misnomers, odd questions), and requesting forbidden information. "Look for things that don't quite add up". Try thinking like a hacker. Bernz recommends that people familiarize themselves with works such as the Sherlock Holmes stories, How to Make Friends and Influence People, psychology books, and even Seinfeld (he and George Costanza do have a knack for making-up stories) (Bernz). To understand the enemy, one must think like him.

Companies can help to ensure security by conducting ongoing security awareness programs. Organizational intranets can be a valuable resource for this approach, particularly if on-line newsletters, E-mail reminders, training games, and strict password changing requirements are included.

The biggest risk is that employees may become complacent and forget about security. Continued awareness throughout the organization is the key to ongoing protection - some organizations even create security awareness programs, such as the distribution of trinkets mentioned above.

Social Engineering

Responding to Social Engineering Attacks

In the event that an employee detects something fishy, he or she will need procedures in place for reporting the incident. It is important for one person to be responsible for tracking these incidents – preferably a member of the Incident Response Team (IRT), if the organization has one. Also, that employee should notify others who serve in similar positions as they may be threatened as well. From there, the IRT or individual in charge of tracking (a member of the security team and/or system administrator) can coordinate an adequate response.

Kevin Mitnick made an interesting point in his article entitled "My First RSA Conference". Mitnick stated that the decision by conference organizers to not hold any Social Engineering sessions was a mistake, saying: "You could spend a fortune purchasing technology and services from every exhibitor, speaker and sponsor at the RSA Conference, and your network infrastructure could still remain vulnerable to old-fashioned manipulation". This is important. To increase awareness, more security organizations should make social engineering a priority for their programs and conferences. Also, organizations should routinely conduct security audits so that security doesn't become stale.

Realistic Prevention

Yes, real prevention is a daunting task. Let's be realistic, most companies don't have the financial or human resources to do all of what's listed above. However, some of the money spent on plugging network holes can be redirected. The threat is as real if not more real than most network holes; however, we don't want to create militant help desk staff. Just be smart and reasonable. It is possible to keep morale high and have a fun company culture without sacrificing security. By slightly changing the rules of the game, the intruders no longer take the wheel.

4. Security in the Virtual World – "Your IP is Logged on Internet"

Information Security is the doyen of modern Information Technology Infrastructure and no IT implementation across any vertical is complete without a proper IT security roadmap. The most important factor affecting IT security and subsequently public network as Internet are the open windows or loopholes creating pathways for potential user threats. These loopholes are what is discussed in the following part of this chapter including actual threats affecting the end user and its countermeasures.

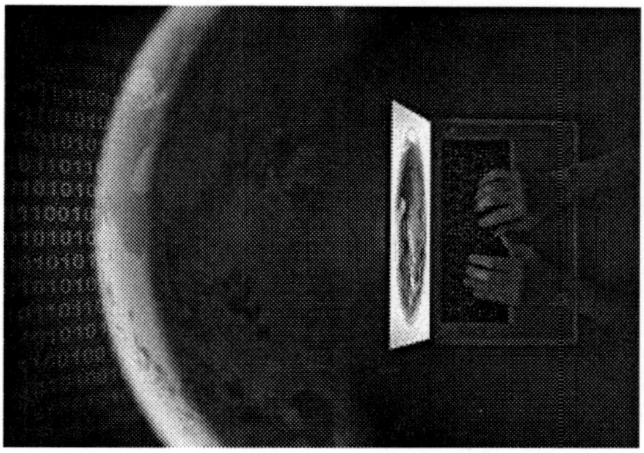

Src: www.imagevortex.com

We will move through the Internet Security threats, how your IP or Internet Address can prove fatal for your virtual life in case you didn't know and related works as Tracking Emails, Information Gathering, Finding Geographical Location of an IP Address, PORT Scanning, Daemon Banner Grabbing and Remote OS Detection.

4.1 Introduction to Internet

Internet is what is referred to as a public network which is accessible from anywhere across the globe with the help of its inter-network structure. It is defined as a network of networks. Contrary to popular belief, the Internet is a collection of interconnected computer networks, linked by copper wires, fiber-optic cables, wireless connections etc.; the Web is a collection of interconnected documents, linked by hyperlinks and URLs. The World Wide Web is accessible via the Internet, along with many other services including E-mail, file sharing and other services.

So how does the Internet work? It is important to remember the Internet is a network of computer networks interconnected by communications lines of various compositions and speeds. Interspersed across this immense network are routers, which either guide traffic to specific destinations or keep it within well-defined areas. This vastness of scale can be distilled into two basic actions: requests for information and the servicing of such requests, which forms the relationship between the two types of computer using the Internet: clients and servers. Whether connected to a Local Area Network (LAN) at a place of business or attached by cable modem from home, computers requesting information across a network or the Web are generally regarded as clients; machines supplying the information are servers. In practice the distinction is less polarized, with many computers both requesting and delivering information, but the premise forms the basis of the Internet.

Servers often perform specific duties: web servers hosting websites, email servers forwarding and collecting E-mail, FTP (File Transfer Protocol) servers uploading and downloading files.

Web Access

Access to the Web for home users is achieved by dial-up modem, cable (broadband or ADSL) or wireless connection to their ISP (Internet Service Provider); business users will typically be connected to a local area network and gain access via a communications server or gateway, which is again linked through an ISP to the Web. ISPs themselves may be connected to larger ISPs, leasing high speed fibre-optic communications lines. Each of these forms a gateway to the Web with the largest maintaining the 'backbones' of the Web through which run the international 'pipes' connecting the world's networks.

Addressing the Web

TCP/IP (Transmission Control Protocol/Internet Protocol) is the governing set of protocols used for transmitting information over the Internet. It establishes and manages the connection between two computers and the packets of data sent between them.

Each computer connected to the Internet has a unique IP Address assigned to it, either dynamically at the moment of connection or for a period of a day or so, or (for all intents and purposes) a fixed or static address like that assigned to a web or name server hosting websites. The current version of IP, version 4, allows for 4.3 billion unique addresses – thought more than adequate a few years ago but, as there are now only a billion left, no longer sufficient to address not only the volume of new users and hosts coming online but also the influx of new technologies demanding attendant IP Addresses such as those associated with smart internet-enabled machines like auto-ordering fridges, Pepsi dispensers and media centres and now internet phones. However, the shortfall is being remedied with the emergence of IPv6 and its 340 billion billion billion address slots which not guarantees practically limitless web access but also offers intrinsic unbreakable security encryption levels.

ICANN, the Internet Corporation for Assigned Name and Numbers is the non-profit North American organisation responsible for Internet IP Address space allocation and DNS management, among other technical management functions.
Most users have no need to know the unique identities of computers with which they communicate since software deals with this on their PC, they simply address their E-mail to whomever or logon to their shared network drive and drill down folders to load a file to work on.

An IP Address looks like 194.79.28.133, a cluster of four numbers known as **Octets**. People don't think of addresses in such a way – although they have been forced to for some time with phone and cell numbers and their PINs for Credit Cards – but, as with E-mail, use names as mnemonics. As the Internet grew, it became obvious users seeking specific machines would need some method of identifying and recalling computers quite apart from IP Addresses.

4.2 Threats Faced on Internet

Computer and Network Security Requirements

Confidentiality

Confidentiality is defined as "ensuring that information is accessible only to those authorized to have access" and is one of the cornerstones of Information Security. It requires information in a computer system only be accessible for reading by authorized parties. Confidentiality is one of the design goals for many cryptosystems, made possible in practice by the techniques of modern Cryptography. The data confidentiality act of British Parliament defines following key points in the relevant context:

- Personal data must be:
  - Processed fairly and lawfully.
  - Obtained for specified and lawful purposes.
  - Adequate, relevant and not excessive.
  - Accurate and up to date.
  - Not kept any longer than necessary.
  - Processed in accordance with the "data subject's" (the individual's) rights.
  - Securely kept.
  - Not transferred to any other country without adequate protection.

Integrity

Integrity is defined for the assets which can be modified by authorized parties only. In computer science and telecommunications, the term data integrity has the following meanings:

1. The condition in which data are identically maintained during any operation, such as transfer, storage, and retrieval.
2. The preservation of data for their intended use.
3. Relative to specified operations, the a priori expectation of data quality.

Another aspect of data integrity is the assurance that data can only be accessed and altered by those authorized to do so. Often such integrity is ensured by use of a number referred to as a Message Integrity Code or Message Authentication Code. These are abbreviated MIC and MAC respectively. In Cryptography and Information Security in general, integrity refers to the validity of data. Integrity can be compromised in two main ways:

- Malicious Altering:

    a. An attacker alters the account number in a bank transaction
    a. Forging an identity document

- Accidental Altering:

    a. Transmission Errors
    b. Hard Disk Crash

Specifically, data integrity in a relational database is concerned with three aspects of the data in a database:

- Accuracy
- Correctness
- Validity

Availability

It is defined as the Assets to be available to authorized parties whenever and however needed. It forms one of the major parts of comprehensive internet threats report due to the fact that without proper availability of the data at the right instance, its existence becomes miniscule.

Authenticity

It requires that a computer system be able to verify the identity of a user. In computer security, authentication is the process of attempting to verify the digital identity of the sender of a communication such as a request to log in. The sender being authenticated may be a person using a computer, a computer itself or a computer program. A blind credential, in contrast, does not establish identity at all, but only a narrow right or status of the user or program.

The problem of authorization is often thought to be identical to that of authentication; many widely adopted standard security protocols, obligatory regulations, and even statutes are based on this assumption. However, more precise usage describes authentication as the process of verifying a person's identity, while authorization is the process of verifying that a known person has the authority to perform a certain operation. Authentication, therefore, must precede authorization. For example, when you show proper identification to a bank teller, the teller could authenticate you, and you would be authorized to access information about your bank accounts. You would not be authorized to access accounts that are not your own.

Types of Threats

Interruption

An asset of the system is destroyed or becomes unavailable or unusable (AOG).

Attack on Availability

Destruction of hardware

Cutting of a Communication Line

Disabling the file management system

Interception

An unauthorized party gains access to an asset

Attack on Confidentiality

Wiretapping to capture data in a network
Illicit copying of files or programs

Modification

An unauthorized party not only gains access but tampers with an asset

Attack on Integrity

Changing values in a data file
Altering a program so that it performs differently
Modifying the content of messages being transmitted in a network

Fabrication

An unauthorized party inserts counterfeit objects into the system

Attack on Authenticity

Insertion of spurious messages in a network
Addition of records to a file

4.3 Case Studies

David L. Smith, a 31-year old New Jersey programmer was accused of unleashing the "Melissa" computer virus, a Visual Basic for Application or VBA based worm. This virus was propagated by deliberately posting an infected document to an alt.sex usenet newsgroup from a stolen AOL account. He constructed the virus to evade anti-virus software and to infect computers using Microsoft Windows and Word programs. The Melissa virus appeared on thousands of email systems on March 26, 1999, disguised as an important message from a colleague or friend. The virus was designed to send an infected E-mail to the first 50 E-mail addresses on the users' Microsoft Outlook address book. Each infected computer would infect 50 additional computers, which in turn would infect another 50 computers. The virus proliferated rapidly and exponentially, resulting in substantial interruption and impairment of pubic communications and services. Many system administrators had to disconnect their computer system from the internet. Companies such as Microsoft, Intel, Lockheed Martin and Lucent Technologies were forced to shut down their E-mail gateways due to the vast amount of email the virus was generating. To date, the Melissa virus is the most costly outbreak, causing more than $400 million in damages to North American businesses.
Smith was one of the first persons ever to be prosecuted for writing a virus. He was sentenced to 20 months in federal prison and a fine of $5,000. He was also ordered to serve three years of supervised release after completion of his prison sentence.

The investigation was conducted by members of the New Jersey State Police High Technology Crime Unit, the Federal Bureau of Investigations

(FBI), the Justice Department's Computer Crime and Intellectual Property Section, and the Defense Criminal Investigative service.

Melissa can spread on word processor Microsoft Word 97 and Word 2000. It can mass-mail itself from E-mail client (MUA) Microsoft Outlook 97 or Outlook 98. The worm does not work on any other versions of Word, including Word 95, nor can it mass-mail itself via any other e-mail client, even Outlook Express.

If a Word Document containing the virus, either LIST.DOC or another infected file, is downloaded and opened, then the macro in the document runs and attempts to mass mail itself.

4.4 Introduction to IP Addresses

The key to understanding IP, and all of the issues related to IP, is knowing what a routing table looks like and the effects each IP topic has on the entries in a routing table. To begin with, let's review the basics. IP Addresses are 32 bit numbers, most commonly represented in dotted decimal notation (xxx.xxx.xxx.xxx). Each decimal number represents eight bits of binary data, and therefore can have a decimal value between 0 and 255. IP Addresses most commonly come as class A, B, or C. It's the value of the first number of the IP Address that determines the class to which a given IP Address belongs. Class D Addresses are used for multi-cast applications.

The class of an address defines which portion of the address identifies the Network number and which portion identifies the Host, as illustrated above, as N and H.

So, without any subnetting, a routing table will keep track of a) network numbers, b) the next hop router to use to get to that network, and c) the interface this next hop router is reachable through. A simple network with the corresponding routing table for a Cisco router is illustrated below.

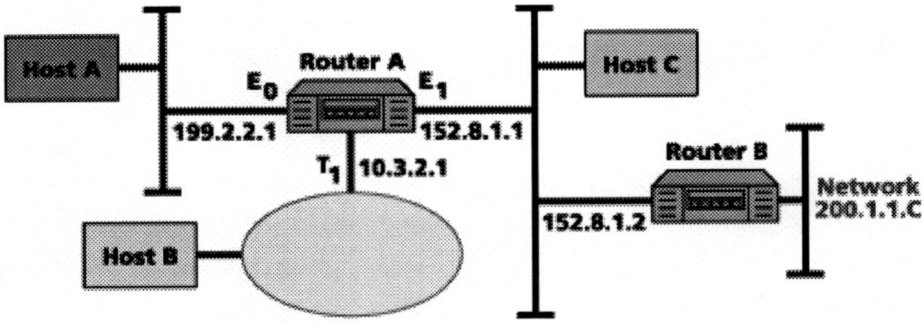

Src: www.scunetix.com

The first column of the routing table indicates how the network number was discovered. C stands for Connected and I indicates the network was learned from the IGRP routing protocol. The important thing to realize is that while a routing table keeps track of network numbers, no one assigns a network number to any piece of equipment. Every interface of a router or host connected on the network must have an IP Address and a subnet mask defined (many pieces of equipment will assign a default subnet mask if none is applied). From this IP Address and subnet mask, the network number is derived by the IP stack and tracked in the routing table.

Routing tables can get very large. Internet backbone routers can have over 40,000 routes defined in them. In most corporate networks, the routing table is much smaller, as there are not so many subnets that need to be reached.

IP Addresses are used to deliver packets of data across a network and have what is termed end-to-end significance. This means that the source and destination IP Address remains constant as the packet traverses a network. Each time a packet travels through a router, the router will reference it's routing table to see if it can match the network number of the destination IP Address with an entry in its routing table. If a match is found, the packet is forwarded to the next hop router for the destination network in question (note that a router does not necessarily know the complete path from source to destination--it just knows the next hop router to go to). If a match is not found, one of two things happens. The packet may be forwarded to the router defined as the default gateway, or the packet may be dropped by the router. (In the language of TCP/IP, a gateway is a router.)

Packets are forwarded to a default router in the belief that the default router has more network information in its routing table and will therefore be able to route the packet correctly on to its final destination. This is typically used when connecting a LAN with PCs on it to the Internet. Each PC will have the router that connects the LAN to the Internet defined as its default gateway.

A default gateway is seen in a routing table of a host as follows: the default route 0.0.0.0 will be listed as the destination network, and the IP Address of the default gateway will be listed as the next hop router.

If the source and destination IP Addresses remain constant as the packet works its way through the network, how is the next hop router addressed? In a LAN environment this is handled by the MAC (Media Access Control) address, as illustrated below. The key point is that the MAC Addresses will change every time a packet travels though a router, however, the IP Addresses will remain constant.

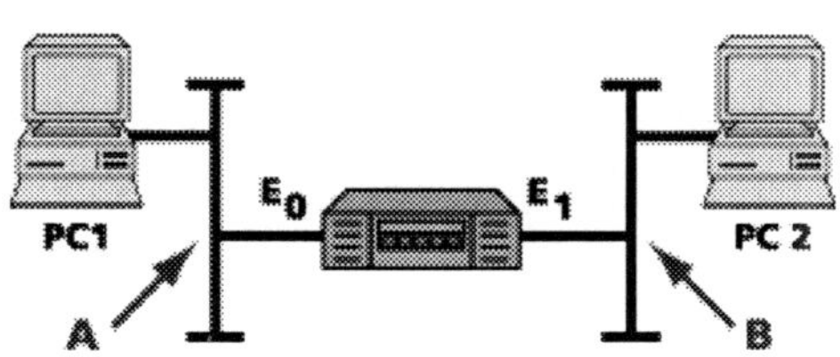

Src: www.acunetix.com

4.5 Finding IP Address of a Remote System

To trace the originating IP Address of an E-mail message, first you need to examine the Internet header of the mail message. This information is generally not visible by default when an E-mail message is printed: see the preceding tip for suggestions on viewing Internet Headers in E-mail messages.

After you identify the originating IP Address, the next question is: to whom does this IP Address belong, and what user was assigned to use it at the time the mail message was sent? The first question can be answered using free Internet search tools. One free option is SmartWhoIs. This Web tool is nice because in addition to identifying the company or organization that owns the originating IP Address, it also provides contact address info and the E-mail address of a network administrator.

After identifying the organization that owns an IP Address, don't jump to conclusions: this information may actually tell you very little. This is because IP Addresses are owned by companies that may lease them to users in many different locations across the United States. The owning ISP will have records showing what user was assigned that IP Address at the time the E-mail in question was sent, but this information is protected by law and may not be releasable unless law enforcement agents are requesting it, with necessary warrants or court orders. The recording industry's efforts to sue peer-to-peer file sharers has demonstrated this recently: the RCAA has petitioned the courts (successfully in some cases, unsuccessfully in others) to force ISPs to release identity information for people who used specific IP Addresses to illegally share copyrighted files.

Another possible way of gathering geographic information about IP tracing is through the Visualroute software or by typing trcerte command in the dos prompt followed by the IP Address as given in the figure.

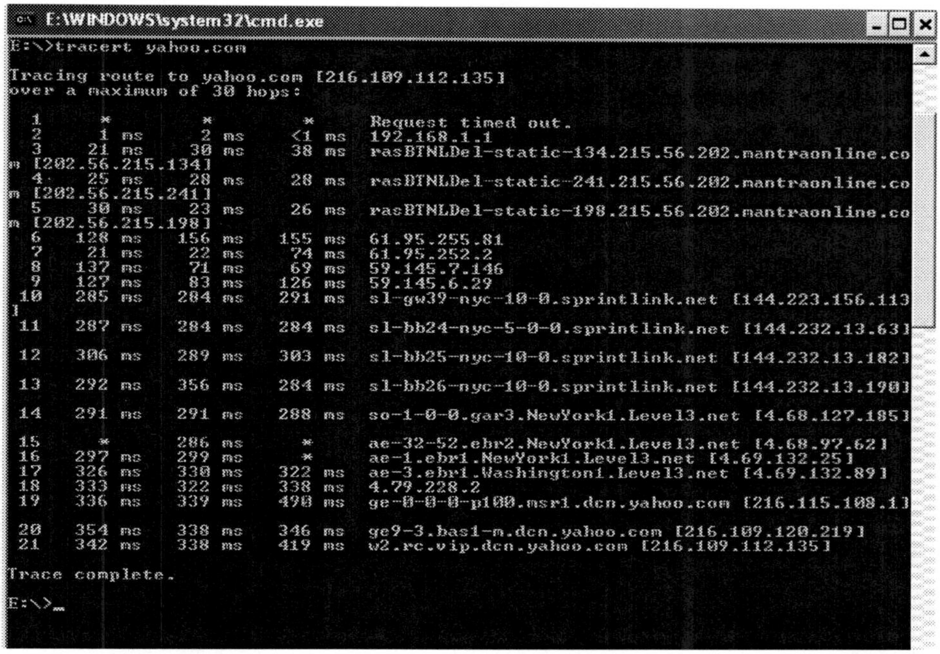

```
E:\WINDOWS\system32\cmd.exe
E:\>tracert yahoo.com

Tracing route to yahoo.com [216.109.112.135]
over a maximum of 30 hops:

  1     *        *        *     Request timed out.
  2     1 ms     2 ms    <1 ms  192.168.1.1
  3    21 ms    30 ms    38 ms  rasBTNLDel-static-134.215.56.202.mantraonline.co
m [202.56.215.134]
  4    25 ms    28 ms    28 ms  rasBTNLDel-static-241.215.56.202.mantraonline.co
m [202.56.215.241]
  5    30 ms    23 ms    26 ms  rasBTNLDel-static-198.215.56.202.mantraonline.co
m [202.56.215.198]
  6   128 ms   156 ms   155 ms  61.95.255.81
  7    21 ms    22 ms    74 ms  61.95.252.2
  8   137 ms    71 ms    69 ms  59.145.7.146
  9   127 ms    83 ms   126 ms  59.145.6.29
 10   285 ms   284 ms   291 ms  sl-gw39-nyc-10-0.sprintlink.net [144.223.156.113
]
 11   287 ms   284 ms   284 ms  sl-bb24-nyc-5-0-0.sprintlink.net [144.232.13.63]

 12   306 ms   289 ms   303 ms  sl-bb25-nyc-10-0.sprintlink.net [144.232.13.182]

 13   292 ms   356 ms   284 ms  sl-bb26-nyc-10-0.sprintlink.net [144.232.13.190]

 14   291 ms   291 ms   288 ms  so-1-0-0.gar3.NewYork1.Level3.net [4.68.127.185]

 15     *      286 ms     *     ae-32-52.ebr2.NewYork1.Level3.net [4.68.97.62]
 16   297 ms   299 ms     *     ae-1.ebr1.NewYork1.Level3.net [4.69.132.25]
 17   326 ms   330 ms   322 ms  ae-3.ebr1.Washington1.Level3.net [4.69.132.89]
 18   333 ms   322 ms   338 ms  4.79.228.2
 19   336 ms   339 ms   490 ms  ge-0-0-0-p100.msr1.dcn.yahoo.com [216.115.108.1]

 20   354 ms   338 ms   346 ms  ge9-3.bas1-m.dcn.yahoo.com [216.109.120.219]
 21   342 ms   338 ms   419 ms  w2.rc.vip.dcn.yahoo.com [216.109.112.135]

Trace complete.

E:\>_
```

traceroute works by increasing the "time-to-live" value of each successive batch of packets sent. The first three packets have a time-to-live (TTL) value of one (implying that they make a single hop). The next three packets have a TTL value of 2, and so on. When a packet passes through a host, normally the host decrements the TTL value by one, and forwards the packet to the next host. When a packet with a TTL of one reaches a host, the host discards the packet and sends an ICMP time exceeded (type 11) packet to the sender. The traceroute utility uses these returning packets to produce a list of hosts that the packets have traversed en route to the destination. traceroute may not list the real hosts, it indicates that the first host is at one hop, the second host at two hops. IP does not guarantee that all the packets take the same route.

On modern Unix and Linux-based operating systems, the traceroute utility by default uses UDP datagrams with a destination port number starting at 33434. The traceroute utility usually has an option to specify use of ICMP echo request (type 8) instead, as used by the Windows tracert utility. There are also traceroute implementations that use TCP packets, such as tcptraceroute or Layer Four Trace. A new utility, pathping, was introduced with Windows NT, combining ping and traceroute functionality. Matt's Trace Route (MTR) is an enhanced version of icmp traceroute available for UNIX and Windows systems under a GNU GPL license. All implementations of traceroute rely on ICMP (type 11) packets being sent to the originator.

4.6 Hiding Your Identity

Anonymous web browsing is browsing the World Wide Web without making one's IP Address or any other personally identifiable information available to the websites that one is visiting.

A degree of anonymity can be achieved by using a proxy server. If the proxy server is trusted, anonymity will be retained because only the information on the proxy server is visible to outsiders.

Anonymous web browsing is generally useful to anyone who wants to ensure that their sessions can not be monitored. For instance, it is used to circumvent traffic monitoring by organizations which want to find out or control which web sites employees visit.

When communicating with others over the Internet, it is frequently preferred to not use any sort of identifiable handle (such as a "user name" or other arbitrary way of identifying who is speaking). The most popular worldwide example of this is within the Japanese forum 2channel. The forum prides itself on the total anonymity of those who post to the channel. The administrators of 2channel see the anonymous posting as a real benefit to those who post to the forum, because it is the argument, not the credibility of the author that is being debated. This is in stark contrast to other Internet forums, such as Slashdot. In Slashdot-style forums, the ability to post anonymously is available, but other users of the forum tend to hold the content of the post in a lower regard than they would if the same post was sent by a user with a registered username. The Slashdot forum encourages this tendency by attributing posts like this to "Anonymous Coward", implying that the poster lacks the courage to stand by his or her statement.

When sending messages over the Internet, many people enjoy a sense of anonymity (or at least pseudonymity). Many popular systems, such as Usenet, e-mail, instant messaging, and web forums, and P2P systems, foster this perception because there is often no obvious way for a casual user to connect other users with a "real world" identity.

On a technical level, all computers on the Internet use the Internet Protocol to speak to each other. Two-way communication at the protocol level requires that both parties know the IP Address of the other. If communications are logged (for example, by the owner of a web-based bulletin board) or intercepted, the IP Address of otherwise anonymous recipients may be discovered. Sometimes IP Addresses are exposed directly as a feature of the communication system (often the case on Internet Relay Chat networks). Casual users often do not feel that knowledge of their IP Address is enough for other participants to connect their online activities to their "real world" identities. Depending on their technical, physical, and legal access, a determined party (such a government prosecutor or plaintiff in a lawsuit, or a determined stalker) may be able to do so, especially if they are assisted by the records of the Internet Service Provider which has assigned the IP Address. Some IP Addresses represent a specific computer. Others, due to proxies and Network Address Translation may represent any number of computers or users. It is usually easy to identify which ISP assigned the address, and this may reveal some identifying information about a person, such as geographic location or with the use of geo software the affiliation with a certain organization.

To achieve strong anonymity, intermediate services may be employed to thwart attempts at identification, even by governments. These attempts to use cryptography, passage through multiple legal jurisdictions, and various methods to thwart traffic analysis to achieve this. Examples include anonymous remailers, Anonymous P2P systems, and services of the Anonymizer Company, among others.

Anonymizer is shareware software, which can help to protect the IP Address identity over the web and offer a variety of consumer information security services including:

- Web Proxying
- Encrypted E-mail Services
- Anti-Spyware
- Anti-Phishing / Anti-Pharming
- Enterprise Class Competitive Intelligence Tools

Anonymity through proxy servers is also debatable issue over its relative nature for the following reasons. In using a proxy server (for example, anonymizing HTTP proxy), all data sent to the service being used (for example, HTTP server in a website) must pass through the proxy server before being sent to the service, mostly in unencrypted form. It is therefore possible, and has been demonstrated (see, for example, Sugarcane) for a malicious proxy server to record everything sent to the proxy: including unencrypted logins and passwords.

By chaining proxies which do not reveal data about the original requestor, it is possible to obfuscate activities from the eyes of the user's destination. However, more traces will be left on the intermediate hops, which could be used or offered up to trace the user's activities. If the policies and administrators of these other proxies are unknown, the user may fall victim to a false sense of security just because those details are out of sight and mind.

The bottom line of this is to be wary when using proxy servers, and only use proxy servers of known integrity (e.g., the owner is known and trusted, has a clear privacy policy, etc.), and never use proxy servers of unknown integrity. If there is no choice but to use unknown proxy servers, do not pass any private information (unless it is properly encrypted) through the proxy.

More of an inconvenience than a risk, proxy users may find themselves being blocked from certain websites, as numerous forums and websites block IP Addresses from proxies known to have spammed or trolled the site.

4.7 Analyzing E-mail Headers

Reading E-mail Headers

E-mail headers are the most interesting art of an E-mail message for System Administrators and Engineers. This is arguable but what isn't the fact that headers are the most important part of an E-mail for tracing and diagnosing problems. Headers may look garbled and incomprehensible but that can be said of anything upon first contact.

The ability to read and decipher E-mail headers is a useful skill to learn for tracing messages to their original source and diagnosing many other problems. Headers may contain a lot of information but the most important information will always be contained in every E-mail header. Pragmatically the 'Received' header lines are the most important.

Each intervening MTA adds a Received header.

During all the E-mail processing, headers will be added to the message three times: At composition time, by whatever E-mail program rth is using; when that program hands control off to mail.bieberdorf.edu; and at the transfer from Bieberdorf to Immense. (Normally, the dialup node that retrieves the message doesn't add any headers). Let's watch the evolution of these headers.

As generated by rth's mailer and handed off to mail.bieberdorf.edu:

From: rth@bieberdorf.edu (R.T. Hood)
To: tmh@immense-isp.com
Date: Tue, Mar 18 1997 14:36:14 PST
X-Mailer: Loris v2.32
Subject: Lunch today?

As they are when mail.bieberdorf.edu transmits the message to mailhost.immense-isp.com:

Received: from alpha.bieberdorf.edu (alpha.bieberdorf.edu [124.211.3.11]) by mail.bieberdorf.edu (8.8.5) id 004A21; Tue, Mar 18 1997 14:36:17 -0800 (PST)
From: rth@bieberdorf.edu (R.T. Hood)
To: tmh@immense-isp.com
Date: Tue, Mar 18 1997 14:36:14 PST
Message-Id: <rth031897143614-00000298@mail.bieberdorf.edu>
X-Mailer: Loris v2.32
Subject: Lunch today?

As they are when mailhost.immense-isp.com finishes processing the message and stores it for tmh to retrieve:

Received: from mail.bieberdorf.edu (mail.bieberdorf.edu [124.211.3.78]) by mailhost.immense-isp.com (8.8.5/8.7.2) with ESMTP id LAA20869 for <tmh@immense-isp.com>; Tue, 18 Mar 1997 14:39:24 -0800 (PST)
Received: from alpha.bieberdorf.edu (alpha.bieberdorf.edu [124.211.3.11]) by mail.bieberdorf.edu (8.8.5) id 004A21; Tue, Mar 18 1997 14:36:17 -0800 (PST)
From: rth@bieberdorf.edu (R.T. Hood)
To: tmh@immense-isp.com
Date: Tue, Mar 18 1997 14:36:14 PST
Message-Id: <rth031897143614-00000298@mail.bieberdorf.edu>
X-Mailer: Loris v2.32
Subject: Lunch today?

This last set of headers is the one that tmh sees on the letter when he downloads and reads his mail. Here's a line-by-line analysis of these headers and exactly what each one means.

Received: from mail.bieberdorf.edu

This piece of mail was received from a machine calling itself mail.bieberdorf.edu...
(mail.bieberdorf.edu [124.211.3.78])
...which is really named mail.bieberdorf.edu (i.e., it identified itself correctly---see Section whatever for more on this) and has the IP Address 124.211.3.78.

by mailhost.immense-isp.com (8.8.5/8.7.2)

The machine that did the receiving was mailhost.immense-isp.com; it's running a mail program called sendmail, version 8.8.5/8.7.2 (don't worry about what the version numbers mean unless you already know).

with ESMTP id LAA20869

The receiving machine assigned the ID number LAA20869 to the message. (This is used internally by the machine---it's something an administrator would need to know to look up the message in the machine's log files, but it's not usually meaningful to anyone else).

for <tmh@immense-isp.com>;

The message was addressed to tmh@immense-isp.com. Note that this header is not related to the To: line (see Section Whatever).

Tue, 18 Mar 1997 14:39:24 -0800 (PST)

This mail transfer happened on Tuesday, March 18, 1997, at 14:39:24 (2:39:24 in the afternoon) Pacific Standard Time (which is 8 hours behind Greenwich Mean Time; hence the "-0800").

Received: from alpha.bieberdorf.edu (alpha.bieberdorf.edu [124.211.3.11]) by mail.bieberdorf.edu (8.8.5) id 004A21; Tue, Mar 18 1997 14:36:17 -0800 (PST)

This line documents the mail handoff from alpha.bieberdorf.edu (rth's workstation) to mail.bieberdorf.edu; this handoff happened at 14:36:17 Pacific Standard Time. The sending machine called itself alpha.bieberdorf.edu; it really is called alpha.bieberdorf.edu, and its IP Address is 124.211.3.11. Bieberdorf's mail server is running sendmail version 8.8.5, and it assigned the ID number 004A21 to this letter for internal processing.

From: rth@bieberdorf.edu (R.T. Hood)

The mail was sent by rth@bieberdorf.edu, who gives his real name as R.T. Hood.

To: tmh@immense-isp.com

The letter is addressed to tmh@immense-isp.com.

Date: Tue, Mar 18 1997 14:36:14 PST

The message was composed at 14:36:14 Pacific Standard Time on Tuesday, March 18, 1997.

Message-Id: <rth031897143614-00000298@mail.bieberdorf.edu>

The message has been given this number (by mail.bieberdorf.edu) to identify it. This ID is different from the SMTP and ESMTP ID numbers in the Received: headers because it is attached to this message for life; the other IDs are only associated with specific mail transactions at specific machines, so that one machine's ID number means nothing to another machine. Sometimes (as in this example) the Message-ID has the sender's E-mail address embedded in it; more often it has no intelligible meaning of its own.

X-Mailer: Loris v2.32

The message was sent using a program called Loris, version 2.32.
Subject: Lunch today?
Self-explanatory

4.8 Tracking E-mails

Tracing an E-mail Address is possible in the following ways even If you do not have an actual E-mail message, but only have an E-mail address, you can trace the address its E-mail Server. However it should be noted that E-mail addresses can be easily forged, the results from tracing an E-mail address may not be related to the true sender.

In most cases, using an E-mail-tracking tool like eMailTrackerPro to trace an E-mail message you have received is your best option. To trace an E-mail message received by someone else, have them forward the message to you as an attachment (just forwarding the message itself will show them as the sender). You can then open the attached message and copy the email header, start eMailTrackerPro and paste the header for analysis.

Every received E-mail has Internet Headers. Using Microsoft Outlook as an example (other mail programs are very similar), just follow these steps to view the headers:

Right-click on the mail message that is still in your Outlook Inbox
Select 'Options...' from the resulting popup menu
Examine the 'Internet Headers' in the resulting 'Message Options' dialog

TIP: Right-click in the 'Internet Headers' field and click on 'Select All' in the popup menu (or type Ctrl-A). Then right-click again and click on 'Copy' in the popup menu (or type Ctrl-C). Finally, paste all the Internet Headers into your favorite text editor for full examination (such as 'Notepad', included with Windows).

Example: What you see will be very similar to the following (with 'line numbers' added for clarity and discussion in following sections):

1: Received: from tes1a623.OneMail.com.sg ([203.127.89.129]) by visualroute.com (8.11.6) id f9CIVSk24480; Tue, 12 Oct 2004 12:31:29 -0600 (MDT)
2: Message-Id: <200110121831.f9CIVSk24480@s2.domain.com>
3: Received: from drb.com (IIM1608 [203.127.89.138]) by tes1a623.OneMail.com.sg with SMTP (Microsoft Exchange Internet Mail Service Version 5.5.2448.0)
4: id 4XNK9ATR; Wed, 13 Oct 2004 01:19:10 +0800
5: From: paylesslongdistance@somedomain.com
6: To: <>
7: Subject: Long Distance - 4.9 cents per min - NO FEES!
8: Date: Tue, 12 Oct 2004 13:24:26 -0400
9: X-Sender: paylesslongdistance@yahoo.com

10: X-Mailer: QUALCOMM Windows Eudora Pro Version 4.1
11: Content-Type: text/plain; charset="us-ascii"
12: X-Priority: 3
13: X-MSMail-Priority: Normal
14: X-UIDL: 8`Y!!0GR!!"?H"!k:O!!
15: Status: U

Header Line Syntax: The Internet Header Fields are just a series of text lines, where each line looks like:

Header-Name: Header-Value

And if a line starts with a tab or spaces, like line 4 above, that line is a continuation of the previous Header-Value line. So, the Header-Name Received in line 3 has a Header-Value that spans lines 3 and 4.

The most important header field for tracking purposes is the Received header field, which usually has syntax similar to:

Received: from ? by ? via ? with ? id ? for ? ; date-time

Where from, by, via, with, id, and for are all tokens with values within a single Header-Value, which may span multiple lines. Note: Some mail servers may not include all of these tokens -- or additional tokens/values may be added to this field, but now you are prepared to break it apart and understand it.

Every time an E-mail moves through a new mail server, a new Received header line (and
possibly other header lines, like line 2 above) is added to the beginning of the headers list. This is similar to FedEx package tracking, when your package enters a new sorting facility and is 'swiped' through a tracking machine.

This means that as you read the Received headers from top to bottom, that you are gradually moving closer to the computer/person that sent you the E-mail.

But please note that as you read through the Received header fields and get closer to the computer/person that sent you the E-mail, you need to consider the possibility that the sender added one or more false Received header lines to the list (at the time, the senders beginning of the list) in an attempt to redirect you to another location and prevent you from finding the true sender. But, now that you know false header lines are possible, just stay alert.

You will probably find it very useful to break a single Received line into multiple lines, with one token per line. Namely, the header line:

Received: from tes1a623.OneMail.com.sg ([203.127.89.129]) by visualroute.com (8.11.6) id f9CIVSk24480; Tue, 12 Oct 2004 12:31:29 -0600 (MDT)

is much easier to read and understand when formatted so that each token is on a new line, as in:

Received:

from tes1a623.OneMail.com.sg ([203.127.89.129])
by visualroute.com (8.11.6)
id f9CIVSk24480
; Tue, 12 Oct 2004 12:31:29 -0600 (MDT)

For tracking purposes, we are most interested in the form and by tokens in the Received header field. In general, you are looking for a pattern similar to:

Received: from BBB (dns-name [ip-address]) by AAA ...
Received: from CCC (dns-name [ip-address]) by BBB ...
Received: from DDD (dns-name [ip-address]) by CCC ...

In other words, mail server AAA received the E-mail from BBB and provides as much information about BBB, including the IP Address BBB used to connect to AAA. This patterns repeats itself on each Received line. The syntax of the from token most times looks like:

name (dns-name [ip-address])

Where: name is the name the computer has named itself. Most of the time we never look at this name because it can be intentionally misnamed in an attempt to foil your tracking (but it may leak the windows computer name). dns-name is the reverse dns lookup on the IP-Address. IP-Address is the IP-Address of the computer used to connect to the mail server that generated this Received header line. So, the IP-Address is gold to us for tracking purposes.

The by token syntax just provides us with the name that the mail server gives itself. But since the last mail server could be under the control of a spammer, we should not trust this name.

So, what is crucial for tracking, is to pay attention to the trail of IP-Address in the from tokens and not necessarily the host name provided to us in the by tokens. Hopefully an example will make the reason why very clear:

1: Received: from tes1a623.OneMail.com.sg ([203.127.89.129]) by visualroute.com (8.11.6) id f9CIVSk24480; Tue, 12 Oct 2004 12:31:29 -0600 (MDT)
3: Received: from drb.com (IIM1608 [203.127.89.138]) by tes1a623.OneMail.com.sg with SMTP (Microsoft Exchange Internet Mail Service Version 5.5.2448.0)

If you ignore line 1, you would conclude from line 3 that mail server tes1a623.OneMail.com.sg sent you an E-mail, but this would be wrong. When you trace to the host name tes1a623.OneMail.com.sg, you are actually tracing to the IP Address lookup on that host name, which is 192.9.200.230. But as you can see from line 1, the IP Address used was really 203.127.89.129. Do not be fooled by this attempted misdirection by spammers and fraudsters.

Determine the IP Address of the Sender: Using the example email headers above and analyzing the Received header lines we can conclude:

A Visualware employee received an email

which came from visualroute.com (line 1)
which came from tes1a623.OneMail.com.sg (line 1; line 3 confirms)
but whose ip-address used was 203.127.89.129 (line 1)
which came from drb.com/IIM1608 (line 3)
but whose ip-address used was 203.127.89.138 (line 3)
So, we have just tracked this email to the source -- IP Address 203.127.89.138.

4.9 Information Gathering

There are a number of techniques and processes available when carrying out a Passive Information Gathering exercise. Here we will detail the most relevant techniques and endeavour to elaborate both the thought processes necessary to identify the leaked information, and to evaluate the relative security risks associated with the leakage.

A lot of important information can be passively harvested and subsequently used in a direct attack or to reinforce other attacks targeted at an organisation. Depending upon the source, information such as current service patching levels, internal network architecture layout and account details can be easily obtained. Just as importantly, with a little insight as to where this information is obtained and the level of detail of information, an organisation can often rectify this information leakage simply and quickly.

The most critical phases or investigation processes revolve around the accessibility of various online resources such as:

- **Internet Service Registration:** The global registration and maintenance of IP Address information.
- **Domain Name System:** Local and global registration and maintenance of host naming.
- **Search Engines:** The specialist retrieval of distributed material relating to an organization or their employees.
- **E-mail Systems:** The information contained within each email delivery process.

- **Naming Conventions:** The way an organization encodes or categorises the services their online hosts provide.
- **Website Analysis:** The information intentionally made public that may pose a risk to security.

Internet Service Registration

In order to access networked resources over the Internet, every accessible host must have a unique and routable IP Address. Whilst there is slow take-up of IPv6, IPv4 is still the de-facto standard and will be considered in this document. This IP Address takes the form of xxx.xxx.xxx.xxx, where "xxx" may be some value between 0 and 255. In order to simplify host addressing, and to make hosts more memorable, services exist that associate IP Addresses to a unique domain name (for instance www.abcexample.com).
Both the registration of IP Addresses and domain names are coordinated at an international level. In order to administer these IP Addresses (or address ranges) and domain names, organizations must supply administrative details including physical billing addresses and technical contact information. By necessity, this information is publicly available and may be requested by anyone over the Internet. Consequently, these international databases may are queried and form the first stages of the Passive Information Gathering exercise.

Dividing the responsibility between them, there are exist four Regional Internet Registries (RIR). These RIRs provide allocation and registration services and support the operation of the Internet globally. Responsibilities include the allocation of Internet (IP) address space, autonomous system numbers (ASNs) and the management of reverse domain name space.

WHOIS

There are two primary WHOIS resources – Network Service-Based and Name Service-Based. As the names suggest, one focuses upon the registration and management of individual/blocks of IP Addresses (note that a block or range of IP Addresses is commonly referred to as a "netblock"), while the other focuses upon the registration and management of domain names.

The core RIR WHOIS services provide a mechanism for finding contact and registration information for resources registered with the individual registries. These databases contain IP Addresses, Autonomous System (AS) numbers, organisations or customers that are associated with these resources, and related Points of Contact (POC).

The RIR WHOIS services will typically not locate any domain-related information or any information relating to military networks. For domain name lookups, various online resources exist – however www.internic.net/whois.html and www.uwhois.com are recommended for non-military, and whois.nic.mil for military network information.

Domain Name System

Since host names are easier to remember than IP Addresses, they are the preferred method of addressing hosts. The Domain Name System (DNS) is a service designed to provide a link between an IP Address and a unique host name.

Several implementations of DNS are used on the Internet and for internal corporate name resolution. The most common DNS service is BIND (named after "The Berkeley Internet Name Daemon"), and most other DNS services provide BIND level functionality/compatibility by default.

Although multiple security vulnerabilities have been identified with the protocol and coded implementation of the service, exploitation of these vulnerabilities is not in any way "passive". Instead, in this section we will focus upon the methods available to query these services, and evaluate the significance of the information returned.

Given the nature of the service, querying DNS records can provide a wealth of information to an attacker in a few short moments. Most critical to the service is the disclosure of multiple IP and naming records for a single queried domain. Loosely implemented name services may also yield more information than expected.

Querying DNS

The most common (and popular) method of querying BIND services is through the use of the "dig" tool. This tool is freely distributed as part of BIND and is installed by default on most UNIX based operating systems. Dig can be used to resolve the names of hosts into IP Addresses, and reverse resolve IP Addresses into names. In addition, dig can also be used to gather version information from name servers which may be used to aid exploitation of the host.

Utilities such as dig can perform other DNS services, such as a Zone Transfers. Authoritative name-servers for a domain retrieve zone files (complete records) from other name-servers using Zone Transfers. By manually conducting a zone transfer, an attacker can gain valuable information about all systems and addresses in the domain from the domain name server.

Another query tool in the arsenal of passive information gathering tools is nslookup (short for "Name Service Lookup"), and comes as standard on most operating systems. Nslookup is almost as flexible as dig, but provides a simpler default method of identifying primary hosts such as Mail and DNS servers.

Search Engines

The use of Search Engines is vital for harvesting the often widely distributed cache of public material relating to the organization under analysis. There is a popular saying in the computer underground when it comes to passive information gathering: "Google is your friend". It is surprising what can be unearthed using an advanced public Search Engine, particularly one as sophisticated as Google. Not only will Google allow you to search for specific text strings, it can also cache page content. Therefore, even after an offending or insecure page has been withdrawn from a web site, an attacker can still call up and analyze the cached page content.

Quite often other informational gems appear through conventional searching techniques. Past investigational queries have discovered client firewall configuration manuals, internal auditing manuals and confidential financial analysis documents when searching for different permutations of the organization's name, and restricting the search to .doc and .xls file extensions.

Searching newsgroups and other public posting areas often reveals infrastructure details as the organisation's administrators pose or answer questions relating to specific components of their network or software.

For example, one organisation had a public posting providing advice on getting a new security patch for AIX systems to work - telling the members of the newsgroup that the only way they managed to get a service functioning was by removing certain other "less likely to be exploited" security patches. Not only did this describe the type and patch level of their server, but also went on to explain what patches they had removed. In other cases, the details can be used for Social Engineering or extortion purposes.

Network Investigation Search Engines

There are a number of specialist search engines that focus upon information gathered about the health of the Internet and hosts that are frequently accessed. One popular site is Netcraft (http://www.netcraft.com), which specializes in the analysis of web hosts, the versions of the software they are running, and system uptime. One particular tool allows you to search for a particular string in the host's name (e.g., Microsoft. or .cisco.com etc.) – and retrieve a list of all known web-enabled systems. An example screenshot is shown below:

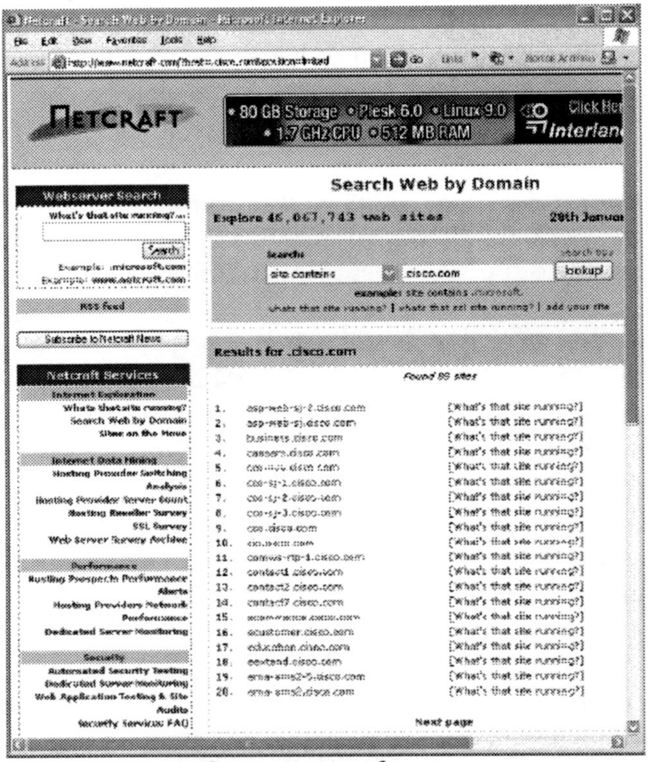

Src: www.netcraft.com

E-mail Systems

E-mail hosts are probably the most important business critical systems organisations operate which are exposed to the Internet. While web sites present the public face of the organisation or services to their customers, their mail systems provide the essential business communications. In general, mail systems are often poorly secured and probably less understood by their administrators than web services.

A lot of information about an organisation can be gathered through passive analysis of the mail systems. In particular, enumeration of user accounts and mapping of the internal network.

SMTP Headers

During a Passive Information Gathering exercise, a lot of information may be obtained from the analysis of E-mail headers. The SMTP protocol stipulates that E-mail headers contain routing and address information for the safe delivery (and consequently reply) of the E-mail message.

To manage E-mail within a global organisation, multiple E-mail servers are frequently utilized. As an E-mail is routed internally, STMP headers are appended to the E-mail message. E-mail headers are valuable for providing insight into internal server naming, IP numbering schemes, the type and version of content filter or anti-virus solution, service patch levels and even the version of the client's mail client.

Naming Conventions

An important aspect of passive information gathering, and more subtle than many of the techniques described previously, is the observation and analysis of the actual names used to define each networked host or service. The naming convention used by an organisation can provide valuable insight to the use and position of hosts within an organisation. In extreme cases, poor naming conventions can even reveal the type of hardware used.

The most common mistakes include:

- The use of physical location information (e.g., London.example.com and HQOffice034.example.com) or common location shorthand (e.g., LONmail.example.com and ATLmail.example.com).
- The use of operations system information (e.g., the Microsoft Windows 2000 host w2k034.example.com and the HP Unix server HPUXserver.example.com).
- The use of functional information (e.g., FW.example.com for the firewall and OWA.example.com for the Outlook Web-mail Application server).
- The use of hardware manufacturer information (e.g., a Dell CPx laptop called DELLCPX002.example.com, or Cisco6100.example.com for a Cisco 6100 network manageable switch).

- The use of network location information (e.g., fwDMZ1.example.com and fwDMZ2.example.com)
- The use of common sequences – such as naming all servers after the planets (e.g., mars.example.com and venus.example.com) or ancient gods (e.g., titan.example.com and zeus.example.com)

For internal naming conventions, even smaller organisations should resist the temptation to use host names such as "johnscomputer" or "reception". Although such conventions make management easier in the short term, they can also raise the temptation for internal users to go snooping through Network Neighbourhood for the finance directors' computer or the personnel departments system holding salary details. Additionally, location based names are of limited value when office layouts change.

The naming conventions used and implemented by an organisation will always be a compromise between attacker obscurity and something internal users can remember. Most organisations will settle on a host naming convention that is memorable and easy to predict, thus information will always be leaked in some form. It is important however, to ensure that valuable information about the host's role or importance within the organisation is not readily discernable.

Trace Route

The importance of choosing a good naming convention is most valuable when seen from an attacker's perspective, using tools that rely upon reverse lookups. One such tool is Traceroute.

Traceroute is supplied with almost all operating systems although the actual name may differ depending on the particular flavour of operating system (e.g., most UNIX systems use the tool name "traceroute" while Microsoft operating systems use the shortened name of "tracert"). The tool is designed to show all the "hops" (intermediary network devices) that network traffic must go through to reach the final destination as discussed in the given sections of the book.

Web Site Analysis

As most organisations maintain large or complex Internet visible websites, the opportunity to inadvertently leak internal information is usually high. As such, detailed analysis of website content is valuable to an attacker.

The most effective way of analyzing an organisations web site is to create a local mirror of the site content. This often requires the use of an automated tool to navigate the site and pull across a copy of every file referenced or linked to by the website. Obviously, such a task requires many consecutive connections and could be interpreted as intrusive. However, this type of activity is fairly common as both search engines and "offline web readers" will frequently perform this task. Therefore, from a passive information gathering perspective, such an activity is unlikely to be discovered or perceived as a threat or prelude to attack. In fact, for many organisations this type of activity may be perceived favourably as it increases the number of "hits" against the site and pleases internal PR staff.

The process of automatically retrieving web site content and analyzing the content is commonly referred to as "Web Scraping". Web scraping, along with other manual investigation techniques can reveal a great deal of information about the organisation. Typical findings include:

- The harvesting of names and E-mail addresses that can be later used for automated brute-force attacks or Social Engineering.
- The observation of internal developer's comments pertaining to the coding or operation of the sites content.
- Signatures of development tools contained within Meta-tags or other "hidden" fields.
- Commented or disabled code - linking to normally inaccessible site content or hosts.
- Links to data file URL's or other in-appropriately secured content (e.g., Form submission log files).
- References to internal development hosts or connectivity methods.

- The inclusion of badly coded site content that includes snippets of server interpreted code.
- The detail and nature of error pages in response to non-existent content requests and "dead" URL's.
- Links to external affiliated sites and hosts that may prove "softer" targets in later attacks.
- The existence of documents and other binary data that may contain internal information (e.g., auditing guides, network layout diagrams).

It is thus important that all content posted by an organization be analyzed for any unintentional disclosure. Any analysis is largely dependant upon the volume of information presented by the organization.

Passive information gathering is a vital stage in any black-box or zero-knowledge pen testing exercise, and consequently should form an important phase of any security assessment. The leaked information discovered during this analysis is often used by attackers to coordinate or plan more advanced attacks. Consequently, every effort should be taken by an organisation to ensure that the information leakage is limited as much as practically possible.

4.10 PORT Scanning

In TCP/IP terminology, a port is a software identifier that corresponds to a specific application or protocol running on a host. For example, by default HTTP uses port 80. An edge router typically provides the only IP Address for an internal network. All packets for hosts on the internal network are addressed to the router's WAN IP Address. Therefore, the router determines where to deliver a packet on its local network in part by looking at the port requested by the packet and then sending the packet to the host running the corresponding application. (It's actually a little more complicated than this because more than one computer may be using the same protocol or application, in which case the router needs to examine the destination host name as well.)

More Information

An open port is any port for which packets will be accepted. Packets for closed ports are dropped. Because packets for open ports are passed through the edge router not an internal network, they provide an access tunnel through any defenses the router might have. If a cracker can determine which ports are open through an edge router, he or she has identified potential avenues for system attacks. The port numbers used by protocols and applications are generally not kept secret. In fact, those ports that are used by TCP/IP are called well known ports.

It is possible, and sometimes desirable, to use a port other than the well known port for a protocol. For example, if you have multiple Web servers on a network (and they are not clones of one another), then you want only one of those servers to use port 80. The others need to use a different port -- which you can code into its IP Address -- so that each Web server can receive the correct packets. If you see an IP Address in the form X.X.X.X:9999, where the 9s are replaced with a number, then you know you're seeing a redirection from a standard port. For example, http://192.168.1.101:8080 indicates that HTTP traffic is intended for port 8080 on the host with IP Address 192.168.1.101. (Don't try this address; as you probably recognize, it's an internal, nonrouteable address used just for this example).

As a first example of a port scan, take a look at the following figure, which contains the result of a port scan on a host that has open ports for the most common TCP/IP protocols. The scan result shows the port numbers along with the protocols or applications that are listening for traffic on each port.

```
Port Scanning host: 192.168.1.100

     open Port:                    21          ftp
     open Port:                    22          ssh
     open Port:                    80          http
     open Port:                    139         netbis-ssn
     open Port:                    427         svrlc
     open Port:                    515         printer
     open Port:                    548         afpvertcp
     open Port:                    631         ipp
     open Port:                    3031        eppc
Port Scan has cmpleted ...
```

A port scan of a wide open host

```
Port Scanning host: 192.168.1.1

     open Port:                    80          http
     open Port:                    2468        qip-msgd
     open Port:                    5678        rrac
     open Port:                    6688
Port Scan has cmpleted ...
```

The result of a port scan on an edge router

Today, network administrators know better than to leave unused ports open. A port scan on an edge router, such as that in the given figure, is likely to show very few open ports. This particular router allows Web traffic through, but little else.

One of the ironies of computer security work is that the tools that crackers use to perform port scans and other information gathering activities are also useful for troubleshooting networks and performing penetration testing. Therefore, the tools are widely and legally available, and, in some cases, are actually supplied with an operating system.

This means that to defend against a port scan, you need to be very proactive. First, on all hosts close all ports that will not be used. To do so, you shut down the services (the applications or operating system daemons) that run on those ports. Also block traffic for all unnecessary ports using a firewall on your edge router.

Reality Check: If you have a good, well-configured firewall on your edge router or as a stand-alone firewall appliance, do you need firewalls on the hosts on your internal network? Probably not. However, home users that are connected directly to the Internet without going through a firewall-equipped router do need their own firewalls. Even a dial-up connection isn't safe from port scans. The ranges of IP Addresses used by major ISPs are well known at this point, and script kiddies run software that attempts port scans through the entire range of addresses automatically.

4.11 Daemon Banner Grabbing

Daemon is basically a program that listens for incoming connections on a specific port. Some daemons may receive commands from you and interact with you, others may simply spew out some text/binary and quit.

We will describe Daemon Banner Grabbing with a reference example. We will use the Sendmail command to summarize Dameon Banner and related commands. Through the Sendmail programs we would be able to solve the following riddle: How can I create authentically looking fake mails?
Sending mail does not require you to have an account on the machine you're sending the mail from (the mail server, not your computer). All you need to know is the IP Address/ Hostname of the mail server and Sendmail commands.

So far we assume that you know the IP/hostname of your target. If you still don't know this important detail, please find out from the previous sections of the book.

Our target outgoing mail server is mailgw.someone.com on port 25.

First, let's telnet into that port by either typing 'telnet mailgw.someone.com 25' (without the quotes) on a standard Unix text-based system, running C:\Windows\telnet.exe or any telnet application and typing in mailgw.someone.com in the host field and 25 in the port field, or executing your favorite telnet application from XWindows (a graphical interface for Unix. If you're smart enough to be running some version of Unix you shouldn't have a hard time finding one. If you don't like the default telnet programs you could always go to www.linuxberg.com and grab one) and typing in the correct details (host and port).

Note about VT: you might be asked to choose a terminal type during the connection process. Something with VT and some number in it.

VT stands for Virtual Terminal. Since there are several types of terminals (all sorts of monitors, old printer terminals etc') you are asked to choose a terminal type (compatibility issues). VT100 should suite most people just fine.

Note about shell accounts: if you're not running Unix and you wish to use Unix tools on Unix systems while you work, telnet to nether.net on port 23, login as newuser and get yourself a free shell account. If you'd rather user Window's tools go ahead (things will work faster since the tools are actually located on your machine, not on some distant computer which runs a shell account), but we still recommend that you will get a shell account at nether.net (in fact they teach you a lot of great Unix-newbies stuff when you sign up).

Note about Telneting from Macintosh: Macintosh does not come with a Telnet program. However, you can download one from: http://www.ncsa.uiuc.edu/SDG/Software/MacTelnet/ (thanks to little_v for this one!).

Now, let's see what we get after we telnet to mailgw.someone.com:25 (in this case, the character: stands for 'on port', so mailgw.someone.com:25 means mailgw.someone.com on port 25).

220 alpha.someone.com ESMTP Sendmail 8.9.3/8.8.6; Thu, 8 Jul 1999 21:46:04 +0000 (GMT).

This is a Daemon Banner and it just gave us tons of valuable pieces of information!
Normally, this info is intended for a client program to determine what version of Sendmail the target is running and how to communicate with it

(the program should know that, for example, every Sendmail version below 7.0.0 uses the command 'halb' instead of the command 'blah', etc').

This daemon banner thing is also great for hackers and crackers, since we can determine what version our target is running.

Analyzing what we have got,
220... we don't know what this is right now...

alpha.someone.com... no luck, can't make anything out of it so far...
ESMTP... SMTP stands for Simple Mail Transfer Protocol. It is the protocol used by E-mail clients to communicate with Sendmail daemons, and this is what we're trying to learn right now. ESMTP is Extended SMTP. It's the same as SMTP, only it contains some more commands. Let's leave this alone for the time being.

Sendmail 8.9.3/8.8.6 – There's something interesting. We got the version of the Sendmail daemon!

The rest is not worth considering as of now.
How do I communicate with this thing?
Let's try typing 'help' (without the quotes). It is normal not to see what you type when you talk to Sendmail since it won't send back your keystrokes. You have to turn on "local echo" in your telnet program in order to see what you type.

```
214-This is Sendmail version 8.9.3
214-Topics:
214-   HELO   EHLO   MAIL   RCPT   DATA
214-   RSET   NOOP   QUIT   HELP   VRFY
214-   EXPN   VERB   ETRN   DSN
214-For more info use "HELP <topic>".
214-To report bugs in the implementation send E-mail to
214-   sendmail-bugs@sendmail.org.
214-For local information send email to Postmaster at your site.
214 End of HELP info
```

By this time you should have guessed that this number (the 220 in the Daemon Banner and the 214 here) is actually a 'message type'. It states the type of the message you got. Each type of message (error because of this, error because of that, help page for this, confirmation message for that etc') has it's own number.
Let's try typing 'help helo'.

214-HELO <hostname>
214-   Introduce yourself.
214 End of HELP info

214 is the message type number for help messages.
So that way you can practically teach yourself what every Sendmail command does. Stop right now, read all the help pages and then continue. It is important that you'll learn how to learn things by yourself. You might see some notes concerning the word RFC(24) and some numbers.
Note about ESMTP: remember that ESMTP thing we came across? You'll be able to get a good clue on what ESMTP is by reading the help pages. They contain tons of great information for newbies as well as pros.

First we need to enter a sender. We do this by typing 'MAIL FROM: <fake E-mail address>' (remove the quotes and replace fake E-mail address with the fake E-mail address of your choice, say... bgates@microsoft.com (but leave the < and the >)).

The mail server should reply with this message:

250 bgates@microsoft.com... Sender ok

Next we type 'RCPT TO: <recipient>'. Replace recipient with the target, say victim@victim.com. We should get

250 victim@victim.com... Recipient ok

You can add recipient by simply doing this command several times, only with different recipients.

Now, let's move on to the actual message body. Type 'data' to start writing the body of the message.

354 Enter mail, end with "." on a line by itself

Now let's type in some stuff...

Subject: fake message (note about this line: in this line you get to determine what subject you want to give for your message).
Hello. This is a fake E-mail message.
I'm bored.
Gimme something to hack!!
.

Now we get this

250 CAA15313 Message accepted for delivery

You must be wondering right now what the heck is that number after the 250. This is called the message ID (or MID). It's just a number, but we'll use them later.

Now, if you were the recepient you would have got a 100% reliably-looking fake mail. OR IS IT?

Let's take a look at what the recepient would get...
Looks like an ordinary message. At least it does to the ordinary user.
Now let's look at the headers.
Headers are a couple of lines which come with every E-mail address. Most of today's E-mail clients show only the simpler parts of the header (sender, subject, date and time etc'), but right now we need the full header.

On Netscape Messanger displaying the full headers is done by going to View ==> Headers ==> All.
On Eudora this is done by clicking on the button which displays the caption when you put your mouse cursor above it for a second or two.

Compuserve automatically displays the full header.

On Outlook, right click the message on your inbox, choose properties and choose details.

On pine, you should have an option somewhere in the configuration screens that let's you choose what kind of header you want to view (full or briefed).

Now let's take a look at the full header.

Received: from alpha.netvision.net.il (alpha.netvision.net.il [194.90.1.13]) by cmx.netvision.net.il (8.9.3/8.9.3) with ESMTP id CAA15313 for victim@victim.com>; Sat, 10 Jul 1999 02:49:59 +0300 (IDT)
From: bgates@microsoft.com
Received: from some.hostname.crap.com (some.hostname.crap.com [62.0.146.225]) by alpha.someone.com (8.9.3/8.8.6) with SMTP id CAA15313 for victim@victim.com; Sat, 10 Jul 1999 02:55:46 +0300 (IDT)
Date: Sat, 10 Jul 1999 02:55:46 +0300 (IDT)
Message-ID: <199907092355. CAA15313@alpha.someone.com>
X-Authentication-Warning: alpha.someone.com: some.hostname.crap.com [62.0.146.225] didn't use HELO protocol
Subject: Fake mail
Status:
X-Mozilla-Status: 8001
X-Mozilla-Status2: 00000000
X-UIDL: 3752da3b000002ff

We will start from the top.

Received: from alpha.someone.com (alpha.someone.com [194.90.1.13]) by cmx.someone.com (8.9.3/8.9.3) with ESMTP id CAA16970 for >; Sat, 10 Jul 1999 02:49:59 +0000 (GMT)

Okay, so the mail was received from alpha.someone.com (alpha.someone.com [194.90.1.13]). What does that mean?

A quick checkup on InterNIC(25)'s databases (type 'whois alpha.someone.com' without the quotes on a Unix system or download SamSpade for Windows at www.samspade.org) reveals that it is owned by someone.com. This is probably some kind of a sub-server they use to send mail. Let's leave it alone, it's not important to us right now. The (alpha.someone.com [194.90.1.13]) part shows you the hostname (10) and the IP Address (9) of the server the E-mail was sent from.

Wasn't the mail supposed to be sent from microsoft.com? The sender being bgates@microsoft.com!

If we did the mail forging thing on microsoft.com instead of on someone.com this wouldn't have happened, now would it? It would have seemed like an ordinary E-mail... from Bill Gates... well, at least so far.
Anyway, the rest is just the MID (which we will get to later) and the date of the message (the sending date) according to the server which the message was sent from. The +0000 (GMT) part means that it was sent from the Greenwich time zone. If it was sent, for example, from the +0200 time zone it would have meant that this time zone's time is actually Greenwich time plus 2 hours. Find our your time zone first so you'll be able to switch time zones and find out when was the message sent in your time.
Now, on to more important things.

From: bgates@microsoft.com

Received: from some.hostname.crap.com (some.hostname.crap.com [62.0.146.225]) by alpha.someone.com (8.9.3/8.8.6) with SMTP id CAA15313 for victim@victim.com; Sat, 10 Jul 1999 02:55:46 +0300 (IDT)

Now this is really interesting. Now we get the sender's hostname and IP Address.
Note about the hostname: a dial-up user will have a long and twisted hostname. For example: my hostname right now (at least when I was writing these lines) is RAS4-p97.hfa.netvision.net.il. Netvision.net.il is our ISP.

You must have noticed by now that the hostname we got is certainly not from microsoft.com, and that the mail server who sent this isn't exactly microsoft.com or a microsoft sub-domain either, which clearly shows that this E-mail is completely fake.

Another note about the hostname: sometimes you might not get a hostname, but you will always get an IP Address. You can find the IP's hostname (most IP Addresses do have a hostname) by doing 'nslookup IP-Address' without the quotes on a Unix system or going to http://www.samspade.org and using their DNSLookup Tool. If you still can't get it, try doing a whois.

To overcome this problem, you need to do two things:

1) Send this mail from Microsoft's Sendmail server.
2) Send this mail from an account that is connected to the web through Microsoft. If you can't get one, it will clearly show in the headers that the mail wasn't sent from Microsoft.

Note: nice trick to pull on someone: if your ISP is blah.com, you can send your friends an Email from admin@blah.com which will look 100% authentic!

Anyway, the next few characters give us the MID (Message ID), as well as other pieces of info. I promised we'll get to the MID, didn't I?

If you think someone is trying to trick you into thinking he's somebody else, send an E-mail to abuse@your.ISP.com or abuse@the.ISP.where.the.message.came.from.com (in this case Microsoft.com) or abuse@the.server.who.stores.the.MID.com.

To know which server stores the MID, we'll need to skip a few lines (two lines actually - time and date) and get straight to this:

Message-ID: <199907092355. CAA15313@alpha.someone.com>

Aha! Look at these interesting numbers! And check this out: CAA15313@alpha.someone.com! This means all the info regarding the MID is stored at alpha.someone.com! Let's send an E-mail to abuse@alpha.someone.com and tell them that we think we received a fake mail, and include the entire header. Next thing we'll do the same with the ISP of the sender (in our case, the sender is some.hostname.crap.com [62.0.146.225], meaning his ISP is probably crap.com).

Now, on to the next line:

X-Authentication-Warning: alpha.someone.com: some.hostname.crap.com [62.0.146.225] didn't use HELO protocol

We forgot something. Now let's do it all over again, but this time we'll type HELO microsoft.com at the beginning.

HELO microsoft.com

We get this:

250 mailgw1.netvision.net.il Hello some.hostname.crap.com [62.0.146.225], pleased to meet you

The rest is exactly like in the last time (sender, rcpt to, etc' etc'). Now let's see what victim@victim.com would have gotten.

No X-Authentication-Warning! That's it and our fake mail is sent!!!
Daemons typically do not have any existing parent process, but reside directly under init in the process hierarchy. Daemons usually become daemons by forking a child process and then making the parent process kill itself, thus making init adopt the child. This practice is commonly known as "fork off and die".

Systems often start (or "launch") daemons at boot time: they often serve the function of responding to network requests, hardware activity, or other programs by performing some task. Daemons can also configure hardware (like devfsd on some Linux systems), run scheduled tasks (like cron), and perform a variety of other tasks.

In a strictly technical sense, Unix recognises as a daemon any process that has process number 1 (init) as its parent process. The init process adopts any process whose parent dies without waiting for the child's status, so the common method for launching a daemon involves forking once or twice, and making the parent (and possibly the grandparent) die while the child (or grandchild) process begins performing its normal function. The idiom is sometimes summarized with the phrase "fork off and die".

In common Unix usage a daemon may be any background process, whether a child of init or not. UNIX users sometimes spell daemon as demon, and most usually pronounce the word that way.

In the DOS environment, such programs were written as Terminate and Stay Resident (TSR) Software. On Microsoft Windows systems, programs called "services" perform the functions of daemons, though the term "daemon" has started to creep into common usage on that platform as well. On the original Mac OS similar systems were known as extensions. Mac OS X, being a UNIX-like system, has daemons. There are "services" as well, but these are completely different in concept.

4.12 Remote OS Detection

Next thing we'll try to determine the OS (Operating System) which this daemon runs on. If Sendmail's banner won't tell us, the Telnet daemon will. First telnet to port 23 and wiat for the response. If there's a daemon on that port, it's probably the Telnet daemon, and it'll probably give you the name and version of the OS. If not, you can either:

1) Try looking for a guest account (username: guest, password: guest or username: newuser, password: newuser), since some systems give you these details only after you log in.
2) E-mail admin@your-target.com and ask him (We recommend opening a mailbox on one of those free mailbox services such as Hotmail and E-mailing them from there, since some admins might get a little suspicious).

3) Try going to your target's website. This kind of information might be there, somewhere.

If you still didn't find the OS, fear not! We might still be able to do a cool hack without this information, but still this information might come in handy, so do all you can to get your hands on it.

4.13 Internet Attacks

Security and Systems Design

Most current real-world computer security efforts focus on external threats, and generally treat the computer system itself as a trusted system. Some knowledgeable observers consider this to be a disastrous mistake, and point out that this distinction is the cause of much of the insecurity of current computer systems - once an attacker has subverted one part of a system without fine-grained security, he or she usually has access to most or all of the features of that system. Because computer systems can be very complex, and cannot be guaranteed to be free of defects, this security stance tends to produce insecure systems.

The 'trusted systems' approach has been predominant in the design of many Microsoft software products, due to the long-standing Microsoft policy of emphasizing functionality and 'ease of use' over security. Since Microsoft products currently dominate the desktop and home computing markets, this has led to unfortunate effects. However, the problems described here derive from the security stance taken by software and hardware vendors generally, rather than the failing of a single vendor. Microsoft is not out of line in this respect, just far more prominent with respect to its consumer marketshare.

It should be noted that the Windows NT line of operating systems from Microsoft contained mechanisms to limit this, such as services that ran under dedicated user accounts, and Role-Based Access Control (RBAC) with user/group rights, but the Windows 95 line of products lacked most of these functions. Before the release of Windows 2003 Microsoft has changed their official stance, taking a more locked down approach. On 15 January 2002, Bill Gates sent out a memo on Trustworthy Computing, marking the official change in company stance. Regardless, Microsoft's latest operating system Windows XP is still plagued by complaints about lack of local security and inability to use the fine-grained user access controls together with certain software (esp. certain popular computer games).

Financial Cost

Severe financial damage has been caused by computer security breaches, but estimating reliable costs is quite difficult. Figures in the billions of dollars have been quoted in relation to the damage caused by malware such as computer worms like the Code Red worm, but such estimates may be exaggerated. However, other losses, such as those caused by the compromise of credit card information, can be more easily determined, and they have been substantial, as measured by millions of individual victims of identity theft each year in each of several nations, and the severe hardship imposed on each victim, that can wipe out all of their finances, prevent them from getting a job, plus be treated as if they were the criminal. Volumes of victims of phishing and other scams may not be known.

On a personal level, people who have been infected with spyware or other types of malware have to go through a stressful and time-consuming process of cleaning their systems. If they decide that they must re-install an operating system, and they did not keep registration or product keys for proprietary software on their system, they sometimes have to pay for software that they already bought. The cost can therefore be days of time, and hundreds or even thousands of dollars. The problem with spyware and malware is considered to be largely a Microsoft Windows-specific problem, however this can be explained somewhat by the fact that they control a major share of the PC market and thus represent the most prominent target.

Reasons

There are many similarities (yet many fundamental differences) between computer and physical security. Just like real-world security, the motivations for breaches of computer security vary between attackers, sometimes called hackers or crackers. Some are teenage thrill-seekers or vandals (the kind often responsible for defacing web sites); similarly, some web site defacements are done to make political statements. However, some attackers are highly skilled and motivated with the goal of compromising computers for financial gain or espionage. An example of the latter is *Markus Hess* who spied for the KGB and was ultimately caught because of the efforts of Clifford Stoll, who wrote an amusing and accurate book, "The Cuckoo's Egg" about his experiences. For those seeking to prevent security breaches, the first step is usually to attempt to identify what might motivate an attack on the system, how much the continued operation and information security of the system are worth, and who might be motivated to breach it. The precautions required for a home PC are very different for those of banks' Internet banking system, and different again for a classified military network. Other computer security writers suggest that, since an attacker using a network need know nothing about you or what you have on your computer, attacker motivation is inherently impossible to determine beyond guessing. If true, blocking all possible attacks is the only plausible action to take.

Vulnerabilities

To understand something about techniques for securing a computer system, it is important to first understand the various types of "attacks" that can be made against it. These threats can typically be classified into a number of categories:

Exploits

Software flaws, especially buffer overflows, are often exploited to gain control of a computer, or to cause it to operate in an unexpected manner. Many development methodologies rely on testing to ensure the quality of any code released; this process often fails to discover extremely unusual potential exploits. The term "exploit" generally refers to small programs designed to take advantage of a software flaw that has been discovered, either remote or local. The code from the exploit program is frequently reused in Trojan horses and computer viruses. In some cases, a vulnerability can lie in a certain programs processing of a specific file type, such as a non-executable media file.

Eavesdropping

Any data that is transmitted over a network is at some risk of being eavesdropped, or even modified by a malicious person. Even machines that operate as a closed system (i.e., with no contact to the outside world) can be eavesdropped upon via monitoring the faint electro-magnetic transmissions generated by the hardware such as TEMPEST. The FBI's proposed Carnivore program was intended to act as a system of eavesdropping protocols built into the systems of internet service providers.

Social Engineering and Human Error

A computer system is no more secure than the human systems responsible for its operation. Malicious individuals have regularly penetrated well-designed, secure computer systems by taking advantage of the carelessness of trusted individuals, or by deliberately deceiving them, for example sending messages that they are the system administrator and asking for passwords. This deception is known as Social Engineering.

Denial of Service Attacks

Denial of service attacks differ slightly from those listed above, in that they are not primarily a means to gain unauthorized access or control of a system. They are instead designed to overload the capabilities of a machine or network, and thereby render it unusable. This type of attack is, in practice, very hard to prevent, because the behavior of whole networks needs to be analyzed, not only of small pieces of code. Distributed denial of service attacks are common, where a large number of compromised hosts (commonly referred to as "zombie computers") are used to flood a target system with network requests, thus attempting to render it unusable through resource exhaustion. There are also commonly vulnerabilities in applications that cannot be used to take control over a computer, but merely make the target application malfunction or crash. This is known as a Denial-of-Service Exploit.

Indirect Attacks

Attacks in which one or more of the attack types above are launched from a third party computer which has been taken over remotely. By using someone else's computer to launch an attack, it becomes far more difficult to track down the actual attacker. There have also been cases where attackers took advantage of public anonymizing systems, such as the tor onion router system.

Backdoors

Methods of bypassing normal authentication or giving remote access to a computer to somebody who knows about the backdoor, while intended to remain hidden to casual inspection. The backdoor may take the form of an installed program (e.g., Back Orifice) or could be in the form of an existing "legitimate" program, or executable file. A specific form of backdoors are rootkits, which replaces system binaries and/or hooks into the function calls of the operating system to hide the presence of other programs, users, services and open ports. It may also fake information about disk and memory usage.

Direct Access Attacks

Common consumer devices that can be used to transfer data surreptitiously. Someone gaining physical access to a computer can install all manner of devices to compromise security, including operating system modifications, software worms, keyboard loggers, and covert listening devices. The attacker can also easily download large quantities of data onto backup media, for instance CD-R/DVD-R, tape; or portable devices such as keydrives, digital cameras or digital audio players. Another common technique is to boot an operating system contained on a CD-ROM or other bootable media and read the data from the harddrive(s) this way. The only way to defeat this is to encrypt the storage media and store the key separate from the system.

We will see other specific internet attacks in the following sections.

Reducing Vulnerabilities

Computer code is regarded by some as just a form of mathematics. It is theoretically possible to prove the correctness of computer programs (within very limited circumstances) though the likelihood of actually achieving this in large-scale practical systems is regarded as unlikely in the extreme by most with practical experience in the industry -- see Bruce Schneier et al.

It's also possible to protect messages in transit (i.e., communications) by means of Cryptography. One method of encryption —the one-time pad —has been proven to be unbreakable when correctly used. This method was used by the Soviet Union during the Cold War, though flaws in their implementation allowed some cryptanalysis (See Venona Project). The method uses a matching pair of key-codes, securely distributed, which are used once-and-only-once to encode and decode a single message. For transmitted computer encryption this method is difficult to use properly (securely), and highly inconvenient as well. Other methods of encryption, while breakable in theory, are often virtually impossible to directly break by any means publicly known today. Breaking them requires some non-cryptographic input, such as a stolen key, stolen plaintext (at either end of the transmission), or some other extra cryptanalytic information.

Social Engineering and direct computer access (physical) attacks can only be prevented by non-computer means, which can be difficult to enforce, relative to the sensitivity of the information. Even in a highly disciplined environment, such as in military organizations, social engineering attacks can still be difficult to foresee and prevent.
In practice, only a small fraction of computer program code is mathematically proven, or even goes through comprehensive information technology audits or inexpensive but extremely valuable computer security audits, so it's usually possible for a determined cracker to read, copy, alter or destroy data in well secured computers, albeit at the cost of great time and resources. Extremely few, if any, attackers would audit applications for vulnerabilities just to attack a single specific system. You can reduce a cracker's chances by keeping your systems up to date, using a security scanner or/and hiring competent people responsible for security.

The effects of data loss/damage can be reduced by careful backing up and insurance.

Security Measures

A state of computer "security" is the conceptual ideal, attained by the use of the three processes:

Prevention, Detection, and Response

User account access controls and Cryptography can protect systems files and data, respectively.

Firewalls are by far the most common prevention systems from a network security perspective as they can (if properly configured) shield access to internal network services, and block certain kinds of attacks through packet filtering.

Intrusion Detection Systems (IDS's) are designed to detect network attacks in progress and assist in post-attack forensics, while audit trails and logs serve a similar function for individual systems.

"Response" is necessarily defined by the assessed security requirements of an individual system and may cover the range from simple upgrade of protections to notification of legal authorities, counter-attacks, and the like. In some special cases, a complete destruction of the compromised system is favored.

Today, computer security comprises mainly "preventive" measures, like firewalls or an Exit Procedure. A firewall can be defined as a way of filtering network data between a host or a network and another network, such as the Internet, and is normally implemented as software running on the machine, hooking into the network stack (or, in the case of most UNIX-based operating systems such as LINUX, built into the operating system kernel) to provide realtime filtering and blocking. Another implementation is a so called physical firewall which consists of a separate machine filtering network traffic. Firewalls are common amongst machines that are permanently connected to the Internet (though not universal, as demonstrated by the large numbers of machines "cracked" by worms like the Code Red worm which would have been protected by a properly-configured firewall). However, relatively few organisations maintain computer systems with effective detection systems, and fewer still have organized response mechanisms in place.

Difficulty with Response

Responding forcefully to attempted security breaches (in the manner that one would for attempted physical security breaches) is often very difficult for a variety of reasons:

Identifying attackers is difficult, as they are often in a different jurisdiction to the systems they attempt to breach, and operate through proxies, temporary anonymous dial-up accounts, wireless connections, and other anonymising procedures which make backtracing difficult and are often located in yet another jurisdiction. If they successfully breach security, they are often able to delete logs to cover their tracks.

The sheer number of attempted attacks is so large that organisations cannot spend time pursuing each attacker (a typical home user with a permanent (e.g., cable modem) connection will be attacked at least several times per day, so more attractive targets could be presumed to see many more). Note however, that most of the sheer bulks of these attacks are made by automated vulnerability scanners and computer worms.

Law enforcement officers are often unfamiliar with information technology, and so lack the skills and interest in pursuing attackers. There are also budgetary constraints. It has been argued that the high cost of technology, such as DNA testing, and improved forensics mean less money for other kinds of law enforcement, so the overall rate of criminals not getting dealt with goes up as the cost of the technology increases.

4.13.1 KeyLoggers

Keylogger is intended for interception and recording in a file of everything that is entered from the keyboard. The program is able to work in the hidden mode and to emerge on pressing a combination of keys. Keylogger is able to present the recorded data in a neat way that is easy to read but at the same time fixing exactly every event that has been done. By constantly using this program you will save your time by preventing accidental data damage and loss that is frequently caused by the use of Internet. You can immediately restore the text which was typed yesterday, the day before yesterday, or one week ago. Keylogger will also help to recollect passwords that you have forgotten or to recover lost E-mail.

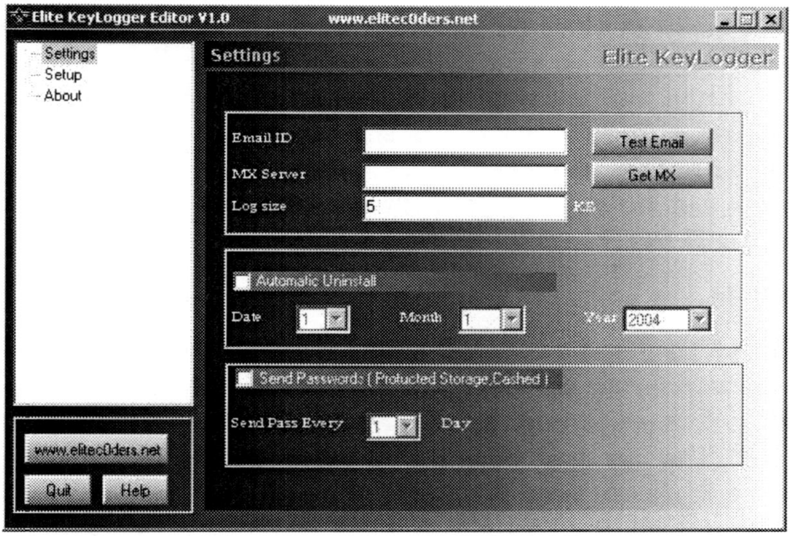

Keystroke logging (often called key logging) is a diagnostic used in software development that captures the user's keystrokes. It can be useful to determine sources of error in computer systems. Such systems are also highly useful for law enforcement and espionage—for instance, providing a means to obtain passwords or encryption keys and thus bypassing other security measures. However, Keyloggers are widely available on the internet and can be used by anyone for the same purposes.

Writing software applications for key logging is trivial, and like any computer program can be distributed as a Trojan horse or as part of a virus or worm. What is not trivial however, is installing a keystroke logger without getting caught and downloading data that has been logged without being traced. An attacker that manually connects to a host machine to download logged keystrokes risks being traced. A Trojan that sends keylogged data to a fixed E-mail address or IP Address risks exposing the attacker.

Trojan

Young and Yung devised several methods for solving this problem and presented them in their 1997 IEEE Security and Privacy paper[1] (their paper from '96 touches on it as well). They presented a deniable password snatching attack in which the keystroke logging Trojan is installed using a virus (or worm). An attacker that is caught with the virus or worm can claim to be a victim. The cryptotrojan asymmetrically encrypts the pilfered login/password pairs using the public key of the Trojan author and covertly broadcasts the resulting ciphertext. They mentioned that the ciphertext can be steganographically encoded and posted to a public bulletin board (e.g., Usenet).

Ciphertext

Young and Yung also mentioned having the cryptotrojan unconditionally write the asymmetric ciphertexts to the last few unused sectors of every writable disk that is inserted into the machine. The sectors remain marked as unused. This can done using a USB token. So, the Trojan author may be one of dozens or even thousands of people that are given the stolen information. Only the Trojan author can decrypt the ciphertext because only the author knows the needed private decryption key. This attack is from the field known as Cryptovirology.

4.13.2 DOS Attack

Denial of Service attack is the process by which requests are sent across a network from a singular attack point to a single or multiple target (destination) server and over-whelming it with requests that are bogus. By over-whelming the request, genuine requests are not entertain and thus – denial of service is experienced.

DoS Attack

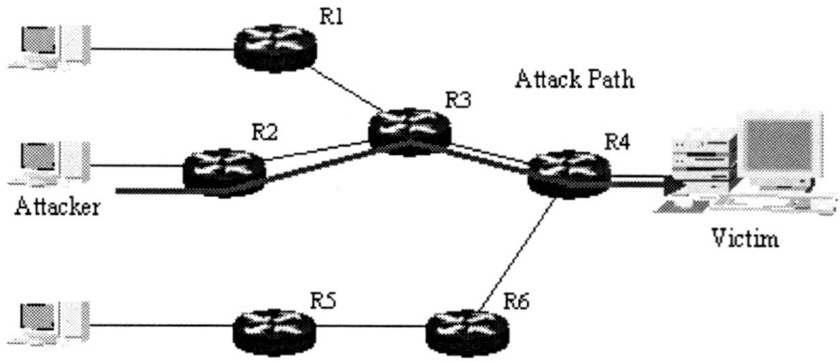

A real world example (sort of) would be…

Suppose you are able to clone yourself…now you make a 10,000 clones and start calling 411 (Directory Assistance):

Clone: [Calls Directory Assistance]
Operator: "Hello, Directory Assistance, what city please?"
Clone: [You say nothing]
Operator: "Hello?"
Clone: [You still say nothing!]
Operator: [She hangs up after 5 seconds into your call]

Now imagine that this Directory Assistance Center only has like 25 operators. Can you picture 10,000 callers (your clones) calling up Directory Assistance and keep each line busy for 5 seconds and then hanging up.

Now a "genuine" user Mary needs the number of a garage shop. She calls Directory Assistance and finds its constantly busy. As she is a real-person, she dials and dials and dials, but after 20 tries, she simply gives up in frustration!

Have the same scenario applicable to say George, Alice, Mike, Bertha, etc. All these users will keep on trying and eventually give up. The problem? Well very simply, the 10,000 clones who are dialing the Directory Assistance have made it impossible for others to get through. Its simply mathematics. They have a higher chance in getting through (because of their sheer number) than an average user has.

You (as a genuine caller) have just experienced Denial of Service. The denial of service attack was directed at the Directory Assistance.

In the computing world…this can happen as follows:

Let's say you are an owner of an online store and you sell iPods. You have a few competitors but nothing so serious. However, there is essentially "one" company that you would not only call a competitor but a threat (and they too have an online store).

Now let's alter the scenario a little bit… Sales are hurting because your so-called competitor/threat is taking chunks of your business away because of their sleek marketing and advertising campaign, etc. You are simply jealous.

You are an evil person with a powerful Server and a T3 bandwidth all to yourself.

You decide to write a program on your machine that will open an HTTP request to a certain domain name and then that's it. The program simply keeps on opening an HTTP request and then forgets it. The program you write is able to open say 1,000 requests per second.

Your target? – your competitors website.

Your competitor is hosted on say a 10Mbps line with some carrier/data center.

You send in your request number 1 – your competitor's server acknowledges the HTTP request and says "Hi – Come on in!" (in computing terms) and waits for say 300 seconds (keeping the door open for you to come on in). After 300 seconds – the door is closed.

After the first second…(with 1000 requests per second throughput rate).

Your competitor's server now has 1000 HTTP requests (or better known as Sessions) OPEN – for the next 299 seconds.

At the 2nd second – 2,000 Sessions are open for 298 seconds (approximately).

Six seconds later – 6,000 Sessions are open for 297 seconds (approximately).

Ten seconds later – your competitor's server dies!

It's RAM and allots a bit of space to each session, so does your CPU and hard disk, with so many sessions coming in – RAM runs out of space, and the CPU and other computing resources cannot keep up with the incoming requests and crashes or denies any further requests from coming in.

All this is automated. All requests are coming in from a "single" source – you!

All this is preventing any one else from trying to buy from your competitor's website!

Since they cannot buy from your competitor's website (actually they cannot even open it), they wait and wait and nothing happens and then Google or Yahoo! again for other sources who sell iPods and come across your website and decide to buy it from there.

What you just did was give your competitor a Denial of Service Attack.

DDos

Distributed Denial of Service (DDoS) Attacks are the same thing pretty much as a Denial of Service (DoS) attacks, except more than one attack computer is used, thus the word distributed attack. Most of these "attacking" computers are usually compromised systems and the owners have usually no idea that their machines are being used for an attack.

Reflective DoS Attacks are also classified as Distributed Denial of Service Attacks.

Architecture of a DDoS Attack

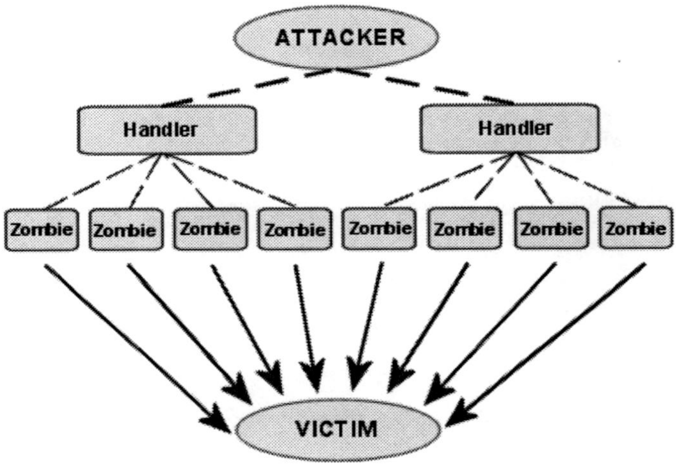

Another way of saying it is that DDoS attacks are more punishing than DoS attacks as they come in from multiple sources, hundreds if not thousands of sources.

On the Internet, a Distributed Denial-of-Service (DDoS) attack is one in which a multitude of compromised systems attack a single target, thereby causing denial of service for users of the targeted system. The flood of incoming messages to the target system essentially forces it to shut down, thereby denying service to the system to legitimate users.

A hacker (or, if you prefer, cracker) begins a DDoS attack by exploiting a vulnerability in one computer system and making it the DDoS "master".

It is from the master system that the intruder identifies and communicates with other systems that can be compromised. The intruder loads cracking tools available on the Internet on multiple -- sometimes thousands of -- compromised systems. With a single command, the intruder instructs the controlled machines to launch one of many flood attacks against a specified target. The inundation of packets to the target causes a denial of service.

While the press tends to focus on the target of DDoS attacks as the victim, in reality there are many victims in a DDoS attack -- the final target and as well the systems controlled by the intruder.

Attacks

DoS/DDoS attacks come in many flavors. They are getting complex as the days go by and sometimes classification of the different types of attacks is a matter of opinion. One vendor may classify only 5 types, whilst the other 10 types. It really is a matter of interpretation as far as vendors go (not to mention marketing as well).

Attacks are generally based on ICMP (Internet Control Message Protocol) Floods, Smurf Attacks (which are also ICMP floods, but uses the broadcast address), UDP (User Datagram Protocol) Flood, TCP (Transmission Control Protocol) Flood, TCP SYN Flood, Spoofing (by falsifying the IP Address and attacking), Ping of Death (pretty much outdated now), Application Attack (attacking a vulnerability in an application), Teardrop (IP fragmentation, again pretty much outdated now), Fraggle Attack (which is similar in nature to a Smurf Attack, except it uses UDP as opposed to TCP).

In any case, the main thing to learn about DoS/DDoS attacks is that the goal is to overwhelm the network and the server resources, denying genuine users access to a particular service (or services).

For example someone can do a DDoS attack on a DNS Server and make it inoperable for other DNS servers to collect information from, or for visitors to be redirected to the correct IP Address where the information being sought is.

DoS/DDoS attacks typically are done on Port 80 (HTTP Service) as that is perhaps the most common of all service. However, this does not mean that SMTP or POP ports are exempted or that you will never experience a DDoS attack on Port 443 (HTTPS Service). It really depends on three things:

- What the attacker wants to do? (Teach you a lesson? Make you pay? Bring your network down to its knees? etc.)
- What sort of services can the attacker attack on?
- How your security gear (if at all present) will handle all this? (Will it succumb to the attack pressure? Will it 100% mitigate it? Will it agitate the attacker in increasing size of the attack?)

With so many attack tools under development and being written by the hacker community and the novices, etc. almost every conceivable service can now be attacked.

How the Attacks Work?

First, it was Yahoo.

Then Buy.com, on the day the discount E-tailer went public. One by one, leading sites on the Web have been brought to their knees by so-called Denial of Service Attacks. Such attacks flood a Web server with false requests for information, overwhelming the system and ultimately crashing it. The following graphics explain how such attacks work and how companies can possibly prevent them.

In a typical connection, the user sends a message asking the server to authenticate it. The server returns the authentication approval to the user. The user acknowledges this approval and then is allowed onto the server.

In a denial of service attack, the user sends several authentication requests to the server, filling it up. All requests have false return addresses, so the server can't find the user when it tries to send the authentication approval. The server waits, sometimes more than a minute, before closing the connection. When it does close the connection, the attacker sends a new batch of forged requests, and the process begins again--tying up the service indefinitely.

4.13.3 Ping of Death Attack

A Ping of Death (abbreviated "POD") is a type of attack on a computer that involves sending a malformed or otherwise malicious ping to a computer. A ping is normally 64 bytes in size; many computer systems cannot handle a ping larger than the maximum IP packet size which is 65,535 bytes. Sending a ping of this size often crashes the target computer.

This bug has traditionally been relatively easy to exploit. Generally, sending a ping packet of a size such as 65,536 bytes is illegal according to networking protocol, but a packet of such a size can be sent if it is fragmented; when the target computer reassembles the packet, a buffer overflow can occur, which often causes a system crash.

This exploit has affected a wide variety of systems, including UNIX, LINUX, Mac, Windows, printers, and routers. However most systems since 1997-1998 or so have been fixed, so this bug is mostly historical.

It should be noted that in the recent years a different kind of ping attack has become wide-spread, ping flooding. The idea there is to simply flood the victim with so much ping traffic that normal traffic will fail to reach the system.

4.13.4 Cross Site Scripting Attack

Cross Site Scripting (XSS) is a type of computer security vulnerability typically found in web applications which can be used by an attacker to compromise the same origin policy of client-side scripting languages.

There are three distinct known types of XSS vulnerability to date. (These will be labeled Type 0, Type 1, and Type 2 for the purposes of this discussion, but these names are by no means industry standard nomenclature. Where possible, other names for these will be provided).

Type 0

This form of XSS vulnerability has been referred to as DOM-based or Local cross-site scripting, and while it isn't new by any means, a recent paper (DOM-Based cross-site scripting) does a good job of defining its characteristics. With Type 0 cross-site scripting vulnerabilities, the problem exists within a page's client-side script itself. For instance, if a piece of JavaScript accesses a URL request parameter and uses this information to write some HTML to its own page, and this information is not encoded using HTML entities, a XSS hole will likely be present, since this written data will be re-interpreted by browsers as HTML which could include additional client-side script.

In practice, exploiting such a hole would be very similar to the exploit of Type 1 vulnerabilities (see below), except in one very important situation. Because of the way Internet Explorer treats client-side script in objects located in the "local zone" (for instance, on the client's local hard drive), a XSS hole of this kind in a local page can result in remote execution vulnerabilities. For example, if an attacker hosts a malicious website, which contains a link to a vulnerable page on a client's local system, a script could be injected and would run with privileges of that user's browser on their system. This bypasses the entire client-side sandbox, not just the cross-domain restrictions that are normally bypassed with XSS exploits.

Type 1

This kind of cross-site scripting hole is also referred to as a non-persistent or reflected vulnerability, and is by far the most common type. These holes show up when data provided by a web client is used immediately by server-side scripts to generate a page of results for that user. If unvalidated user supplied data is included in the resulting page without HTML encoding, this will allow client-side code to be injected into the dynamic page. A classic example of this is in site search engines: if one searches for a string which includes some HTML special characters, often the search string will be redisplayed on the result page to indicate what was searched for, or will at least include the search terms in the text box for easier editing. If all occurrences of the search terms aren't HTML entity encoded, an XSS hole will result.

At first blush, this doesn't appear to be a serious problem since users can only inject code into their own pages. However, with a small amount of social engineering, an attacker could convince a user to follow a malicious URL which injects code into the results page, giving the attacker full access to that page's content. Due to the general requirement of the use of some social engineering in this case (and normally in Type 0 vulnerabilities as well), many programmers have disregarded these holes as not terribly important. This misconception is sometimes applied to XSS holes in general (even though this is only one type of XSS) and there is often disagreement in the security community as to the importance of cross-site scripting vulnerabilities.

Type 2

This type of XSS vulnerability is also referred to as a stored or persistent or second-order vulnerability and it allows the most powerful kinds of attacks. A type 2 XSS vulnerability exists when data provided to a web application by a user is first stored persistently on the server (in a database, filesystem, or other location), and later displayed to users in a web page without being encoded using HTML entities. A classic example of this is with online message boards, where users are allowed to post HTML formatted messages for other users to read. These vulnerabilities are usually more significant than other types because an attacker can inject the script just once, and could potentially hit a large number of other users with little need for Social Engineering. The methods of injection can vary a great deal, and an attacker may not need to use the web application itself to exploit such a hole. Any data received by the web application (via E-mail, system logs, etc.) that can be controlled by an attacker must be encoded prior to re-display in a dynamic page, else a XSS vulnerability of this type could result.

Exploit Scenarios

Attackers intending to exploit cross-site scripting vulnerabilities must approach each class of vulnerability differently. For each class, a specific attack vector is described here. (The names below come from the cast of characters commonly used in computer security).

Type-0 Attack

Mallory sends a URL to Alice (via E-mail or another mechanism) of a maliciously constructed web page.

Alice clicks on the link.

The malicious web page's JavaScript opens a vulnerable HTML page installed locally on Alice's computer.

The vulnerable HTML page is tricked into executing JavaScript in the computer's local zone.

Mallory's malicious script now may run commands with the privileges Alice holds on her own computer.

Type-1 Attack

Alice often visits a particular website, which is hosted by Bob. Bob's website allows Alice to log in with a username/password pair and store sensitive information, such as billing information.

Mallory observes that Bob's website contains a reflected XSS vulnerability.

Mallory crafts a URL to exploit the vulnerability, and sends Alice an E-mail, making it look as if it came from Bob.

Alice visits the URL provided by Mallory while logged into Bob's website. The malicious script embedded in the URL executes in Alice's browser, as if it came directly from Bob's server. The script steals sensitive information (authentication credentials, billing info, etc.) and sends this to Mallory's web server without Alice's knowledge.

Type-2 Attack

Bob hosts a web site which allows users to post messages and other content to the site for later viewing by other members.

Mallory notices that Bob's website is vulnerable to a type 2 XSS attack. Mallory posts a message, controversial in nature, which may encourage many other users of the site to view it.

Upon merely viewing the posted message, site users' session cookies or other credentials could be taken and sent to Mallory's webserver without their knowledge.

Later, Mallory logs in as other site users and posts messages on their behalf....

Please note the preceding examples are merely a representation of common methods of exploit and are not meant to encompass all vectors of attack.

Real World Examples

There are literally hundreds of examples of cross-site scripting vulnerabilities available publicly. Just a few examples to illustrate the different types of holes will be listed here.

An example of type-0 vulnerability was once found in an error page produced by Bugzilla where JavaScript was used to write the current URL, through the document.location variable, to the page without any filtering or encoding. In this case, an attacker who controlled the URL might have been able to inject script, depending on the behavior of the browser in use. This vulnerability was fixed by encoding the special characters in the document.location string prior to writing it to the page.

A recent type-1 vulnerability can be found in older versions of ATutor, an Open Source Web-based Learning Content Management System (LCMS) written in PHP. This vulnerability exists in the application's site search page. Script could be injected into nearly every URL request parameter, and the result page would include the malicious script.

Finally, an example of type 2 vulnerability was found in Hotmail, in October of 2001 by Marc Slemko, which allowed an attacker to steal a user's Microsoft .NET Passport session cookies. The exploit for this vulnerability consisted of sending a malicious E-mail to a Hotmail user, which contained malformed HTML. The script filtering code in Hotmail's site failed to remove the broken HTML and Internet Explorer's parsing algorithm happily interpreted the malicious code. This problem was quickly fixed, but multiple similar problems were found in Hotmail and other Passport sites later on.

A similar example, which was more fatal, was found in Indiatimes E-mail portal by Sandeep Giri. This example demonstrated that if a mailing service is vulnerable to such kind of attack a victim's inbox can be hijacked even if victim doesn't open the mail sent by malicious user.

On October 13, 2005 Samy exploited a security flaw in MySpace resulting in over one million friend requests being made to its creator's profile. Qualifying as type 2 vulnerability, it used multiple XMLHttpRequests to propogate itself.

Netcraft announced on June 16, 2006. A security flaw in the PayPal web site is being actively exploited by fraudsters to steal credit card numbers and other personal information belonging to PayPal users. The issue was reported to Netcraft via their own anti-phishing toolbar. Soon after, Paypal reported that a "change in some of the code" on the Paypal website had removed the vulnerability.

4.13.5 Input Validation Attack

Input Validation Attack is the root cause of most web hacks. All inputs received should be validated for the following attributes in order to check the input validation vulnerability:

- Data types
- Data ranges (e.g., –ve or fractional numbers)
- Buffer size and bounds
- Metacharacters

In fact input validation is the tampering with the hidden fields and is thus a highly intense web security attack. It can bypass client side checking as in Javascript etc. The countermeasures are almost none and they are the worst to deal with. The only abstract countermeasure to them is efficient code practice.

4.13.6 SQL Injection Attack

What is SQL Injection?

SQL Injection is a hacking technique which attempts to pass SQL commands through a web application for execution by a backend database. This is one of the most common application layer attacks currently being used on the Internet. The technologies vulnerable to this attack are dynamic script languages like ASP, ASP.NET, PHP, JSP, CGI, and so on.

To be able to perform SQL Injection hacking, all an attacker needs is a web browser and some guess work to find important table and field names. This is why SQL Injection attacks are so popular.

This kind of attack is not a technological security hole in the Operating System or server software, but rather it depends on the way that a website is developed. Some developers are unaware of this kind of attack and unknowingly develop web applications which open doors for hackers to inject SQL Queries/Commands into the system.

Any web page which passes parameters to a database can be vulnerable to SQL Injection hacking. Usually these vulnerabilities are present in Login forms, Forgot Password forms, etc…

What an attacker can do if your site is vulnerable?

Once an attacker realizes that a system is vulnerable to SQL Injection, he is able to inject SQL Query/Commands through an input form field. This is equivalent to handing the attacker the Query Browser, allowing him to send any SQL command like SELECT, INSERT, DELETE and DROP TABLE to the database!

Whether an attacker is able to see the data stored on the database or not, depends on how the website is coded to display the results of the queries sent. What is certain is that the attacker will be able to execute arbitrary SQL Commands on the vulnerable system, either to compromise it or else to obtain information.

What an attacker gains access to also depends on the level of security set by the database. The database could be set to restrict to certain commands only. A read access normally is enabled for use by web application back ends. So even if an attacker is not able to modify the system, he would still be able to read valuable information.

Example of a SQL Injection Attack

Here is a sample basic HTML form with two inputs, login and password.

```
<form method="post" action="login.php">
<input type="text" name="username">
<input type="password" name="password">
</form>
```

The easiest way for the login.php to work is by building a database query that looks like this:

```
"SELECT id
FROM logins
WHERE username = '$username'
AND password = '$password'";
```

If the variables $username and $password are requested directly from the user's input, this can easily be compromised. Suppose that we gave "Joe" as a username and that the following string was provided as a password: anything' OR 'x'='x

```
"SELECT id
FROM logins
WHERE username = 'Joe'
AND password = 'anything' OR 'x'='x'";
```

Because the application is not really thinking about the query, but just constructing a string, the use of the single quotes has turned the WHERE

:'x' part guarantees to be true

he login form without actually

›ination!

abilities

web site and applications are
by using a Web Vulnerability
:rawls your entire website and
› SQL Injection attacks. It will
ble to SQL injection attack so
:asily. Besides SQL injection
will also check for Cross site

scans for SQL injection, Cross
more vulnerabilities. For more
:.

injection attacks it to filter
One should "remove everything
characters from the user input.
be entered in the field will be

:k

ınetix staff using Acunetix Web
can your website simulating
L injection, cross site scripting,
identify vulnerabilities in your
u will receive a summary report
indicating what - if any - vulnerabilities exist on your site.

SQL Injection has become a common issue with database-driven web sites. The flaw is easily detected, and easily exploited, and as such, any site or software package with even a minimal user base is likely to be subject to an attempted attack of this kind.

Essentially, the attack is accomplished by placing a meta character into data input to then place SQL commands in the control plane, which did not exist there before. This flaw depends on the fact that SQL makes no real distinction between the control and data planes.

How to avoid SQL Injection?

Filter out character like single quote, double quote, slash, back slash, semi colon, extended character like NULL, carry return, new line, etc, in all strings from:

- Input from users
- Parameters from URL
- Values from cookie

For numeric value, convert it to an integer before parsing it into SQL statement. Or using ISNUMERIC to make sure it is an integer.

Change "Startup and run SQL Server" using low privilege user in SQL Server Security tab.

Delete stored procedures that you are not using like:

master..Xp_cmdshell, xp_startmail, xp_sendmail, sp_makewebtask

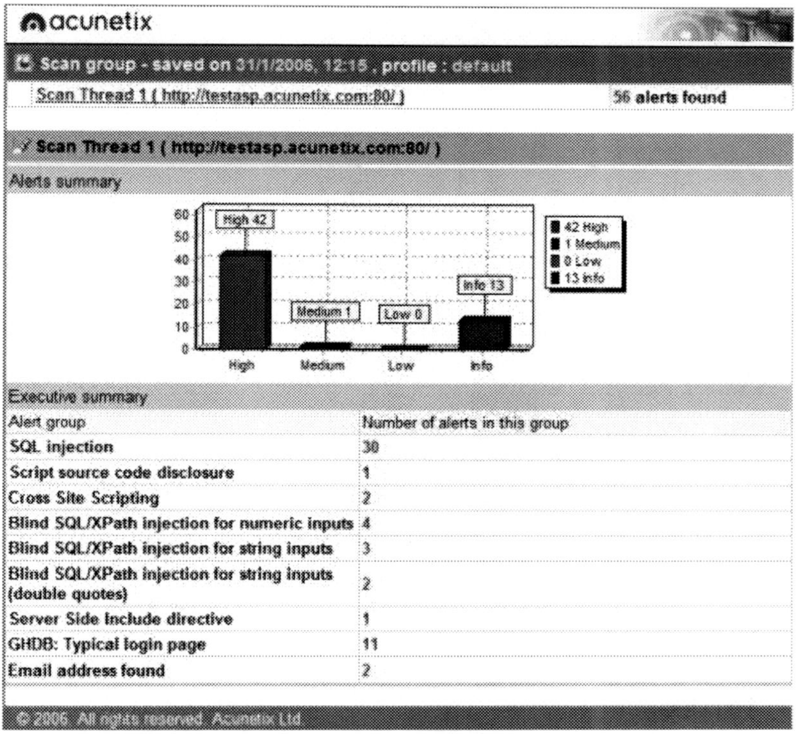

Src: www.acunetix.com

4.13.7 Sniffing Attack

Packet Sniffers (also known as network or protocol analyzers or Ethernet Sniffers) are computer software (usually) or computer hardware that can intercept and log traffic passing over a digital network or part of a network. As data streams travel back and forth over the network, the sniffer captures each packet and eventually decodes and analyzes its content according to the appropriate RFC or other specifications. Depending on the network structure (hub or switch) one can sniff all or just parts of the traffic from a single machine within the network; however, there are some methods to avoid traffic narrowing by switches to gain access to traffic from other systems on the network (e.g. ARP spoofing). For network monitoring purposes it may also be desirable to monitor all data packets in a LAN by using a network switch with a so-called monitoring port (it mirrors all packets passing through all ports of the switch).

The special network device driver used for some packet sniffing software is said to operate in "promiscuous mode" as it listens to everything on the wire.

The versatility of packet sniffers means they can be used to:

- Analyse network problems.
- Detect network intrusion attempts.
- Gain information for effecting a network intrusion.
- Monitor network usage.
- Gather and report network statistics.
- Filter suspect content from network traffic.
- Spy on other network users and collect sensitive information such as passwords (depending on any content encryption methods which may be in use)
- Reverse engineer protocols used over the network.
- Debug client/server communications.

4.13.8 Phishing

The UK today is one of the main attack targets by phishing organized crime groups, globally.

Globally, phishing damages will amount to about two billions USD in 2006. Not counting risk management measures such as preventative measures, counter-measures, incident response and PR damages. In most cases, phishing is caused by the fault of the users, either by entering the wrong web page, not keeping their computers secure or falling for cheap scams. Often this is due to lack of awareness or ability in the realm of Internet use rather than incompetence by the users. Still, these attacks are aimed at the banks and the financial institutions themselves, just because they are done in a distributed fashion on the micro level, attacking multiple users rather than on one centralized point (the web page) does not change that.

In Britain, by law, the risk of phishing is on the banks alone. Any damages caused by phishing attacks are to be reimbursed completely. In other countries the risk is on the clients alone, a combination of both bank and client, or no legislation exists yet. In all these countries the banks mostly offer complete assurance and/or completely reimburse clients regardless, as protecting the web channel for banking (being the cheapest one) is very important to them. This is about maintaining the effectiveness and trust of the populace in eCommerce. In very rare cases, banks choose to manage their risk differently and they abandon the web channel, likely due to very low usage. Banks are often short-term sighted with their risk management compared to the current revenue loss vs. gain when it comes to technological risks. The acceptable risk in the banking world changes constantly and what could have been prevented years ago was very smartly managed, but not fine-tuned for the technology risks involved.

Phishing Techniques

Most methods of phishing use some form of technical deception designed to make a link in an E-mail appear to belong to the spoofed organization. Misspelled URLs or the use of subdomains are common tricks used by phishers, such as this example URL, http://www.yourbank.com.example.com/. One method of spoofing links used web addresses containing the @ symbol, which were used to include a username and password in a web URL (contrary to the standard[11]). For example, the link http://www.google.com@members.tripod.com/ might deceive a casual observer into believing that the link will open a page on www.google.com, whereas the link actually directs the browser to a page on members.tripod.com, using a username of www.google.com; were there no such user, the page would open normally. This method has since been closed off in the Mozilla[12] and Internet Explorer[13] web browsers, while Opera provides a warning message and the option not to follow the link.

Some phishing scams use JavaScript commands in order to alter the address bar. This is done either by placing a picture of the legitimate entity's URL over the address bar, or by closing the original address bar and opening a new one containing the legitimate URL[14].

In another popular method of phishing, an attacker uses a bank or service's own scripts against the victim[15]. These types of attacks (known as cross-site scripting) are particularly problematic, because they direct the user to sign in at their bank or service's own web page, where everything from the web address to the security certificates appears correct. In reality, the link to the website is crafted to carry out the attack, although it is very difficult to spot without specialist knowledge. Just such a flaw was used in 2006 against PayPal[16].

A further problem with URLs has been found in the handling of Internationalized domain names (IDN) in web browsers, that might allow visually identical web addresses to lead to different, possibly malicious, websites. Despite the publicity surrounding the flaw, known as IDN spoofing[17] (or a homograph attack[18]), no known phishing attacks have yet taken advantage of it.

Not all phishing attacks require a fake website. In an incident in 2006[19], messages that claimed to be from a bank told users to dial a phone number regarding a problem with their bank account. Once the phone number was dialed, prompts told users to enter their account numbers and PIN. The number was provided by a Voice over IP provider.

Anti-Phishing Tips Debunked

Today every other online banking website features the "anti-phishing tips" page intended to teach an ordinary computer user how to fight those annoying emails collecting your personal data. While this educational initiative is praiseworthy, many of the tips, and some of them originate from security experts, are in fact questionable, incorrect, or misleading.

Myth #1: Secure, encrypted web page indicates a valid website.

Contrary to a popular advise, never rely solely on "https://" prefix or padlock icon that indicate a "secure" page. It is possible for a phishing website to have a valid SSL certificate. You might want to check certificate details to see if the "Common Name" field of the certificate matches the host name of the organization's website, but it requires some level of technical expertise.

Myth #2: Secured by [insert authority name]. Click here to verify.

Have you seen those? Well, they are worthless. The splash window you get by clicking on the link does not guarantee that you are on a legitimate website.

Myth #3: Address bar always shows a correct URL.

Another faulty advice is to check if the address bar contains a correct URL. It is not enough to ensure validity of a website. Vulnerabilities in browser software could allow Phishers to spoof information in the address bar. There is another type of attack (DNS Spoofing) that can also trick you to think you are visiting a valid website.

Myth #4: Moving mouse over a link shows the real URL in the status bar.

Status bar text can easily be changed. In fact, it is even easier that spoofing the address bar content.

Myth #5: Anti-phishing software prevents scams.

Similarly to antiviral software's inability to detect new malicious code, your Anti-phishing browser plug-in (often offered for free by internet providers) is incapable of detecting all phishing attempts. On the contrary, by adding software (sometimes of questionable quality) to your browser you make yourself vulnerable to the malware that specifically targets that software.

Myth #6: An E-mail containing your personal data is legitimate.

If you receive the message from your bank and it contains your name and your account number (or a part of it), it might as well be a fraudulent email. Phishers can get access to some of your personal data by using public databases or data leaked from other organizations.

Myth #7: It is safe to log in once you know the website is legitimate.

NO! Website vulnerabilities (called Cross-Site Scripting) could allow a sophisticated attacker to use the form on company's website to capture your credentials by redirecting you to attacker's website as soon as you click "Login" button or hit "Enter".

What to do to avoid getting scammed?

Tip #1: Do not click on links in your E-mail.

If you receive a message from your bank asking you to do something, do not click on links in the E-mail and do not use forms in the E-mail to log in. Instead, open your browser, go directly to your bank's website, log in, and continue there. Even if the E-mail is from someone you know, DO NOT CLICK ON THE LINKS.

Tip #2: Invalid credentials usually work on impersonated websites.

If you feel there is something wrong with a website, use invalid username and invalid password to log in. If the website then presents you with the "Logon failed" page, you are possibly on a legitimate website. It may not always work as sometimes impersonators simulate failed logons for double-checking victim's input or redirect to a legitimate website after collecting credentials. But if your invalid credentials get you right through - it is definitely a phishing attempt.

Tip #3: Report the message to the company impersonated in the email.

Most financial organizations have guidelines and dedicated E-mail addresses where to report security problems. If you suspect a message is a phishing attempt, forward it to the organization. You can find E-mail address to forward suspicious emails to in our Scam Reporting Database. You should include all email headers. Do not expect a reply from the organization as they receive thousands of those reports.

4.13.9 Pharming

What is this thing called "Pharming"? Put simply, it's redirection of web traffic, so that the server you think you're talking to actually belongs to a criminal. For example: you think you're talking to http://www.examplebank.com because it says so in the browser's address bar, but actually you're connected to http://www.mafia-R-us.ru.

This can happen in three main ways:

- **DNS Hijack:** A Social Engineering attack on the Internet infrastructure. Criminals pretend to be the domain owner and have the bank's name re-pointed to their servers.
- **DNS Poisoning:** As above, but a technical attack, taking advantage of possible bugs in the DNS.
- **Malware:** A virus, worm, Trojan, or piece of spyware could redirect traffic, usually by writing to the Hosts file, thus circumventing the DNS altogether.

None of these issues are new. This is unlikely to become as big a problem as phishing. So this isn't as big a problem as some people believe. Let's examine the reasons in more detail, and provide some actionable recommendations for organizations. We will also take the lazier banks to task for not doing more to protect their customers from phishing and pharming attacks.

The fundamental reason that this isn't as big a problem as some believe is that it's not a new problem. In other words, we're not starting from ground zero. It's not like the phishing problem, in that respect.

Here's why we needn't worry too much about each of the three redirection methods above:

There were two high-profile DNS hijacking cases recently: suffered by Panix and eBay Germany. Neither of these cases would have happened if the correct, standard procedures had been followed by the respective domain registrars. The very fact that they did happen will cause domain registrars the world over to more carefully follow existing procedures.

DNS poisoning relies on hackers finding security holes in the DNS infrastructure. Such potential security problems are rare, and tend to be quickly fixed. The weakest point is likely to be local DNS caches in firewall products. Organizations using such features should ensure that they have processes in-place to ensure that they are always up to date with security patches.

Most organizations and individual consumers now recognize the need for anti-virus scanning. Increasingly, they are also recognizing the need for anti-spyware scanning. Such scanners mitigate the malware risk. Organizations without a strategy to filter all types of malware (not just classic viruses) should develop and implement one.

Finally, and perhaps most importantly, we should critically examine the security of the banks and other websites that pharming and phishing seek to attack. For example, a surprisingly large number of banks still rely on a simple username/password combination; many of them claim that users will not accept the additional burden of stronger authentication methods. This is a lazy and complacent attitude. While malicious redirection is a significant potential issue for internet users, recent PR-led activities risk blowing the severity out of proportion.

5. Penetration Testing – "Evaluate Your Information System's Security"

5.1 Introduction

A penetration test is a method of evaluating the security of a computer system or network by simulating an attack by a malicious cracker. The process involves an active analysis of the system for any weaknesses, technical flaws or vulnerabilities. This analysis is carried out from the position of a potential attacker, and can involve active exploitation of security vulnerabilities. Any security issues that are found will be presented to the system owner together with an assessment of their impact and often with a proposal for mitigation or a technical solution.

1. What is a Penetration Test?

A Penetration Test is the process of actively evaluating your information security measures. There are a number of ways that this can be undertaken, but the most common procedure is that the security measures are actively analyzed for design weaknesses, technical flaws and vulnerabilities; the results are then delivered comprehensively in a report, to Executive, Management and Technical audiences.

Src: www.imagevortex.com

2. Why Penetration Testing: Why would you want it?

There are several reasons why organizations choose to perform a penetration test; they range from technical to commercial but the most common are:

- Identify the threats facing your organization's information assets so that you can quantify your information risk and provide adequate information security expenditure.
- Reduce your organization's IT security costs and provide a better Return on IT Security Investment (ROSI) by identifying and resolving vulnerabilities and weaknesses. These may be known vulnerabilities in the underlying technologies or weaknesses in the design or implementation.
- Provide your organization with assurance - a thorough and comprehensive assessment of organizational security covering policy, procedure, design and implementation.
- Gain and maintain certification to an industry regulation (BS7799, HIPAA etc).
- Adopt best practice by conforming to legal and industry regulations.

3. Choosing a service: What are the different types of tests available?

External Penetration Testing is the traditional approach to penetration testing. The testing is focused on the servers, infrastructure and the underlying software comprising the target. It may be performed with no prior knowledge of the site (black box) or with full disclosure of the topology and environment (crystal box). This type of testing should typically involve a comprehensive analysis of publicly available information about the target, a network enumeration phase where target hosts are identified and analyzed and the behaviour of security devices such as screening routers and firewalls are analyzed. Vulnerabilities within the target hosts should then be identified, verified and the implications assessed.

Internal Security Assessment follows a similar methodology to external testing, but provides a more complete view of the site security. Testing will typically be performed from a number of network access points, representing each logical and physical segment. For example, this may include tiers and DMZ's within the environment, the corporate network or partner company connections.

Application Security Assessment is designed to identify and assess threats to the organization through bespoke, proprietary applications or systems. These applications may provide interactive access to potentially sensitive materials, for example. It is vital that they be assessed to ensure that, firstly, the application doesn't expose the underlying servers and software to attack, and secondly that a malicious user cannot access, modify or destroy data or services within the system. Even in a well-deployed and secured infrastructure, a weak application can expose the organization's crown-jewels to unacceptable risk.

Wireless/Remote Access Assessment (RAS) Security Assessment addresses the security risks associated with an increasingly mobile workforce. Home-working, broadband always-on Internet access, 802.11 wireless networking and a plethora of emerging remote access technologies have greatly increased the exposure of companies by extended the traditional perimeter ever further. It is vital that the architecture, design and deployment of such solutions is secure and sound, to ensure the associated risks are managed effectively.

Telephony Security Assessment addresses security concerns relating to corporate voice technologies. This includes abuse of PBX's by outsiders to route calls at the targets expense, mailbox deployment and security, Voice over IP (VoIP) integration, unauthorized modem use and associated risks.

Social Engineering addresses a non-technical kind of intrusion; it relies heavily on human interaction and often involves tricking other people into breaking normal security procedures. Social engineering usually involves a scam; trying to gain the confidence of a trusted source by relying on the natural helpfulness of people as well as their weaknesses, appealing to their vanity, their authority and eaves dropping are natural techniques used. Other techniques involve searching refuse bins for valuable information, memorizing access codes by looking over someone's shoulder, or taking advantage of people's natural inclination to choose passwords that are meaningful to them but can be easily guessed.

4. The different types of approach: "Black-box" and "White-box"

Penetration tests can be conducted in one of two ways: Black-box (with no prior knowledge the infrastructure to be tested) or White-box (with complete knowledge of the infrastructure to be tested). As you might expect, there are conflicting opinions about this choice and the value that either approach will bring to a project.

Some Penetration Testing suppliers will suggest that when given the choice, theBlack-box approach is the best because it closely simulates the process of a real hacker. This is an interesting theory, but not particularly true. Firstly it presupposes that an attacker doesn't have any knowledge of your systems, which is actually unlikely. If someone is targeting your organization specifically then there is a strong possibility that they do indeed have detailed knowledge of your systems and procedures (an ex-employee with a grudge for example). In which case it would be wise to assume the worst; that they in fact have complete knowledge of your systems; because if your security relies solely on the secrecy of your designs, then you do not have any tangible security at all. Secondly, a hacker will not be limited to any time constraints that might be applied to a penetration test. For arguments sake, they will not have a week in which to circumvent your security measures, they will happily be able to probe away for years (if undiscovered) until they find a weakness they can exploit.

There is also the question of value for money. In conducting a black-box test it is necessary to spend a reasonable proportion of the time allocated for the project on discovering the nature of the infrastructure and how it connects and interrelates. Obviously, if the time is being spent on discovery, it is not being spent on actually testing for vulnerabilities.

This is not to say that black-box testing has no value, it does. It is useful for finding out how information leaks from your systems that might be utilised by others (such as in mail headers). When choosing a Black-box test it just needs to be born in mind that to get the same amount of time spent on accessing vulnerabilities, you will need to allocate more time overall to the project.

5. Deliverables: What do you get for the money?

A Penetration Test will involve the systematic analysis of all the security measures in place. A full project should include some or all of the following areas, with the exact requirements usually being agreed in a formal scoping document prior to commencing (this list is provided courtesy of the OSSTMM):

- Network Security
- Network Surveying
- Port Scanning
- System Identification
- Services Identification
- Vulnerability Research and Verification
- Application Testing and Code Review
- Router Testing
- Firewall Testing
- Intrusion Detection System Testing
- Trusted Systems Testing
- Password Cracking
- Denial of Service Testing
- Containment Measures Testing
- Information Security
- Document Grinding
- Competitive Intelligence Scouting
- Privacy Review
- Social Engineering
- Request Testing

- Guided Suggestion Testing
- Trust Testing
- Wireless Security
- Wireless Networks Testing
- Cordless Communications Testing
- Privacy Review
- Infrared Systems Testing
- Communications Security
- PBX Testing
- Voicemail Testing
- FAX review
- Modem Testing
- Physical Security
- Access Controls Testing
- Perimeter Review
- Monitoring Review
- Alarm Response Testing
- Location Review
- Environment Review

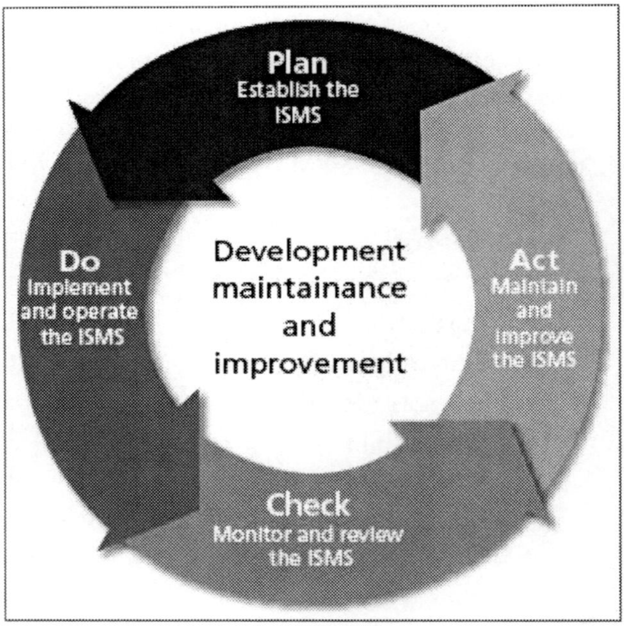

Src: BS7799

Although there is a lot of work involved prior, the real essence and value of a penetration test is in the report and briefings that you receive at the end. If they are not clear and easy to understand, then the whole exercise is of little value. Ideally the report and briefings should be broken into sections that are specifically targeted at their intended audience. Board members need the risks and possible solutions clearly described in layman's terms, technical managers need a broad overview of the situation without getting embroiled in detail, and system administrators need a host-by-host list of technical vulnerabilities to address.

With many IT companies now providing penetration testing services the quality of the reports varies enormously; everything from a page of bullet points, to three-hundred pages of mind numbing repetition (both of which are equally useless). Because of this wide variation, it is always wise to ask for a sample report before proceeding with any new supplier of penetration testing services.

Additionally, some service providers will charge separately to present the findings of the report to your team; clarify this before making a final choice.

6. Special Tips: How can you ensure the project is a success?

One of the first steps to ensure that your project is a success is in determining which supplier to use. When considering a penetration testing partner, first outline your goals for the project and your expectations of the supplier. You will want to choose one with experience in your industry and that has all the expertise you require. Speak to at least two references; and make sure that at least one of these is still working with the supplier.

As an absolute fundamental when choosing a partner, discount the supplier who provided the systems that will be tested; to use them will create a conflict of interests (will they tell you that they installed the products incorrectly, or quietly ignore any issues?).

Detailed below are some suggestions for questions that you should be asking any potential suppliers:

- Is the supplier a specialist first and foremost, or is the security practice a secondary concern?
- Does the supplier offer a comprehensive suite of services, tailored to your specific requirements?
- Does the supplier's methodology follow and exceed those such as OSSTMM, CHECK and OWASP?
- Does the supplier have a policy of employing ex hackers?
- Are the supplier's staff experienced security professionals, holding recognised certifications such as CISSP, CISA, CHECK etc?
- Can they distinguish and articulate between infrastructure and application testing?
- How many technical consultants does the supplier have that work on security and assessments and how many of those are dedicated solely to security?
- Does the supplier present the deliverables, such as the final report, in an informed manner, with concise and practical information for technical and non-technical parties?
- Is the supplier a recognised contributor within the security industry?
- Are references available to attest to the quality of past work performed?

Consultants

The quality of the Penetration Testing service that you will receive is the direct result of the quality of the consultants that will be supplied for the project.

A Penetration Test of a corporate network will examine numerous different hosts (with a number of different operating systems), network architecture, and policies and procedures. To be thorough, each area must be examined in depth; requiring the consultants to possess both a broad spread of experience and also detailed knowledge of the individual areas under scrutiny. It is clear that these kinds of skills cannot be obtained without years of experience in a variety of complementary IT fields, such as development, systems administration or consultancy.

Additionally, because of the interdependence on several other security disciplines, such as architecture, implementation and policy, it is essential that the consultants do not focus exclusively on penetration testing alone. It is logical that concentrating on penetration testing to the exclusion of all else narrows the skill set and is counterproductive when one of the key requirements of the discipline is breadth. For example, when a penetration test encounters vulnerabilities that are rooted in poor network architecture, it is essential that these are quickly identified and solutions suggested that are in keeping with architecture best practice. Without the essential complementary knowledge, this result is unlikely.

When considering a penetration testing supplier, a good measure of their worth is to qualify how they contribute to research and development within the security industry. Research demonstrates a profound understanding of current technologies and a proven ability of the supplier's team to assess, review and audit infrastructure and provide trusted solutions. What is more supplier's that operate in this way are able to deliver real value-add by identifying, remedying and disseminating details of new security flaws discovered; allowing their customers the opportunity to gain both increased security and gain an instant competitive advantage.

A commonly heard complaint when embarking on a penetration testing project is that a high-level consultant will come to the pre-project meetings, but when the project starts a junior consultant or trainee is used. To avoid this kind of issue when choosing a penetration testing partner, insist on being provided with the CV's of all the consultants that will be working on your project, prior to commencing.

Methodology

Although the skills involved in penetration testing are often specialised, the approach shouldn't be. For the most part it is simply the systematic analysis of the security measures at hand; and as we all know, the best way of doing anything systematic is to follow a plan or formal methodology.

A formal methodology doesn't need to be restrictive though; it shouldn't stifle the creativity of the consultants to explore their intuitions. But what it should do is provide a disciplined framework of areas that must be tested in order to provide a complete and accurate penetration test. Like any project, if a penetration test is undertaken without the support of a plan then it is likely that there will be oversights. No methodology also means no consistency. What happens if several consultants from the same organization are testing different sites independently (or the same site at different times); the chances are that without a common methodology they will produce dramatically different results because some areas of testing will be missed.

When selecting a supplier, be sure to ask if they have a formal methodology, and what is more to see documentary evidence of it prior to commencing. Without it, how will you know what you are getting for your money?

Standards Compliance

There are a number of good standards and guidelines in relation to information security in general, and for penetration tests in particular, that provide an excellent framework from which to work. Any provider chosen should at least have a working knowledge of these standards and would ideally be exceeding their recommendations. These include:

Standards for Information Systems Auditing (ISACA): ISACA was established in 1967 and has become a pace-setting global organization for information governance, control, security and audit professionals. Its IS auditing and IS control standards are followed by practitioners worldwide and its research pinpoints professional issues challenging its constituents. CISA, the Certified Information Systems Auditor is ISACA's cornerstone certification. Since 1978, the CISA exam has measured excellence in the area of IS auditing, control and security and has grown to be globally recognized and adopted worldwide as a symbol of achievement.

CHECK

The CESG IT Health Check scheme was instigated to ensure that sensitive government networks and those constituting the GSI (Government Secure Intranet) and CNI (Critical National Infrastructure) were secured and tested to a consistent high level. The methodology aims to identify known vulnerabilities in IT systems and networks which may compromise the confidentiality, integrity or availability of information held on that IT system. CHECK consultants are only required when the assessment for HMG or related parties, and meets the requirements above. In the absence of other standards, CHECK became the de-facto standard for penetration tests and penetration testing in the UK. However, open source methodologies such as the following are providing viable and comprehensive alternatives, without UK Government association.

OSSTMM

The aim of The Open Source Security Testing Methodology Manual is to set forth a standard for Internet security testing. It is intended to form a comprehensive baseline for testing that, if followed, ensures a thorough and comprehensive penetration test has been undertaken. This should enable a client to be certain of the level of technical assessment independently of other organization concerns, such as the corporate profile of the penetration testing provider.

OWASP

The Open Web Application Security Project (OWASP) is an Open Source community project developing software tools and knowledge based documentation that helps people secure web applications and web services. OWASP is an open source reference point for system architects, developers, vendors, consumers and security professionals involved in designing, developing, deploying and testing the security of web applications and Web Services. In short, the Open Web Application Security Project aims to help everyone and anyone build more secure web applications and web services.

The key areas of relevance are the forthcoming Guide to Testing Security of Web Applications and Web Services and the testing tools under the development projects. The Guide to Building Secure Web Applications not only covers design principals, but also is a useful document for setting out criteria by which to assess vendors and test systems.

Tools

Tools are essential for automating the penetration testing process, both for efficiency and for thoroughness; without them the task would not be achievable in a realistic time scale or budget. The tools do not however replace the skills of a security consultant; with the current rate of discovery running at around fifty new vulnerabilities a week, there will always be new vulnerabilities that the tools do not yet detect (and so must be tested for manually).

The tools can be obtained from a number of areas. There are a number of commercial vulnerability assessment tools that can be used, and there are also lots of freely available open-source tools in addition. Specialist penetration testing providers will also develop their own tools, to either automate a laborious task or to test for a new or subtle vulnerability that is not possible with an existing tool.

Commercial tools work by using sets of thousands of pre-defined signatures that can identify vulnerabilities in a system. These signatures are obviously changing and being added to all the time as new vulnerabilities are discovered and new variations come to light. They are often updated on a monthly or weekly basis, and because of this there is always a slight delay between the vulnerabilities being discovered and the automated tools detecting them. Also, some commercial tools are more focused on a particular vulnerability area (such as UNIX or web servers) and so should not be relied upon in isolation to give a good picture of the overall security of a network. A thorough test will overlap multiple commercial tools to ensure nothing is missed.

The open-source tools are often called "hacker tools" because not surprisingly, this is exactly what their heritage is. They tend to be a mixed collection, ranging from very professionally developed and supported tools, all the way through to dodgy scripts that were knocked up in the early hours to perform a specific task. Most can be freely obtained on the Internet, and are generally simple to use (allowing for some background knowledge of the subject). However, they are often made available on "hacker" web sites, where it is not unusual to find they have been pre-infected with a virus or Trojan horse ready to catch out the unwary.

When selecting a penetration testing supplier it is essential to make sure that the tools that are being used are appropriate. Be sure to ask for a full list of all tools that will be used, their source and a brief description of what they will be used for.

If commercial vulnerability assessment software will be used, make sure that there will be multiple tools; they do not overlap with each other 100% so more tools will mean there is less chance of anything being missed.

If "hacker" tools are going to be used, make sure to ask what steps have been taken to ensure that they do not contain a virus or other malicious software that could be introduced to your systems. Do not accept the answer that the tools have been tested with antivirus software and that this enough. Antivirus software will not typically find anything malicious unless it has already been inadvertently activated and reported to the antivirus vendor. Being a pioneer in this situation is not such a good thing.

You should also ask how the latest vulnerabilities will be tested and how false positives are eliminated; if any referral is made back to tools at this point be wary. Vulnerabilities are being discovered at a rate of around fifty per week at the present time. No tool can be completely up-to-date at that pace, and so it is critical to check for all the latest vulnerabilities manually. It is also necessary to manually verify the output of the tools to ensure that no vulnerabilities are missed and also to verify that those that are reported aren't false alarms. Again, the only way to do this is to use the skills of a trained consultant. Without an element of manual testing, the process will be incomplete and inaccurate.

"Confidential" and "Proprietary"

Many security organizations that provide penetration testing services will claim to have a methodology or use custom tools and specialized procedures, but when pressed will retreat behind a barrier of secrecy;

claiming that their methods are "confidential" or "proprietary" and so can not be disclosed. This reaction generally means that there is no methodology, or that there are in fact no custom tools either.

When it comes to the briefings and reports that provide the real value to the penetration testing assignment, a number of suppliers also fail to provide any real detail for the same reasons. We have heard of suppliers that claim not to be able to provide any more than cursory information because they are "government approved". Corsaire have worked for a number of years with government agencies, and are not aware of any such restrictions.

If the organization in question cannot provide transparency in their approach to the assessment, nor evidence of their methodology and tools, then it would be reasonable to view them with suspicion.

Legalities

No matter how much care is taken, actively testing your systems carries with it a small element of risk that there will be an unscheduled outage. Whilst this risk can be reduced through good practices and a comprehensive methodology, it cannot be eliminated entirely. Legacy systems and unreliable applications might not respond well to being tested, and if their presence is not made known beforehand, they are difficult to avoid.

As part of the penetration testing preliminaries, there should be a signed agreement put in place that guarantees that your organizations information will be treated confidentially. It should also provide cover for a number of other key areas, such as negligence and liability in the event of something untoward happening.

Beware of any supplier that seeks to exclude all liabilities, including negligence, from the penetration testing agreement. Without any form of legal protection, you are effectively at greater risk from your penetration testing supplier than from a hacker; at least with the hacker you will have the option of legal recourse!

Additionally, before you embark on a relationship with a new suppler, ensure that they have professional indemnity insurance cover in place to cover at least a million pounds worth of damages. Specialist security companies are often small organisations; without comprehensive insurance policies there is little chance that they would be able to meet any reasonable level of reparation. Ask to see copies of their insurance documents before proceeding.

Prices

Prices for penetration tests, like anything else will vary enormously. Be sure to get at least three quotes from different suppliers and make sure you receive like-for-like pricing. Pricing will usually be based on the number of man days required to fulfill the scope of the project. If you obtain sample reports and three references from reputable organizations that the supplier is and has been dealing with for a period of time you should be able to ascertain which supplier is offering best value for money.

5.2 Case Studies

The General Medical Council - GMC (a registered UK charity) - exists to provide protection for patients and guidance for medical professionals. Its website, www.gmc-uk.org, acts as a portal for stakeholders and the GMC's online presence is set to grow as they move increasingly towards web-based services.

Background

The GMC decided that any profound increase in its online business activity should be marshalled with structured, non-organic architecture growth. It was important for the GMC that any development should be bound to a rigorous security framework. The nature and sensitivity of the information being transacted means that an information security breach is unacceptable. Therefore the development and building processes were carried out to minimise the risk of information leakage and susceptibility to attack.

To further reinforce their security stance the GMC demanded that the concurrent web and application projects be subject to testing. The testing needed to be:

- Methodical (in order to manage it effectively).
- Well documented (so that findings and recommendations could be translated directly into relevant work packages).
- Entirely consistent (as it was planned that testing would be carried out both 'pre' and 'post' rollout).
- Flexible (so that the content, duration, depth and intensity of the testing could exactly match the requirement).
- Transparent (enabling the GMC to scrutinise every minute aspect of the testing being carried out and use this to enhance future development work).

Once the 'testing criteria' (in the loosest sense) had been defined it was a straightforward matter of applying the appropriate methodologies to each testing scenario and carrying out the tests. The components requiring attention were:

The rollout of the PLAB - Professional and Linguistic Assessment Board - online test booking application (carrying an information transaction risk).

PLAB (a two-part test) is the main way in which the GMC obtains objective evidence of the skill and knowledge of a doctor who has qualified outside the EEA (European Economic Area (Austria, Belgium, Denmark, Finland, France, Germany, Greece, Ireland, Italy, Luxembourg, Netherlands, Portugal, Spain, Sweden, United Kingdom, Iceland, Norway, Liechtenstein) and who wishes to practice in the UK. A pass in the test gives a doctor access to a form of registration, which allows employment in the NHS, but only under supervision. Following a period of supervised practice the doctor can apply for full registration, which allows unsupervised practice (more information can be obtained from the GMC web site at www.gmc-uk.org).

The need to take secure online payments (carrying a financial transaction risk).

The provision of a real-time interface via their site (carrying an information leakage risk and authentication issues).

The aforementioned provisions are all 'firsts' for the GMC; this is the first time that the GMC has ventured to provide a system allowing web interaction with a doctor for online transactions.

Details of Service Delivered

After weighing up several options the GMC ultimately chose to use mwr InfoSecurity. The bulk of the testing concentrated on the PLAB application so Application Security Testing was employed. In order to provide thorough and insightful results the application was tested both before and after it went live.

The type of infrastructure testing that the GMC opted for came from mwr InfoSecurity's Modular Penetration Testing bundle. Modules used were:

- Network Surveying
- Port Scanning
- Systems and Services Identification
- Vulnerability Testing Research
- Password Cracking

This gave the GMC the opportunity to tune the testing so that it was needs-specific with no superfluous work being carried out. The added benefit here was that the GMC did not have to carry the unnecessary cost of irrelevant test components- in effect a bespoke test with an 'off-the-shelf' price.

Expectations

As with any web-enabled business activity, is it small or large, public or private sector the GMC rightly identified the key concerns. They centre on the risks to systems and core databases from the necessarily public facing links on its website.

The GMC's own auditor's technical arm had been brought in to advise and it was following their recommendations that the technical architecture was established which was subject to mwr InfoSecurity's testing.

Problems Solved/Outcomes

mwr InfoSecurity won GMC's business because of a straightforward approach to the requirement. The proposal was a clear 'fit' with the GMC's needs. An important factor was also the way in which mwr InfoSecurity approached the GMC – ".explaining [mwr InfoSecurity's] capabilities and relating this to our structure. It's also been important for us that there is a level of flexibility and support throughout the process".

The ultimate impact of the testing however is evident in the GMC's trust in the security of PLAB online bookings.

Testimonial

"The GMC is acutely aware that the information it holds and collects is very sensitive and therefore the security of any interactive web application was critical to its success. Success in this first step toward online services was essential if we are to achieve our aim to place a significant part of our services online by 2005".

"[mwr InfoSecurity] Testing gave us an independent view of the value of the security we had installed and allowed us to make changes which increased our confidence".

5.3 Social Engineering

Because of different ways and natures of attacks involved in Social Engineering there are slightly different definitions but the definition that suits most criteria to our problem is as, "The art and Science of the psychological tricks to get the desired results from human beings and to make them comply accordingly for unauthorized operations is known as Social Engineering (in contrast with computer security)". The goals of the

Social Engineering are same as traditional hacking. But by Social Engineering hackers got these goals by implementing social skills and exploiting human tendencies. By Social Engineering crackers are not the mind controllers of the victim. Victim will not do the things out of his normal behavior. He will perform the usual acts but unconsciously he becomes the asset for cracker. Crackers are exploiting the nature of human beings. Most brilliant crackers of the day study the human psychology with same effort and attention as they learn new bugs in most secure operating systems. They will consider/study all the possibilities according to the nature of attack being performed. And they pay more attention in preparations for social engineering than to perform it like normal technical hacking. And every body knows that time taken in a hack is just a small fraction of the time to gather the proper information regarding the victim for real attack.

To understand the targets of Social Engineering we have to first see the purposes of Social Engineering in contrast with conventional hacking. The basic goals of Social Engineering are to gain unauthorized access to systems, to achieve information to perform illegal operations like fraud, industrial espionage, identity theft, or to take revenge, in case of upset employee, disruption of network and loss of reputation of the target organization and in some cases it can be curiosity of the hacker to see what and how every thing is going on in that particular field of interest. These are the same goals as of conventional hacking, so same are the targets. Typical targets are included computer related industry giants, telecom corporations, highly well known organizations, military and government operated agencies. As tighter security an organization have more prone they are for social engineering, because in the presence of effective security policies and tight technical security, employees start trusting heavily on it and ignores others vectors of security. In the presence of such effective security, an attacker will eventually fail to break security through technical skills and result will be a social engineering approach

Although Social Engineering is one of biggest challenge in today security and most famous successful attack of crackers on big organizations have a story of social engineering attached with it. But it is very difficult to find a publicly accepted example of social engineering attacks. As Social Engineering is not detectable by any automated technical system like IDS or firewalls or any thing else, so there is no chance of automatic detection and eventually record keeping mechanism of these kinds of attacks. This is also one main reason of so many and so easily crafted social engineered attacks. One another important factor is that people consider social engineering attacks directly on their intelligence and character and after success of these attacks they feel socially vulnerable. They hesitate to report such kind of attacks to not stand fool among their co-fellows and society. Of course most of the people don't like that they are called fools among their colleagues. This is reason that mostly social engineering attacks, along with successful attack, remain undocumented or even reported. This is a main reason of wide spread of social engineering attacks. Let's face it bravely and start documenting and reporting these attacks. It is tough reality of life that many highly skilled admins become victims of such attacks once upon a time! Another reason is that organization don't want to lose their reputation, organizations try to avoid publicity of such breaches, as some time confidence and trust is only a basic rule of their business e.g., for a company, who's main business runs accepting credit cards, it is very difficult for that organization to admit that their credit card data have been hacked.

6. The Art of Cryptography – "Behind the Locked Door"

6.1 Introduction

Cryptography is the art or science of keeping messages secret. Cryptography used to protect information of real value against organized criminals, multinational corporations, and major governments. Cryptography used to be only military business; however, in the information society it has become one of the central tools for maintaining privacy and confidentiality. Suppose that someone wants to send a message to a receiver, and wants to be sure that no one else can read the message. However, there is the possibility that someone else opens the letter or hears the electronic communication, so to make sure that something like that never happened we use cryptographic methods. Cryptology is the branch of mathematics that studies the mathematical foundations of cryptographic methods. "Public Key Cryptography", a method for encrypting messages to be transmitted over an insecure channel is emerging as fundamental tools for conducting business securely over the Internet.

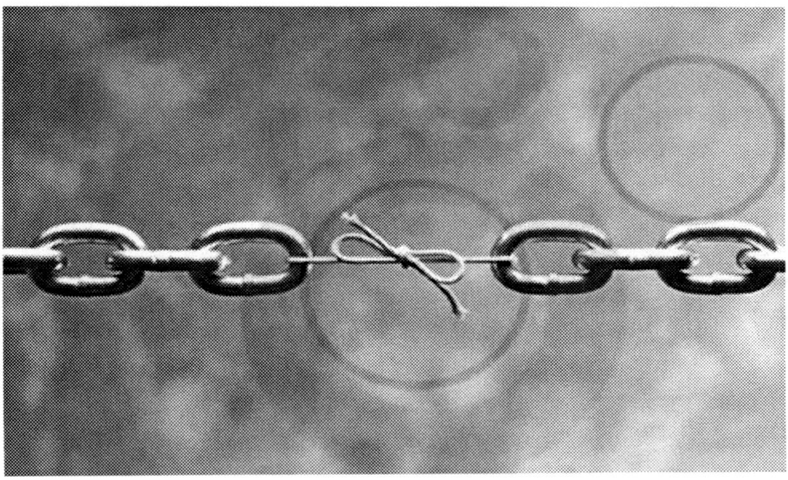

Src:www.imagevortex.com

This technology is widely expected to be used to conduct billions of dollars in electronic commerce within the next few years. As we move into an information society, the technological means for global surveillance of millions of individual people are becoming available to major governments. Cryptography has become one of the main tools for privacy, trust, access control, electronic payments, corporate security, and countless other fields. Cryptography is no longer a military thing that should not be messed with. It is time to demystify cryptography and make full use of the advantages it provides for the modern society.

Widespread cryptography is also one of the few defenses people have against suddenly finding themselves in a totalitarian surveillance society that can monitor and control everything they do. In cryptographic terminology, the message is called plaintext or cleartext. Encoding the contents of the message in such a way that hides its contents from outsiders is called Encryption. The encrypted message is called the ciphertext. The process of retrieving the plaintext from the ciphertext is called Decryption. Encryption and Decryption usually make use of a key, and the coding method is such that decryption can be performed only by knowing the proper key.

Cryptanalysis is the art of breaking ciphers, i.e., retrieving the plaintext without knowing the proper key. People who do cryptography are cryptographers, and practitioners of cryptanalysis are cryptanalysts. Cryptography deals with all aspects of secure messaging, authentication, digital signatures, electronic money, and other applications.

A method of encryption and decryption is called a Cipher. Some cryptographic methods rely on the secrecy of the algorithms; such algorithms are only of historical interest and are not adequate for real-world needs. All modern algorithms use a key to control encryption and decryption; a message can be decrypted only if the key matches the encryption key. The key used for decryption can be different from the encryption key, but for most algorithms they are the same. There are two classes of key-based algorithms, symmetric (or Secret-Key) and asymmetric (or Public-Key) algorithms. The difference is that symmetric algorithms use the same key for encryption and decryption (or the decryption key is easily derived from the encryption key), whereas asymmetric algorithms use a different key for encryption and decryption, and the decryption key cannot be derived from the encryption key.

6.2 Classical Approach

Internet Security Issues

All communication over the Internet uses the Transmission Control Protocol/Internet Protocol (TCP/IP). TCP/IP allows information to be sent from one computer to another through a variety of intermediate computers and separate networks before it reaches its destination.

The great flexibility of TCP/IP has led to its worldwide acceptance as the basic Internet and intranet communications protocol. At the same time, the fact that TCP/IP allows information to pass through intermediate computers makes it possible for a third party to interfere with communications in the following ways:

Eavesdropping: Information remains intact, but its privacy is compromised. For example, someone could learn your credit card number, record a sensitive conversation, or intercept classified information.

Tampering: Information in transit is changed or replaced and then sent on to the recipient. For example, someone could alter an order for goods or change a person's resume.

Impersonation: Information passes to a person who poses as the intended recipient. Impersonation can take two forms:

Spoofing: A person can pretend to be someone else. For example, a person can pretend to have the E-mail address jdoe@mozilla.com, or a computer can identify itself as a site called www.mozilla.com when it is not. This type of impersonation is known as Spoofing.

Misrepresentation: A person or organization can misrepresent itself. For example, suppose the site www.mozilla.com pretends to be a furniture store when it is really just a site that takes credit-card payments but never sends any goods.

Normally, users of the many cooperating computers that make up the Internet or other networks don't monitor or interfere with the network traffic that continuously passes through their machines. However, many sensitive personal and business communications over the Internet require precautions that address the threats listed above. Fortunately, a set of well-established techniques and standards known as Public Key Cryptography make it relatively easy to take such precautions.

Public Key Cryptography facilitates the following tasks:

Encryption and Decryption allow two communicating parties to disguise information they send to each other. The sender encrypts, or scrambles, information before sending it. The receiver decrypts, or unscrambles, the information after receiving it. While in transit, the encrypted information is unintelligible to an intruder.

Tamper detection allows the recipient of information to verify that it has not been modified in transit. Any attempt to modify data or substitute a false message for a legitimate one will be detected.

Authentication allows the recipient of information to determine its origin--that is, to confirm the sender's identity.

Nonrepudiation prevents the sender of information from claiming at a later date that the information was never sent.

The sections that follow introduce the concepts of public-key cryptography that underlie these capabilities.

Encryption and Decryption

Encryption is the process of transforming information so it is unintelligible to anyone but the intended recipient. Decryption is the process of transforming encrypted information so that it is intelligible again. A cryptographic algorithm, also called a Cipher, is a mathematical function used for encryption or decryption. In most cases, two related functions are employed, one for encryption and the other for decryption.

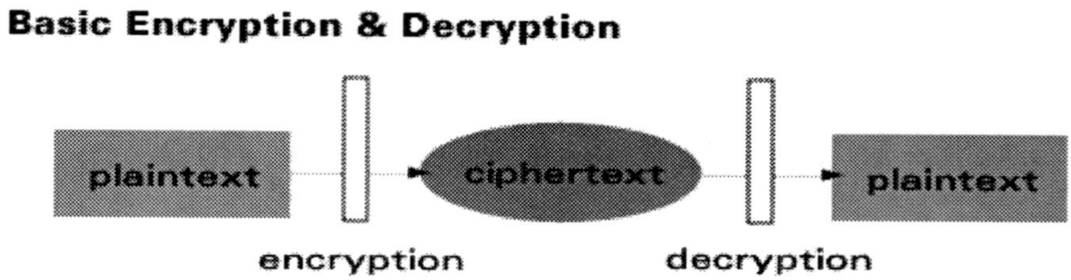

With most modern cryptography, the ability to keep encrypted information secret is based not on the cryptographic algorithm, which is widely known, but on a number called a key that must be used with the algorithm to produce an encrypted result or to decrypt previously encrypted information. Decryption with the correct key is simple. Decryption without the correct key is very difficult, and in some cases impossible for all practical purposes.

The sections that follow introduce the use of keys for encryption and decryption.

- Symmetric Key Encryption
- Public Key Encryption
- Key Length and Encryption Strength

Symmetric Key Encryption

With Symmetric Key Encryption, the encryption key can be calculated from the decryption key and vice versa. With most symmetric algorithms, the same key is used for both encryption and decryption, as shown in *Figure 1*.

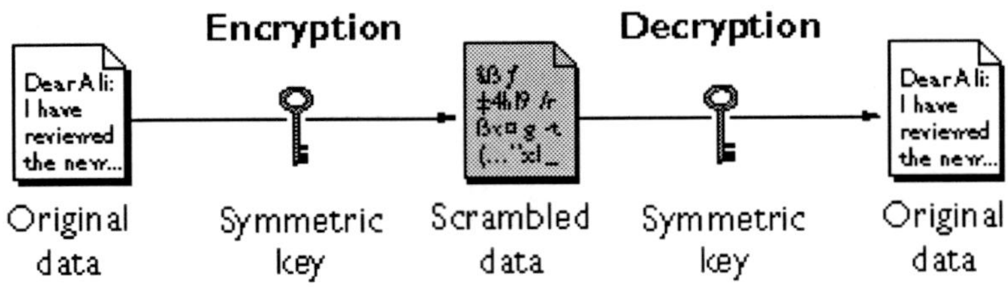

Figure 1: Symmetric Key Encryption

Implementations of Symmetric Key Encryption can be highly efficient, so that users do not experience any significant time delay as a result of the encryption and decryption. Symmetric Key Encryption also provides a degree of authentication, since information encrypted with one symmetric key cannot be decrypted with any other symmetric key. Thus, as long as the symmetric key is kept secret by the two parties using it to encrypt communications, each party can be sure that it is communicating with the other as long as the decrypted messages continue to make sense.

Symmetric Key Encryption is effective only if the symmetric key is kept secret by the two parties involved. If anyone else discovers the key, it affects both confidentiality and authentication. A person with an unauthorized symmetric key not only can decrypt messages sent with that key, but can encrypt new messages and send them as if they came from one of the two parties who were originally using the key.

Symmetric Key Encryption plays an important role in the SSL protocol, which is widely used for authentication, tamper detection, and encryption over TCP/IP networks. SSL also uses techniques of public-key encryption, which is described in the next section.

Public Key Encryption

The most commonly used implementations of Public Key Encryption are based on algorithms patented by RSA Data Security. Therefore, this section describes the RSA approach to Public Key Encryption.

Public Key Encryption (also called Asymmetric Encryption) involves a pair of keys--a public key and a private key--associated with an entity that needs to authenticate its identity electronically or to sign or encrypt data.

Each public key is published, and the corresponding private key is kept secret. (For more information about the way public keys are published, see Certificates and Authentication.) Data encrypted with your public key can be decrypted only with your private key. *Figure 2* shows a simplified view of the way public-key encryption works.

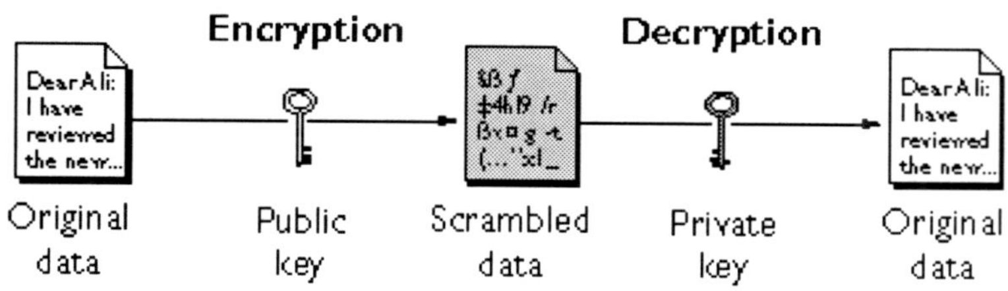

Figure 2: Public Key Encryption

The scheme shown in *Figure 2* lets you freely distribute a public key, and only you will be able to read data encrypted using this key. In general, to send encrypted data to someone, you encrypt the data with that person's public key, and the person receiving the encrypted data decrypts it with the corresponding private key.

Compared with Symmetric Key Encryption, Public Key Encryption requires more computation and is therefore not always appropriate for large amounts of data. However, it's possible to use Public Key Encryption to send a Symmetric Key, which can then be used to encrypt additional data. This is the approach used by the SSL protocol.

As it happens, the reverse of the scheme shown in *Figure 2* also works: data encrypted with your private key can be decrypted only with your public key. This would not be a desirable way to encrypt sensitive data, however, because it means that anyone with your public key, which is by definition published, could decrypt the data. Nevertheless, private-key encryption is useful, because it means you can use your private key to sign data with your Digital Signature--an important requirement for electronic commerce and other commercial applications of Cryptography. Client software such as Communicator can then use your public key to confirm that the message was signed with your private key and that it hasn't been tampered with since being signed. Digital Signatures and subsequent sections describe how this confirmation process works.

Key Length and Encryption Strength

In general, the strength of encryption is related to the difficulty of discovering the key, which in turn depends on both the cipher used and the length of the key. For example, the difficulty of discovering the key for the RSA cipher most commonly used for public-key encryption depends on the difficulty of factoring large numbers, a well-known mathematical problem.

Encryption strength is often described in terms of the size of the keys used to perform the encryption: in general, longer keys provide stronger encryption. Key length is measured in bits. For example, 128-bit keys for use with the RC4 symmetric-key cipher supported by SSL provide significantly better cryptographic protection than 40-bit keys for use with the same cipher. Roughly speaking, 128-bit RC4 encryption is 3 x 1026 times stronger than 40-bit RC4 encryption. (For more information about RC4 and other ciphers used with SSL, see Introduction to SSL.)

Different ciphers may require different key lengths to achieve the same level of encryption strength. The RSA cipher used for public-key encryption, for example, can use only a subset of all possible values for a key of a given length, due to the nature of the mathematical problem on which it is based. Other ciphers, such as those used for symmetric key encryption, can use all possible values for a key of a given length, rather than a subset of those values. Thus a 128-bit key for use with a Symmetric Key Encryption cipher would provide stronger encryption than a 128-bit key for use with the RSA Public Key Encryption cipher.

This difference explains why the RSA Public Key Encryption cipher must use a 512-bit key (or longer) to be considered cryptographically strong, whereas symmetric key ciphers can achieve approximately the same level of strength with a 64-bit key. Even this level of strength may be vulnerable to attacks in the near future.

Because the ability to surreptitiously intercept and decrypt encrypted information has historically been a significant military asset, the U.S. Government restricts export of cryptographic software, including most software that permits use of symmetric encryption keys longer than 40 bits. For detailed information about these restrictions as they apply to Netscape products, see Export Restrictions on International Sales.

Digital Signatures

A major benefit of public key cryptography is that it provides a method for employing *Digital Signatures.* Digital Signatures enable the recipient of information to verify the authenticity of the information's origin, and also verify that the information is intact. Thus, public key digital signatures provide *authentication* and data *integrity.* A digital signature also provides *non-repudiation,* which means that it prevents the sender from claiming that he or she did not actually send the information. These features are every bit as fundamental to cryptography as privacy, if not more.

A Digital Signature serves the same purpose as a handwritten signature. However, a handwritten signature is easy to counterfeit. A digital Signature is superior to a handwritten signature in that it is nearly impossible to counterfeit, plus it attests to the contents of the information as well as to the identity of the signer.

Some people tend to use signatures more than they use encryption. For example, you may not care if anyone knows that you just deposited $1000 in your account, but you do want to be darn sure it was the bank teller you were dealing with.

The basic manner in which digital signatures are created is illustrated in *Figure 3.* Instead of encrypting information using someone else's public key, you encrypt it with your private key. If the information can be decrypted with your public key, then it must have originated with you.

Figure 3: Simple digital signatures

A Certificate Identifies Someone or Something

A certificate is an electronic document used to identify an individual, a server, a company, or some other entity and to associate that identity with a public key. Like a driver's license, a passport, or other commonly used personal IDs, a certificate provides generally recognized proof of a person's identity. Public Key Cryptography uses certificates to address the problem of impersonation (see Internet Security Issues).

To get a driver's license, you typically apply to a government agency, such as the Department of Motor Vehicles, which verifies your identity, your ability to drive, your address, and other information before issuing the license. To get a student ID, you apply to a school or college, which performs different checks (such as whether you have paid your tuition) before issuing the ID. To get a library card, you may need to provide only your name and a utility bill with your address on it.

Certificates work much the same way as any of these familiar forms of identification. Certificate authorities (CAs) are entities that validate identities and issue certificates. They can be either independent third parties or organizations running their own certificate-issuing server software (such as Netscape Certificate Server). The methods used to validate an identity vary depending on the policies of a given CA--just as the methods to validate other forms of identification vary depending on who is issuing the ID and the purpose for which it will be used. In general, before issuing a certificate, the CA must use its published verification procedures for that type of certificate to ensure that an entity requesting a certificate is in fact who it claims to be.

The certificate issued by the CA binds a particular public key to the name of the entity the certificate identifies (such as the name of an employee or a server). Certificates help prevent the use of fake public keys for impersonation. Only the public key certified by the certificate will work with the corresponding private key possessed by the entity identified by the certificate.

In addition to a public key, a certificate always includes the name of the entity it identifies, an expiration date, the name of the CA that issued the certificate, a serial number, and other information. Most importantly, a certificate always includes the digital signature of the issuing CA. The CA's digital signature allows the certificate to function as a "letter of introduction" for users who know and trust the CA but don't know the entity identified by the certificate.

For more information about the role of CAs, see How CA Certificates are Used to Establish Trust.

Authentication Confirms an Identity

Authentication is the process of confirming an identity. In the context of network interactions, authentication involves the confident identification of one party by another party. Authentication over networks can take many forms. Certificates are one way of supporting authentication.

Network interactions typically take place between a client, such as browser software running on a personal computer, and a server, such as the software and hardware used to host a Web site. Client authentication refers to the confident identification of a client by a server (that is, identification of the person assumed to be using the client software). Server authentication refers to the confident identification of a server by a client (that is, identification of the organization assumed to be responsible for the server at a particular network address).

Client and server authentication are not the only forms of authentication that certificates support. For example, the digital signature on an email message, combined with the certificate that identifies the sender, provide strong evidence that the person identified by that certificate did indeed send that message. Similarly, a digital signature on an HTML form, combined with a certificate that identifies the signer, can provide evidence, after the fact, that the person identified by that certificate did agree to the contents of the form. In addition to authentication, the digital signature in both cases ensures a degree of nonrepudiation--that is, a digital signature makes it difficult for the signer to claim later not to have sent the email or the form.

Client authentication is an essential element of network security within most intranets or extranets. The sections that follow contrast two forms of client authentication:

Password-Based Authentication: Almost all server software permits client authentication by means of a name and password. For example, a server might require a user to type a name and password before granting access to the server. The server maintains a list of names and passwords; if a particular name is on the list, and if the user types the correct password, the server grants access.

Certificate-Based Authentication: Client Authentication based on certificates is part of the SSL protocol. The client digitally signs a randomly generated piece of data and sends both the certificate and the signed data across the network. The server uses techniques of public-key cryptography to validate the signature and confirm the validity of the certificate.

Password-Based Authentication

Figure 4 shows the basic steps involved in authenticating a client by means of a name and password. *Figure 4* assumes the following:

- The user has already decided to trust the server, either without authentication or on the basis of server authentication via SSL.
- The user has requested a resource controlled by the server.
- The server requires client authentication before permitting access to the requested resource.

These are the steps shown in Figure 4:

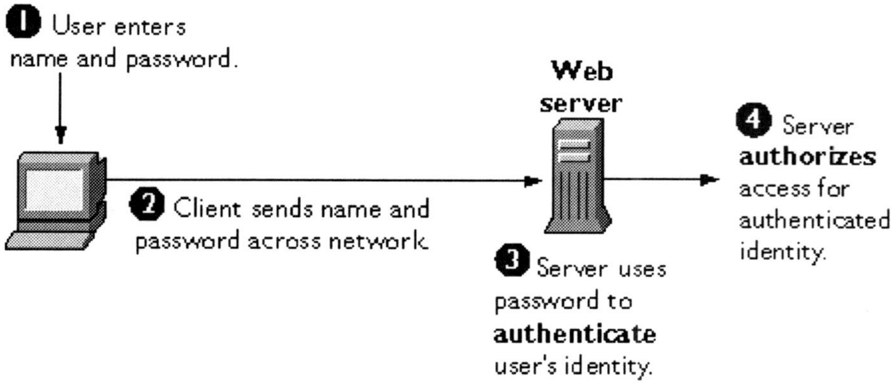

Figure 4: Using a password to authenticate a client to a server

In response to an authentication request from the server, the client displays a dialog box requesting the user's name and password for that server. The user must supply a name and password separately for each new server the user wishes to use during a work session.

The client sends the name and password across the network, either in the clear or over an encrypted SSL connection.

The server looks up the name and password in its local password database and, if they match, accepts them as evidence authenticating the user's identity.

The server determines whether the identified user is permitted to access the requested resource, and if so allows the client to access it.

With this arrangement, the user must supply a new password for each server, and the administrator must keep track of the name and password for each user, typically on separate servers.

As shown in the next section, one of the advantages of Certificate-Based Authentication is that it can be used to replace the first three steps in *Figure 2* with a mechanism that allows the user to supply just one password (which is not sent across the network) and allows the administrator to control user authentication centrally.

Certificate-Based Authentication

Figure 5 shows how client authentication works using certificates and the SSL Protocol. To authenticate a user to a server, a client digitally signs a randomly generated piece of data and sends both the certificate and the signed data across the network. For the purposes of this discussion, the digital signature associated with some data can be thought of as evidence provided by the client to the server. The server authenticates the user's identity on the strength of this evidence.

Like *Figure 4, Figure 5* assumes that the user has already decided to trust the server and has requested a resource, and that the server has requested client authentication in the process of evaluating whether to grant access to the requested resource.

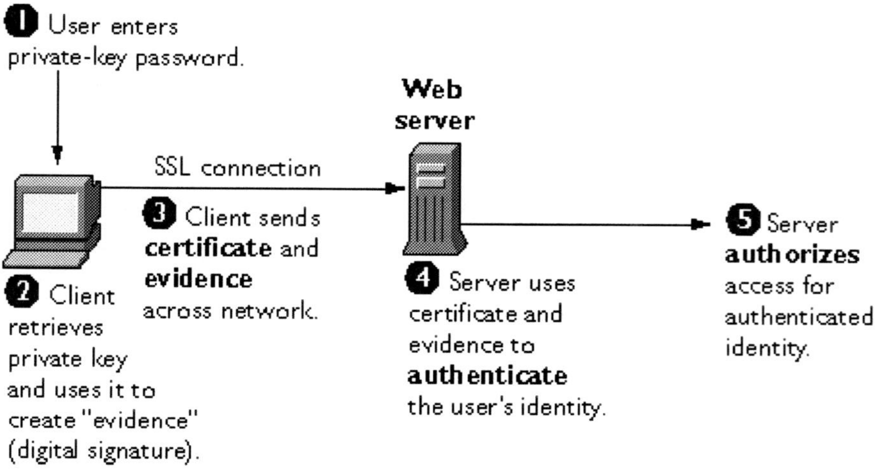

Figure 5: Using a certificate to authenticate a client to a server

Unlike the process shown in *Figure 4, t*he process shown in *Figure 5* requires the use of SSL. *Figure 5* also assumes that the client has a valid certificate that can be used to identify the client to the server. Certificate-based authentication is generally considered preferable to password-based authentication because it is based on what the user has (the private key) as well as what the user knows (the password that protects the private key). However, it's important to note that these two assumptions are true only if unauthorized personnel have not gained access to the user's machine or password, the password for the client software's private key database has been set, and the software is set up to request the password at reasonably frequent intervals.

Important neither Password-Based Authentication nor Certificate-Based Authentication address security issues related to physical access to individual machines or passwords. Public Key Cryptography can only verify that a private key used to sign some data corresponds to the public key in a certificate. It is the user's responsibility to protect a machine's physical security and to keep the private-key password secret.

These are the steps shown in *Figure 3:*

The client software, such as Communicator, maintains a database of the private keys that correspond to the public keys published in any certificates issued for that client. The client asks for the password to this database the first time the client needs to access it during a given session--for example, the first time the user attempts to access an SSL-enabled server that requires certificate-based client authentication. After entering this password once, the user doesn't need to enter it again for the rest of the session, even when accessing other SSL-enabled servers.

The client unlocks the private-key database, retrieves the private key for the user's certificate, and uses that private key to digitally sign some data that has been randomly generated for this purpose on the basis of input from both the client and the server. This data and the digital signature constitute "evidence" of the private key's validity. The digital signature can be created only with that private key and can be validated with the corresponding public key against the signed data, which is unique to the SSL session.

The client sends both the user's certificate and the evidence (the randomly generated piece of data that has been digitally signed) across the network.

The server uses the certificate and the evidence to authenticate the user's identity. (For a detailed discussion of the way this works, see Introduction to SSL.)

At this point the server may optionally perform other authentication tasks, such as checking that the certificate presented by the client is stored in the user's entry in an LDAP directory. The server then continues to evaluate whether the identified user is permitted to access the requested resource. This evaluation process can employ a variety of standard authorization mechanisms, potentially using additional information in an LDAP directory, company databases, and so on. If the result of the evaluation is positive, the server allows the client to access the requested resource.

As you can see by comparing *Figure 5* to *Figure 4,* certificates replace the authentication portion of the interaction between the client and the server. Instead of requiring a user to send passwords across the network throughout the day, single sign-on requires the user to enter the private-key database password just once, without sending it across the network.

For the rest of the session, the client presents the user's certificate to authenticate the user to each new server it encounters. Existing authorization mechanisms based on the authenticated user identity are not affected.

SSL Protocol

The Secure Sockets Layer (SSL) protocol, which was originally developed by Netscape, is a set of rules governing server authentication, client authentication, and encrypted communication between servers and clients. SSL is widely used on the Internet, especially for interactions that involve exchanging confidential information such as credit card numbers.

SSL requires a server SSL certificate, at a minimum. As part of the initial "handshake" process, the server presents its certificate to the client to authenticate the server's identity. The authentication process uses Public Key Encryption and Digital Signatures to confirm that the server is in fact the server it claims to be. Once the server has been authenticated, the client and server use techniques of Symmetric Key Encryption, which is very fast, to encrypt all the information they exchange for the remainder of the session and to detect any tampering that may have occurred.

Servers may optionally be configured to require client authentication as well as server authentication. In this case, after server authentication is successfully completed, the client must also present its certificate to the server to authenticate the client's identity before the encrypted SSL session can be established.

For an overview of client authentication over SSL and how it differs from password-based authentication, see Authentication Confirms an Identity. For more detailed information about SSL, see Introduction to SSL.

Signed and Encrypted E-mail

Some E-mail programs (including Messenger, which is part of Communicator) support digitally signed and encrypted E-mail using a widely accepted protocol known as Secure Multipurpose Internet Mail Extension (S/MIME). Using S/MIME to sign or encrypt E-mail messages requires the sender of the message to have an S/MIME certificate.

An E-mail message that includes a digital signature provides some assurance that it was in fact sent by the person whose name appears in the message header, thus providing authentication of the sender. If the digital signature cannot be validated by the email software on the receiving end, the user will be alerted.

The Digital Signature is unique to the message it accompanies. If the message received differs in any way from the message that was sent--even by the addition or deletion of a comma--the digital signature cannot be validated. Therefore, signed E-mail also provides some assurance that the email has not been tampered with. As discussed at the beginning of this document, this kind of assurance is known as nonrepudiation. In other words, signed E-mail makes it very difficult for the sender to deny having sent the message. This is important for many forms of business communication. (For information about the way digital signatures work, see Digital Signatures.)

S/MIME also makes it possible to encrypt E-mail messages. This is also important for some business users. However, using encryption for email requires careful planning. If the recipient of encrypted email messages loses his or her private key and does not have access to a backup copy of the key, for example, the encrypted messages can never be decrypted.

Issuing Certificates

The process for issuing a certificate depends on the certificate authority that issues it and the purpose for which it will be used. The process for issuing nondigital forms of identification varies in similar ways. For example, if you want to get a generic ID card (not a driver's license) from the Department of Motor Vehicles in California, the requirements are straightforward: you need to present some evidence of your identity, such as a utility bill with your address on it and a student identity card. If you want to get a regular driving license, you also need to take a test--a driving test when you first get the license, and a written test when you renew it. If you want to get a commercial license for an eighteen-wheeler, the requirements are much more stringent. If you live in some other state or country, the requirements for various kinds of licenses will differ.

Similarly, different CAs have different procedures for issuing different kinds of certificates. In some cases the only requirement may be your E-mail address. In other cases, your UNIX or NT login and password may be sufficient. At the other end of the scale, for certificates that identify people who can authorize large expenditures or make other sensitive decisions, the issuing process may require notarized documents, a background check, and a personal interview.

Depending on an organization's policies, the process of issuing certificates can range from being completely transparent for the user to requiring significant user participation and complex procedures. In general, processes for issuing certificates should be highly flexible, so organizations can tailor them to their changing needs.

The Netscape Certificate Server, part of the Mission Control family of products, allows an organization to set up its own certificate authority and issue certificates.

Issuing certificates is one of several managements tasks that can be handled by separate Registration Authorities.

Renewing and Revoking Certificates

Like a driver's license, a certificate specifies a period of time during which it is valid. Attempts to use a certificate for authentication before or after its validity period will fail. Therefore, mechanisms for managing certificate renewal are essential for any certificate management strategy. For example, an administrator may wish to be notified automatically when a certificate is about to expire, so that an appropriate renewal process can be completed in plenty of time without causing the certificate's subject any inconvenience. The renewal process may involve reusing the same public-private key pair or issuing a new one.

A driver's license can be suspended even if it has not expired--for example, as punishment for a serious driving offense. Similarly, it's sometimes necessary to revoke a certificate before it has expired--for example, if an employee leaves a company or moves to a new job within the company.

Certificate revocation can be handled in several different ways. For some organizations, it may be sufficient to set up servers so that the authentication process includes checking the directory for the presence of the certificate being presented. When an administrator revokes a certificate, the certificate can be automatically removed from the directory, and subsequent authentication attempts with that certificate will fail even though the certificate remains valid in every other respect. Another approach involves publishing a certificate revocation list (CRL)--that is, a list of revoked certificates--to the directory at regular intervals and checking the list as part of the authentication process. For some organizations, it may be preferable to check directly with the issuing CA each time a certificate is presented for authentication. This procedure is sometimes called real-time status checking.

6.3 Hashing

Hashing is the transformation of a string of characters into a usually shorter fixed-length value or key that represents the original string. Hashing is used to index and retrieve items in a database because it is faster to find the item using the shorter hashed key than to find it using the original value. It is also used in many encryption algorithms.

As a simple example of the using of hashing in databases, a group of people could be arranged in a database like this:

Abernathy, Sara
Epperdingle, Roscoe
Moore, Wilfred
Smith, David
(and many more sorted into alphabetical order)

Each of these names would be the key in the database for that person's data. A database search mechanism would first have to start looking character-by-character across the name for matches until it found the match (or ruled the other entries out). But if each of the names were hashed, it might be possible (depending on the number of names in the database) to generate a unique four-digit key for each name. For example:

7864 Abernathy, Sara
9802 Epperdingle, Roscoe
1990 Moore, Wilfred
8822 Smith, David
(and so forth)

A search for any name would first consist of computing the hash value (using the same hash function used to store the item) and then comparing for a match using that value. It would, in general, be much faster to find a match across four digits, each having only 10 possibilities, than across an unpredictable value length where each character had 26 possibilities.

The hashing algorithm is called the hash function (and probably the term is derived from the idea that the resulting hash value can be thought of as a "mixed up" version of the represented value). In addition to faster data retrieval, hashing is also used to encrypt and decrypt digital signatures (used to authenticate message senders and receivers). The digital signature is transformed with the hash function and then both the hashed value (known as a message-digest) and the signature are sent in separate transmissions to the receiver. Using the same hash function as the sender, the receiver derives a message-digest from the signature and compares it with the message-digest it also received. They should be the same.

The hash function is used to index the original value or key and then used later each time the data associated with the value or key is to be retrieved. Thus, hashing is always a one-way operation. There's no need to "reverse engineer" the hash function by analyzing the hashed values. In fact, the ideal hash function can't be derived by such analysis. A good hash function also should not produce the same hash value from two different inputs. If it does, this is known as a collision. A hash function that offers an extremely low risk of collision may be considered acceptable.

Here are some relatively simple hash functions that have been used:

- **The division-remainder method:** The size of the number of items in the table is estimated. That number is then used as a divisor into each original value or key to extract a quotient and a remainder. The remainder is the hashed value. (Since this method is liable to produce a number of collisions, any search mechanism would have to be able to recognize a collision and offer an alternate search mechanism.)
- **Folding:** This method divides the original value (digits in this case) into several parts, adds the parts together, and then uses the last four digits (or some other arbitrary number of digits that will work) as the hashed value or key.
- **Radix transformation:** Where the value or key is digital, the number base (or radix) can be changed resulting in a different sequence of digits. (For example, a decimal numbered key could be transformed into a hexadecimal numbered key.) High-order digits could be discarded to fit a hash value of uniform length.
- **Digit rearrangement:** This is simply taking part of the original value or key such as digits in positions 3 through 6, reversing their order, and then using that sequence of digits as the hash value or key.

A hash function that works well for database storage and retrieval might not work as for cryptographic or error-checking purposes. There are several well-known hash functions used in cryptography. These include the message-digest hash functions MD2, MD4, and MD5, used for hashing digital signatures into a shorter value called a message-digest, and the Secure Hash Algorithm (SHA), a standard algorithm, that makes a larger (60-bit) message digest and is similar to MD4.

6.4 Encryption Algorithms(RSA, MD5, IDEA)

RSA

The RSA Algorithm and the RSA Patent

The RSA Algorithm was named after Ronald Rivest, Adi Shamir and Leonard Adelman, who first published the algorithm in April, 1977. Since that time, the algorithm has been employed in the most widely-used Internet electronic communications encryption program, Pretty Good Privacy (PGP). It is also employed in both the Netscape Navigator and Microsoft Explorer web browsing programs in their implementations of the Secure Sockets Layer (SSL), and by MasterCard and VISA in the Secure Electronic Transactions (SET) protocol for credit card transactions.

The RSA Algorithm is claimed in the RSA Patent, which was issued to Drs. Rivest, Shamir and Adelman, who exclusively licensed the patent nine days later to RSA Data Security, Inc., a company which was originally controlled by the inventors but is now a wholly-owned subsidiary of a Boston based company called Security Dynamics Technology, Inc. RSA Data has to date filed three lawsuits alleging infringement of the RSA Patent. Two were settled prior to trial, and the third is still pending. Other litigation threats have been made regarding alleged infringements of the patent, including threats against non-commercial implementations for use by the Internet community. The patent expires on September 20, 2000, but that will be enough time for the patent to have a profound impact on the development of electronic commerce.

The existence of the patent, and RSA Data's aggressive litigation posture, has chilled the interest in both commercial and non-commercial implementations of public key encryption and digital signature technologies. Many have taken for granted the bald assertion that the "RSA Algorithm is patented", without examining the patent itself, or more particularly, the claims of the patent. As we set forth in this article, however, a careful review of the patent reveals that the patent is not necessarily as broad as publicly asserted. More particularly, the decryption operation, standing alone, is not independently claimed at all in the patent. These weaknesses in the patent may be particularly relevant for digital signature operations because they may allow a developer to implement the protocol for verifying an RSA-generated digital signature without infringing the patent. In addition, if one separates the generation of the key pairs from the encryption operation, the claims of the patent do not cover the encryption (or signing) function by itself.

Basic uses of Public Key Encryption and Digital Signatures

The RSA Algorithm is only one implementation of the more general concept of public key cryptography, which permits two parties who have never met and who can only communicate on an insecure channel to nonetheless send secure and verifiable messages to each other. The Internet as currently structured is an insecure communications channel with an obvious use for such technologies. Indeed, the greatest expected growth for public key techniques is in Internet-related communications.

With public key techniques, each user has two different keys, one made available to the public and the other kept secret. One of the keys is used to encrypt a message, and the other is used to decrypt the message. If Alice wants to send a secret message to Bob, for example, she looks up Bob's public key and uses it to encrypt the message. Because Bob's *public* key cannot undo the encryption process, no one who intercepts the message can read it. Only Bob, who possesses the secret key corresponding to his public key, can read the message. Alice never has to meet Bob out of the hearing of others to exchange keys or passwords; this is a substantial improvement over older encryption methods in which an exchange of private keys was necessary.

This system can also be used as a means for Bob to be sure a message comes from Alice. If Alice wants to sign a message, she can encrypt it with her private key. When Bob receives an encrypted message which purports to be from Alice, he can obtain Alice's public key and decrypt the message. If a readable message emerges, Bob can have confidence that the message came from Alice, because Alice's public key would only properly unlock a message which was locked with her private key (known only to Alice).

Of course, digitally signing the message does not make the content of the message private, because anyone with Alice's public key can read a message she encrypted with her private key. Alice can send a private, signed message to Bob, however, by first encrypting the message with Bob's public key (so only Bob can read it with his private key) and then encrypting the message a second time with her private key, forming her signature. Anyone who receives the message can use Alice's public key to undo the second encryption, but only Bob (or someone with Bob's private key) can undo the first encryption step and actually read the message. All of these complex-sounding manipulations can be made quite manageable with well-written software.

The RSA Implementation of Public Key Encryption and Digital Signatures

The Arithmetic in the RSA System

Typical encryption techniques use mathematical operations to transform a message (represented as a number or a series of numbers) into a *ciphertext*. Mathematical operations called *one way functions* are particularly suited to this task. A one way function is one which is comparatively easy to do in one direction but much harder to do in reverse. As a trivial example, it is comparatively easy to square a two digit number; with a little concentration, many people can probably multiply 24 by 24 without using a pencil and paper. One the other hand, calculating the square root of the number 576 is much harder, even with a pencil and paper.

The RSA system uses one way functions of a more complex nature. Specifically, the system uses *modular arithmetic* to transform a message (or pieces of the message, one piece at a time) into unreadable ciphertext. Modular arithmetic is often called "clock" arithmetic, because addition, subtraction, and the like, work like telling time. In a 12-hour system, four hours after 10:00 is not 14:00 (10 + 4 is not equal to 14); it is 2:00. This is because we subtract out 12 (or any multiples of 12) after doing the addition. In modular arithmetic notation, the operation might look like this:

2 = (10+4) mod 12
2 = 14 mod 12

One can do multiplication in modular arithmetic much the same way addition is done in the above example:

2 = (7*2) mod 12
2 = 14 mod 12
This process is sometimes called *modular reduction.* By subtracting out the modulus (and all multiples of the modulus) a number is "reduced" to a much smaller number. When the number 14 is "reduced" to the number 2 in the above example, one can say that "14 is reduced modulo 12".

The RSA system uses multiplication in modular arithmetic. Instead of multiplying one number by a different number (as (7) is multiplied by (2) in the above example), The RSA system multiplies one number (called the *base*) by itself a number of times. The number of times a base is multiplied by itself is called the *exponent*:

16 = 2*2*2*2
16 = 2^4

In this example, the number (2) is the base, and is multiplied by itself four times, making the exponent the number (4).

In the RSA encryption formula, the message (represented by a number M) is multiplied by itself (e) times (called "raising (M) to the power (e)"), and the product is then divided by a modulus (n), leaving the remainder as a ciphertext (C):

$C = M^e \bmod n$

This is a hard operation to undo -- when (n) is very large (200 digits or so) -- even the fastest computers using the fastest known methods could not feasibly recover the message (M) simply from knowing the ciphertext (C) and the key used to create the message ((e) and (n)).

In the decryption operation, a different exponent, (d) is used to convert the ciphertext back into the plain text:

$C = M^d \bmod n$

The modulus (n) is a composite number, constructed by multiplying two prime numbers, (p) and (q), together:

$n = p * q$

The encryption and decryption exponents, (d) and (e), are related to each other and the modulus (n) in the following way:

$d = e^{-1} \bmod ((p-1)\ (q-1))$

To calculate the decryption key, one must know the numbers (p) and (q) (called the factors) used to calculate the modulus (n). When (n) is a sufficiently large number, it is infeasible, using known algorithms and the fastest computing techniques, to calculate the prime number factors of (n).

The RSA Algorithm may be divided, then, into three steps:

***(1) Key Generation*:** In which the factors of the modulus (n) (the prime numbers (p) and (q)) are chosen and multiplied together to form (n), an encryption exponent (e) is chosen, and the decryption exponent (d) is calculated using (e), (p), and (q).
(2) *Encryption*: In which the message (M) is raised to the power (e), and then reduced modulo (n).
(3) *Decryption*: In which the ciphertext (C) is raised to the power (d), and then reduced modulo (n).

Using the RSA Algorithm for Privacy and Digital Signatures

When the RSA Algorithm is used in a public key system, the modulus (n) and one of the exponents (arbitrarily, we can assume (e)) are published. The other exponent (d) is kept secret, as are (p) and (q), the factors of (n). Each user holds his or her own keys, and knows the public key of the other user or users. Alice, for example, knows her own public key (e_{alice}

and n_{alice}), her own private key (d_{alice}), and Bob's public key (e_{bob} and n_{bob}). Bob knows the converse: his public key (e_{bob} and n_{bob}), his private key (d_{bob}) and Alice's public key (e_{alice} and n_{alice}).

For Alice to send Bob a private message only Bob can read, she performs the following operation on the message (M):

$C = M^{ebob} \bmod n_{bob}$

Bob, who is the only one to possess his private key (d_{bob}), performs the following to recover the message (M):

$M = C^{dbob} \bmod n_{bob}$

To sign the message, Alice encrypts with her own private key:

$C = M^{dalice} \bmod n_{alice}$

Because only Alice possesses d_{alice}, only she can create this ciphertext C. Anyone in possession of her public key (e_{alice} and n_{alice}) can verify the signature, however:

$M = C^{ealice} \bmod n_{alice}$

It bears note that (p) and (q), the factors of (n), are not needed for encryption or decryption; they are only used in the key generation step (creating the modulus (n) and the second exponent). In addition, while it is important for key generation purposes that the modulus (n) be the product of two prime numbers, the exponentiation and modular arithmetic operation would work just as well with prime numbers (which are by definition evenly divisible only by themselves and the number 1).

MD5

MD5 Algorithm Description

We begin by supposing that we have a b-bit message as input, and that we wish to find its message digest. Here b is an arbitrary nonnegative integer; b may be zero, it need not be a multiple of eight, and it may be arbitrarily large. We imagine the bits of the message written down as follows:

$m\_0\ m\_1 \ldots m\_\{b-1\}$

The following five steps are performed to compute the message digest of the message.

Step 1: Append Padding Bits

The message is "padded" (extended) so that its length (in bits) is congruent to 448, modulo 512. That is, the message is extended so that it is just 64 bits shy of being a multiple of 512 bits long. Padding is always performed, even if the length of the message is already congruent to 448, modulo 512.

Padding is performed as follows: a single "1" bit is appended to the message, and then "0" bits are appended so that the length in bits of the padded message becomes congruent to 448, modulo 512. In all, at least one bit and at most 512 bits are appended.

Step 2: Append Length

A 64-bit representation of b (the length of the message before the padding bits were added) is appended to the result of the previous step. In the unlikely event that b is greater than 2^64, then only the low-order 64 bits of b are used. (These bits are appended as two32-bit words and appended low-order word first in accordance with the previous conventions).

At this point the resulting message (after padding with bits and with b) has a length that is an exact multiple of 512 bits. Equivalently, this message has a length that is an exact multiple of 16 (32-bit)words. Let M[0 ... N-1] denote the words of the resulting message, where N is a multiple of 16.

Step 3: Initialize MD Buffer

A four-word buffer (A,B,C,D) is used to compute the message digest. Here each of A, B, C, D is a 32-bit register. These registers reinitialized to the following values in hexadecimal, low-order bytes first):

word A: 01 23 45 67
word B: 89 ab cd ef
word C: fe dc ba 98
word D: 76 54 32 10

Step 4: Process Message in 16-Word Blocks

We first define four auxiliary functions that each take as input three 32-bit words and produce as output one 32-bit word.

F(X,Y,Z) = XY v not(X) Z
G(X,Y,Z) = XZ v Y not(Z)
H(X,Y,Z) = X xor Y xor Z
I(X,Y,Z) = Y xor (X v not(Z))

In each bit position F acts as a conditional: if X then Y else Z. The function F could have been defined using + instead of v since XY and not(X)Z will never have 1's in the same bit position). It is interesting to note that if the bits of X, Y, and Z are independent and unbiased, the each bit of F(X,Y,Z) will be independent and unbiased.

The functions G, H, and I are similar to the function F, in that they act in "bitwise parallel" to produce their output from the bits of X, Y, and Z, in such a manner that if the corresponding bits of X, Y, and Z are independent and unbiased, then each bit of G(X,Y,Z),H(X,Y,Z), and I(X,Y,Z) will be independent and unbiased. Note that the function H is the bit-wise "xor" or "parity" function of its inputs.
This step uses a 64-element table T[1 ... 64] constructed from the sine function. Let T[i] denote the i-th element of the table, which is equal to the integer part of 4294967296 times abs(sin(i)), where I is in radians.

Do the following:

```
/* Process each 16-word block. */
For i = 0 to N/16-1 do

   /* Copy block i into X. */
   For j = 0 to 15 do
```

```
  Set X[j] to M[i*16+j].
end /* of loop on j */

/* Save A as AA, B as BB, C as CC, and D as DD. */
AA = A
BB = B

CC = C
DD = D

/* Round 1. */
/* Let [abcd k s i] denote the operation
   a = b + ((a + F(b,c,d) + X[k] + T[i]) <<< s). */
/* Do the following 16 operations. */
[ABCD  0  7  1]  [DABC  1 12  2]  [CDAB  2 17  3]  [BCDA  3 22  4]
[ABCD  4  7  5]  [DABC  5 12  6]  [CDAB  6 17  7]  [BCDA  7 22  8]
[ABCD  8  7  9]  [DABC  9 12 10]  [CDAB 10 17 11]  [BCDA 11 22 12]
[ABCD 12  7 13]  [DABC 13 12 14]  [CDAB 14 17 15]  [BCDA 15 22 16]

/* Round 2. */
/* Let [abcd k s i] denote the operation
   a = b + ((a + G(b,c,d) + X[k] + T[i]) <<< s). */
/* Do the following 16 operations. */
[ABCD  1  5 17]  [DABC  6  9 18]  [CDAB 11 14 19]  [BCDA  0 20 20]
[ABCD  5  5 21]  [DABC 10  9 22]  [CDAB 15 14 23]  [BCDA  4 20 24]
[ABCD  9  5 25]  [DABC 14  9 26]  [CDAB  3 14 27]  [BCDA  8 20 28]
[ABCD 13  5 29]  [DABC  2  9 30]  [CDAB  7 14 31]  [BCDA 12 20 32]

/* Round 3. */
/* Let [abcd k s t] denote the operation
   a = b + ((a + H(b,c,d) + X[k] + T[i]) <<< s). */
/* Do the following 16 operations. */
[ABCD  5  4 33]  [DABC  8 11 34]  [CDAB 11 16 35]  [BCDA 14 23 36]
[ABCD  1  4 37]  [DABC  4 11 38]  [CDAB  7 16 39]  [BCDA 10 23 40]
[ABCD 13  4 41]  [DABC  0 11 42]  [CDAB  3 16 43]  [BCDA  6 23 44]
[ABCD  9  4 45]  [DABC 12 11 46]  [CDAB 15 16 47]  [BCDA  2 23 48]

/* Round 4. */
```

```
/* Let [abcd k s t] denote the operation
    a = b + ((a + I(b,c,d) + X[k] + T[i]) <<< s). */
/* Do the following 16 operations. */
[ABCD  0  6 49]  [DABC  7 10 50]  [CDAB 14 15 51]  [BCDA  5 21 52]
[ABCD 12  6 53]  [DABC  3 10 54]  [CDAB 10 15 55]  [BCDA  1 21 56]
[ABCD  8  6 57]  [DABC 15 10 58]  [CDAB  6 15 59]  [BCDA 13 21 60]
[ABCD  4  6 61]  [DABC 11 10 62]  [CDAB  2 15 63]  [BCDA  9 21 64]

/* Then perform the following additions. (That is increment each
   of the four registers by the value it had before this block
   was started.) */
A = A + AA
B = B + BB
C = C + CC
D = D + DD

end /* of loop on i */
```

Step 5: Output

The message digest produced as output is A, B, C, D. That is, we begin with the low-order byte of A, and end with the high-order byte of D.

This completes the description of MD5. A reference implementation in C is given in the appendix.

Summary

The MD5 message-digest algorithm is simple to implement, and provides a "fingerprint" or message digest of a message of arbitrary length. It is conjectured that the difficulty of coming up with two messages having the same message digest is on the order of 2^64 operations, and that the difficulty of coming up with any message having a given message digest is on the order of 2^128 operations. The MD5 algorithm has been carefully scrutinized for weaknesses.

Differences between MD4 and MD5

The following are the differences between MD4 and MD5:

1. A fourth round has been added.
2. Each step now has a unique additive constant.
3. The function g in round 2 was changed from (XY v XZ v YZ) to (XZ v Y not(Z)) to make g less symmetric.
4. Each step now adds in the result of the previous step. This promotes a faster "avalanche effect".
5. The order in which input words are accessed in rounds 2 and 3 is changed, to make these patterns less like each other.
6. The shift amounts in each round have been approximately optimized, to yield a faster "avalanche effect". The shifts in different rounds are distinct.

IDEA

In cryptography, the International Data Encryption Algorithm (IDEA) is a block cipher designed by Xuejia Lai(□□□) and James L. Massey of ETH-Zürich and was first described in 1991. The algorithm was intended as a replacement for the Data Encryption Standard. IDEA is a minor revision of an earlier cipher, PES (Proposed Encryption Standard); IDEA was originally called IPES (Improved PES).

The cipher was designed under a research contract with the Hasler Foundation, which became part of Ascom-Tech AG. The cipher is patented in a number of countries but is freely available for non-commercial use. The name 'IDEA" is also a trademark. The patents will expire in 2010–2011. Today, IDEA is licensed worldwide by MediaCrypt.

IDEA was used in Pretty Good Privacy (PGP) V2.0, and was incorporated after the original cipher used in v1.0 ('Bass-O-Matic") was found to be insecure. It is an optional algorithm in OpenPGP.

6.5 PGP (Pretty Good Policy)

How PGP Works?

PGP combines some of the best features of both conventional and Public Key Cryptography. PGP is a *Hybrid Cryptosystem.* When a user encrypts plaintext with PGP, PGP first compresses the plaintext. Data compression saves modem transmission time and disk space and, more importantly, strengthens cryptographic security. Most cryptanalysis techniques exploit patterns found in the plaintext to crack the cipher. Compression reduces these patterns in the plaintext, thereby greatly enhancing resistance to cryptanalysis. (Files that are too short to compress or which don't compress well aren't compressed).

PGP then creates a *Session Key,* which is a one-time-only secret key. This key is a random number generated from the random movements of your mouse and the keystrokes you type. This session key works with a very secure, fast conventional encryption algorithm to encrypt the plaintext; the result is ciphertext. Once the data is encrypted, the session key is then encrypted to the recipient's public key. This Public Key Encrypted session key is transmitted along with the ciphertext to the recipient.

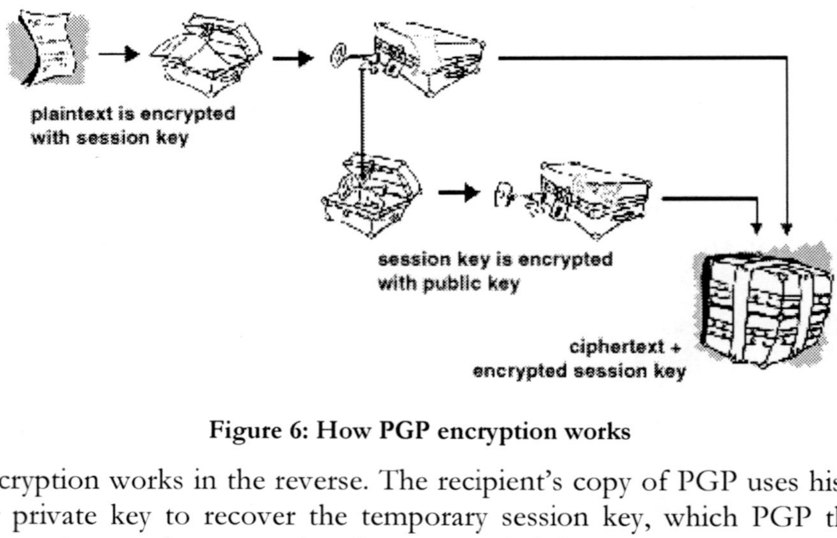

Figure 6: How PGP encryption works

Decryption works in the reverse. The recipient's copy of PGP uses his or her private key to recover the temporary session key, which PGP then uses to decrypt the conventionally-encrypted ciphertext.

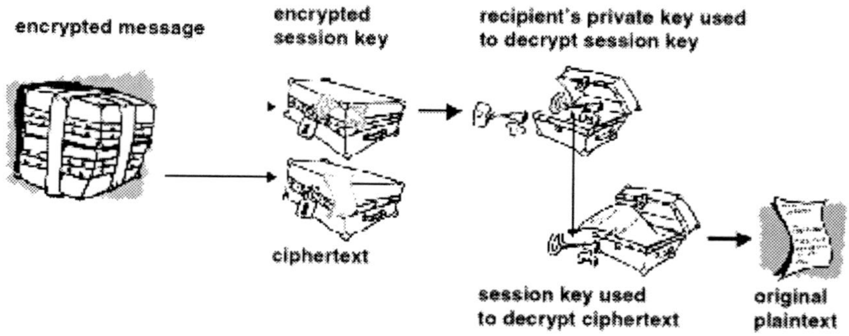

Figure 7: How PGP decryption work

The combination of the two encryption methods combines the convenience of public key encryption with the speed of conventional encryption. Conventional encryption is about 1,000 times faster than Public Key Encryption. Public Key Encryption in turn provides a solution to key distribution and data transmission issues. Used together, performance and key distribution are improved without any sacrifice in security.

Keys

A key is a value that works with a cryptographic algorithm to produce a specific ciphertext. Keys are basically really, really, really big numbers. Key size is measured in bits; the number representing a 1024-bit key is darn huge. In public key cryptography, the bigger the key, the more secure the ciphertext.

However, public key size and conventional cryptography's secret key size are totally unrelated. A conventional 80-bit key has the equivalent strength of a 1024-bit public key. A conventional 128-bit key is equivalent to a 3000-bit public key. Again, the bigger the key, the more secure, but the algorithms used for each type of cryptography are very different and thus comparison is like that of apples to oranges.

While the public and private keys are mathematically related, it's very difficult to derive the private key given only the public key; however, deriving the private key is always possible given enough time and computing power. This makes it very important to pick keys of the right size; large enough to be secure, but small enough to be applied fairly quickly. Additionally, you need to consider who might be trying to read your files, how determined they are, how much time they have, and what their resources might be.

Larger keys will be cryptographically secure for a longer period of time. If what you want to encrypt needs to be hidden for many years, you might want to use a very large key. Of course, who knows how long it will take to determine your key using tomorrow's faster, more efficient computers? There was a time when a 56-bit symmetric key was considered extremely safe.

Keys are stored in encrypted form. PGP stores the keys in two files on your hard disk; one for public keys and one for private keys. These files are called *Keyrings.* As you use PGP, you will typically add the public keys of your recipients to your public Keyring. Your private keys are stored on your private Keyring. If you lose your private Keyring, you will be unable to decrypt any information encrypted to keys on that ring.

6.5.1 Hash Functions

The system described above has some problems. It is slow, and it produces an enormous volume of data — at least double the size of the original information. An improvement on the above scheme is the addition of a one-way *Hash Function* in the process. A one-way hash function takes variable-length input — in this case, a message of any length, even thousands or millions of bits — and produces a fixed-length output; say, 160-bits. The hash function ensures that, if the information is changed in any way — even by just one bit — an entirely different output value is produced.

PGP uses a cryptographically strong hash function on the plaintext the user is signing. This generates a fixed-length data item known as a *message digest.* (Again, any change to the information results in a totally different digest).

Then PGP uses the digest and the private key to create the "signature". PGP transmits the signature and the plaintext together. Upon receipt of the message, the recipient uses PGP to recompute the digest, thus verifying the signature. PGP can encrypt the plaintext or not; signing plaintext is useful if some of the recipients are not interested in or capable of verifying the signature.

As long as a secure hash function is used, there is no way to take someone's signature from one document and attach it to another, or to alter a signed message in any way. The slightest change in a signed document will cause the digital signature verification process to fail.

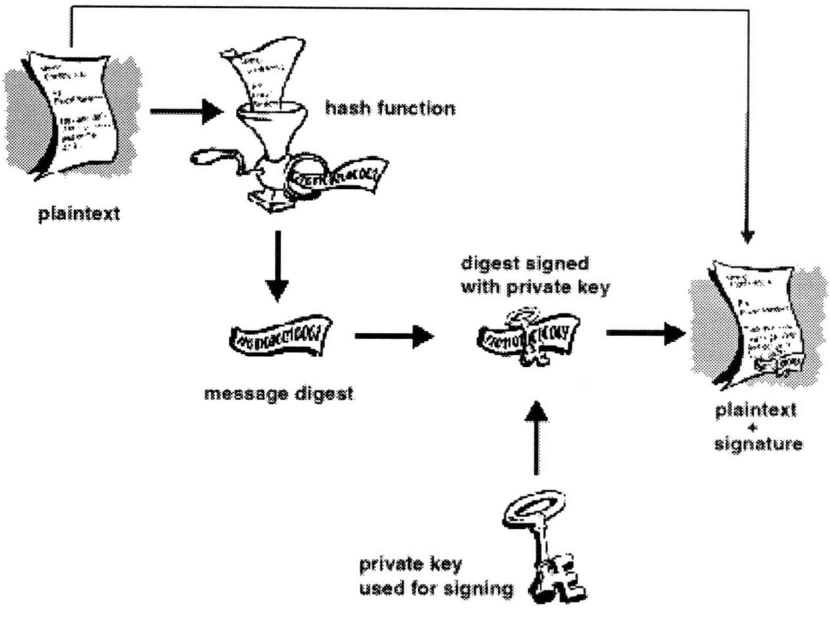

Figure 8: Secure digital signatures

Digital signatures play a major role in authenticating and *validating* other PGP users' keys.

Digital Certificates

One issue with public key cryptosystems is that users must be constantly vigilant to ensure that they are encrypting to the correct person's key. In an environment where it is safe to freely exchange keys via public servers, *man-in-the-middle* attacks are a potential threat. In this type of attack, someone posts a phony key with the name and user ID of the user's intended recipient. Data encrypted to — and intercepted by — the true owner of this bogus key is now in the wrong hands.

In a public key environment, it is vital that you are assured that the public key to which you are encrypting data is in fact the public key of the intended recipient and not a forgery. You could simply encrypt only to those keys which have been physically handed to you. But suppose you need to exchange information with people you have never met; how can you tell that you have the correct key?

Digital certificates, or *certs,* simplify the task of establishing whether a public key truly belongs to the purported owner.

A certificate is a form of credential. Examples might be your driver's license, your social security card, or your birth certificate. Each of these has some information on it identifying you and some authorization stating that someone else has confirmed your identity. Some certificates, such as your passport, are important enough confirmation of your identity that you would not want to lose them, lest someone use them to impersonate you.

A Digital Certificate is data that functions much like a physical certificate. A Digital Certificate is information included with a person's public key that helps others verify that a key is genuine or *valid.* Digital certificates are used to thwart attempts to substitute one person's key for another.
A digital certificate consists of three things:

- A public key.
- Certificate information. ("Identity" information about the user, such as name, user ID, and so on).
- One or more Digital Signatures.

The purpose of the digital signature on a certificate is to state that the certificate information has been attested to by some other person or entity. The digital signature does not attest to the authenticity of the certificate as a whole; it vouches only that the signed identity information goes along with, or *is bound to,* the public key.

Thus, a certificate is basically a public key with one or two forms of ID attached, plus a hearty stamp of approval from some other trusted individual.

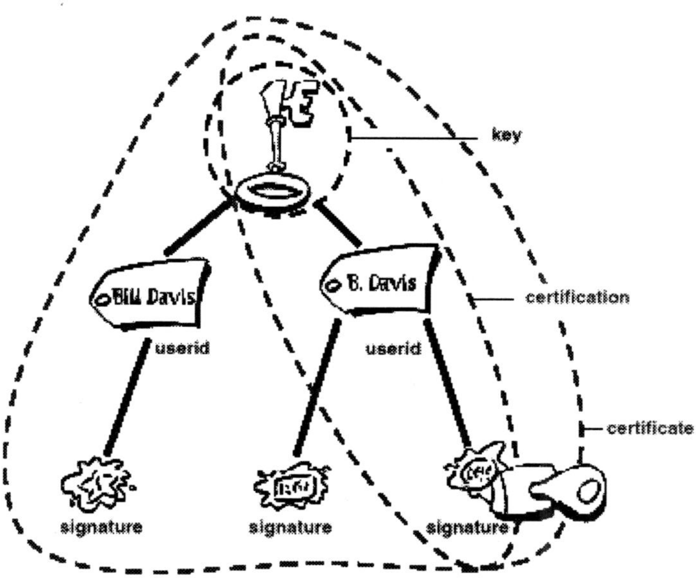

Figure 9: Anatomy of a PGP certificate

6.5.2 Certificate Distribution

Certificates are utilized when it's necessary to exchange public keys with someone else. For small groups of people who wish to communicate securely, it is easy to manually exchange diskettes or emails containing each owner's public key. This is *manual public key distribution,* and it is practical only to a certain point. Beyond that point, it is necessary to put systems into place that can provide the necessary security, storage, and exchange mechanisms so coworkers, business partners, or strangers could communicate if need be. These can come in the form of storage-only repositories called *Certificate Servers,* or more structured systems that provide additional key management features and are called *Public Key Infrastructures (PKIs).*

Certificate Servers

A *Certificate Server,* also called a *Cert Server* or a *Key Server,* is a database that allows users to submit and retrieve digital certificates. A cert server usually provides some administrative features that enable a company to maintain its security policies — for example, allowing only those keys that meet certain requirements to be stored.

Public Key Infrastructures

A PKI contains the certificate storage facilities of a certificate server, but also provides certificate management facilities (the ability to issue, revoke, store, retrieve, and trust certificates). The main feature of a PKI is the introduction of what is known as a *Certification Authority,* or CA, which is a human entity — a person, group, department, company, or other association — that an organization has authorized to issue certificates to its computer users. (A CA's role is analogous to a country's government Passport Office). A CA creates certificates and digitally signs them using the CA's private key. Because of its role in creating certificates, the CA is the central component of a PKI. Using the CA's public key, anyone wanting to verify a certificate's authenticity verifies the issuing CA's digital signature, and hence, the integrity of the contents of the certificate (most importantly, the public key and the identity of the certificate holder).

6.6 Case Study – Real World Example

A Real World Example -- Secure Sockets Client

One of the most common uses of public key technology is in the Secure Sockets Layer (SSL) protocol, used by Netscape Navigator and other web browsers for secure communications over the internet. Secure sockets allows the user -- typically an individual working from a personal computer at home (called the client) -- to communicate with a web site computer (called the server). The server might be operated by a merchant and the user might wish to have the client computer send a credit card number to the server to order goods. The secure sockets protocol uses public key techniques to encrypt the credit card number so that the number is not sent in plaintext over the internet. According to the analysis set forth in this article, the client should be able to perform all of the RSA encryption and verifications steps without infringing the RSA Patent.

In simplified form, the secure sockets protocol using the RSA method works as follows. After a client makes context with the web site server, and a secure session is to be established, the server transmits a message the client containing (1) the server's public key; and (2) a digital signature from a certificate authority certifying that the public key the server claims as its own is, in fact, its own. The client next verifies the server's public key using the signature authority's public key, which is installed with the browser software on the client's computer. In this way, the client can be assured that the server is who it claims to be. The client is then ready to send confidential information (such as a credit card number) to the server.

The client will encrypt the credit card number, but will not use RSA or another public key technique to actually encrypt the data. RSA is much slower than other conventional encryption methods, which use the same key to encrypt and decrypt. While this might not matter if all that is being encrypted is a single credit card number, in practice a secure session with a web browser may involve the transmission of thousands of bytes of information.

To avoid painfully long delays, the client will generate a random number for use as a conventional, symmetric key to encrypt the all of the data being sent during the secure session. The client then encrypts this key using the server's RSA public key transmitted in the opening message from the server. The server receives this encrypted key, and decrypts it using its secret key. Both the client and the server are now in possession of a shared, symmetric key which both use to encrypt and decrypt all subsequent data being sent during the secure session.

In this protocol, the client does only two public key steps, and does not perform any key generation steps. First, the client verifies the server's public key. To perform the verification step, it uses the certificate authority's public key. That key, necessarily generated by the certificate authority, can be assumed reasonably to be generated by a licensed entity.

The second step -- encrypting the symmetric encryption key for the session -- uses the public key supplied by the server. That key also can be presumed to have been generated by a licensed method. Although both decryption (verification) and encryption (of the session key) steps are performed by the client, there is every reason to believe that the key generation steps are performed by licensed methods.

Accordingly, because the client software does not generate any keys, the client does not directly infringe the any of the claims of the RSA patent. Although the client does use two public keys (the server's and the certificate authority) for encryption and decryption, those keys are almost certainly generated licensed means. Accordingly, the client does not contribute to, or induce the infringement of, the RSA Patent.

7. Cyber Laws – "The legal Aspect of Cyberspace"

7.1 Introduction

India became Independent on 15th August, 1947. Since then it has been struggling through to make its stand in the world. Many new technologies were brought and many new are still are to be found. One such revolution was brought about by the introduction of the 'Internet', which is till date considered as the pool of knowledge...the deeper you go in, the more you learn about your world, about yourself.

But who could think of the time when this rich source of knowledge will be misused for criminal activities. There are many such disturbing activities that occurred in past and demanded of some rules and regulations urgently, some set definite patterns that can be put forward while carrying out any business transaction over the net, ranging from a simple friendly e-mail to carrying out the whole set of your work, without which it may go wild and beyond control and it can be used as a tool for the very destruction of mankind.

It was at this point of time that the government of India felt the need to enact the relevant cyber laws which can regulate the internet in India. It denotes all aspects, issues and the legal consequences on the Internet, the World Wide Web and cyber space.

7.2 Need of Cyber Laws

There are numerous factors that stand behind this decision of government.

1. Although India has a very well defined legal system that has been developed with the aim cover all possible situations and cases that have occurred or might take place in future, but it lacks when it comes to the newly developed internet technology. With the arrival of internet many new complex and ticklish issues cropped up which

could not be interpreted (cleared) in the light of existing laws and thus necessitated the enactment of the cyber laws.

2. Also, with the growth of the internet, it became important to give some legal recognition to what is going on the internet. Internet has grown up as one of the dominating resources to carry out one's business in today's world. Most of the world fame companies prefer to outsource their business processes, which has become possible because of the internet. How come a company can carry out its business safely and securely when there is no legal validity or sanction to the activities in the cyberspace?? It is now with the emergence of cyber laws the concept of digital signatures and digital records have come up, with which a business organization can legally carry out its business process; or else even the e-mails were not given the legal recognition in the country.

3. With the growth of the internet and many associated business and friendly activities, grew the cyber crime and cyber terrorism. Here the two terms hold an entirely different meaning. While the cyber crime refers to some activity done with the criminal intentions aiming to harm or completely destruct ones workplace or something similar with or without the use of computer; cyber terrorism is defined as a premeditated use of disruptive activities or the threat thereof, in cyber space, with the intention to further social, ideological, religious, political or similar objectives, or to intimidate any person in furtherance of such objectives. The cyber criminals can employ conventional activities or could use some innovative methods and develop some new ways to achieve destroying their target places. Such crimes may include Virus/worm attack, E-mail spoofing, E-mail bombing, Salami attack or Web Jacking.

4. There were certain issues that required either the existing laws to be amended as they were outdated in the present scenario of the world or required certain new clauses to be added up in the existing cyber laws to check the various criminal activities going on the internet. Among various such cases is the MMS porn case in which the CEO of bazee.com was arrested for allegedly selling the MMS clips

involving school children on its website. Then there was a case where the two actors threatened the Mid-day daily with a defamation suit when the newspaper published the pictures of the Indian actor kissing her boyfriend at the Bombay nightspot. Also Delhi Police has recently taken Krishan Kumar into the judicial custody for 6 days for illegally using the internet account of Col. (Retd.) J.S. Bajwa.

All such activities taking place around the country needed a new discipline that could provide everyone with the safe and secure environment where an illegal encroachment of some cyber criminal, as law calls it, to be prosecuted and punished for his crime. Also these laws were needed to lay the foundation of the legally recognized rules and regulations that a company or an individual must follow while carrying out his business...giving even the business processes carried out by this newly evolved (hot) media even the legal status.

Keeping all these factors in to the consideration, Indian Parliament passed the Information Technology Bill on 17th May 2000 which is known as the Information Technology Act, 2000. It talks about the Cyber laws and forms the legal framework for electronic records and other activities done by electronic means/ways.

7.3 Laws Related to Hacking

With the growing trend of outsourcing world wide, India is continuously focusing towards deepening its roots in the outsourcing market. Undoubtedly one can be assure of the quality and low wages, the prime requirements a company searches for while outsourcing its business processes. This is the reason why India has been successfully able to drive all the big banners to its land and establish itself as the world's biggest software outsourcing destination.

Today, India exports software and services to nearly 95 countries around the world, with North America (U.S. and Canada) leading ahead in India's software exports.

India is this success and growth of the Indian IT industry, which has motivated government to take necessary steps for ensuring the continuous growth of the outsourcing company in India.

India has set up a separate ministry of IT, to expedite swift approval and implementation of IT projects and to streamline the regulatory projects. Also the government has approved a 108 point action plan submitted by the National IT Task Force to promote the IT in the country. This has been done in order to alleviate the situation of the critical shortage of venture capital, especially faced by the small and medium enterprise sector.

India regards the IT sector as one of its top five priorities.

Further, the Indian Parliament has passed the Information Technology Bill in May 2000, notified as the IT Act 2000 in order to bring the E-commerce with in the purview of the law and to accord stringent punishments to cyber criminals. The act will provide legal recognition for transactions carried out by means of electronic data interchange and other means of electronic communication, commonly referred to as "electronic commerce", which involve the use of alternatives to paper-based methods of communication and storage of information, to facilitate electronic filing of documents with the Government agencies and further to amend the Indian Penal Code, the Indian Evidence Act, 1872, the Bankers' Books Evidence Act, 1891 and the Reserve Bank of India Act, 1934 and for matters connected therewith or incidental thereto.

Under this act the government puts forward the legal definitions of many IT related terms and outlaws computer crime. It has given a special emphasis to check the privacy and security of the IT industry by taking up the "security of the electronic records and secure digital signature" in a separate chapter, CHAPTER, of the act.

It defines the secure electronic record as the one in which any security procedure has been applied at any specific point of time, and from such point of time to the time of verification.

Also it regards the digital signatures as the one which are unique and can be used to identify the subscriber. They should be created in the manner or using a means under the exclusive control of the subscriber and is linked to the electronic record to which it relates in such a manner that if the electronic record was altered the digital signature would be invalidated. Or in short we can say that the digital signals have been given as the same legal status as the physical signatures, and thus the documents are acceptable in Indian Courts.

State Governments in India have also got into the action to match the central government's own information age initiatives like the recently passed IT Act 2000. That is why the E-government infrastructure and services sector in India is looked up as a billion dollar market for IT vendors, software and training companies.

Also the E-governance initiatives promote the digital research.

The success of any business is greatly affected by the resources available and the business polices of the nation. The tremendous heights that take the Indian Information Technology industry to the top of the world cannot be only rewarded to the resources, price cut outs, etc factor, but to a great extent it is the encouragement and promotion techniques adopted by the Indian Government to take forth the Indian IT industry. IT Act 2000 was a major development in this respect which laid down a clear picture of the industry, and secures the Indian business, making many domestic and offshore customers to rely over the Indian Industry and many entrepreneurs to securely join or move ahead in the field. Refer Appendix for detailed hacking laws of US Government.

7.4 Laws Related to Phishing

Phishing is an insidious cyber scam perpetrated by identity thieves who use official-looking but bogus E-mail to lure recipients to a dummy Web site ready to steal visitors' personal and bank information (provided they hand it over). Nearly anyone online in the past year has been E-mailed repeatedly by "eBay", "Master Card" or their "private bank", urging them to take urgent action to solve an urgent problem with their account ("Did we mention this is urgent?") by clicking on the provided Web site link.

Of course, like the E-mail, the Web site also looks "official", but is instead a phishing hole, so to speak. And if you aren't careful, you could end up handing over credit card numbers, user names, passwords and other information for Phishers to use or sell.

Lots of people haven't been careful -- the good scams are realistic-looking -- and the number of Americans who fall victim to identity fraud each year runs between seven million and 10 million, according to some estimates.

A scourge indeed. But for many people convicted of identity-theft crimes, punishment often comes in the form of probation, restitution, home confinement and perhaps a stern lecture from the judge -- a reliable recipe for recidivism.

ITPEA tries to toughen things up by establishing a new crime -- aggravated identity theft, which the federal government defines as using a stolen identity to commit other crimes. Convictions for aggravated identity theft would carry a mandatory two-year prison sentence.

Mandatory sentencing usually arises from several factors -- a climate of fear or urgency fueled by genuine frustration about a certain type of widespread crime, pressure on politicians to appear "tough" and the eternal desire for easy solutions.

The trouble with easy solutions is that they're not always "just", and "just" should be the top priority of a "justice" system. The imposition of mandatory sentencing essentially replaces some bad judgment with no judgment, while providing a forum for public representatives to dispense some "sheriff" sound bytes.

So while the president and the ITPEA's congressional sponsors undoubtedly feel good about their tough stand on identity theft, it's not likely that Phishers, especially the many based in Asia and Eastern Europe, will be scared straight.

A better piece of anti-phishing legislation was introduced to the U.S. Senate on July 9 by Sen. Patrick Leahy, D-Vt. The Anti-Phishing Act of 2004 defines phishing as a federal crime. Specifically, the proposed law prohibits spoofing a Web site in order to "induce, request, ask or solicit any person to transmit, submit or provide any means of identification to another".

The bill tackles the "lure" part of the phishing equation by outlawing the transmission of E-mail disguised to look like it's from a legitimate business, but is intended to trick online users into providing personal and financial information with the intent to commit identity theft or fraud.

Convictions under the Anti-Phishing Act of 2004 could mean up to five years in prison -- a stiff sentence -- and a $250,000 fine. Plus the bill is proactive: Charges could be filed against Phishers just for attempting an online scam, so law enforcement doesn't have to wait for a victim to be defrauded.

No legislation is perfect, but as long as criminal elements roam the Internet, clearly we'll need evolving laws to deal with them. In this case, I prefer the Leahy bill because it's tough but flexible and gives federal officials the ability to pre-empt scams.

Refer Appendix

8. Appendix: Hacking Laws

The Computer Fraud and Abuse Act (as amended Oct. 3, 1996) Section 1030. Fraud and related activity in connection with computers

(A) Whoever --

(1) Having knowingly accessed a computer without authorization or exceeding authorized access, and by means of such conduct having obtained information that has been determined by the United States Government pursuant to an Executive order or statute to require protection against unauthorized disclosure for reasons of national defense or foreign relations, or any restricted data, as defined in paragraph y of section 11 of the Atomic Energy Act of 1954, with reason to believe that such information so obtained could be used to the injury of the United States, or to the advantage of any foreign nation, willfully communicates, delivers, transmits, or causes to be communicated, delivered, or transmitted, or attempts to communicate, deliver, transmit or cause to be communicated, delivered, or transmitted the same to any person not entitled to receive it, or willfully retains the same and fails to deliver it to the officer or employee of the United States entitled to receive it;

(2) Intentionally accesses a computer without authorization or exceeds authorized access, and thereby obtains--

(a) Information contained in a financial record of a financial institution, or of a card issuer as defined in section 1602(n) of title 15, or contained in a file of a consumer reporting agency on a consumer, as such terms are defined in the Fair Credit Reporting Act (15 U.S.C. 1681 et seq.);

(b) Information from any department or agency of the United States; or

(c) Information from any protected computer if the conduct involved an interstate or foreign communication;

(3) Intentionally, without authorization to access any nonpublic computer of a department or agency of the United States, accesses such a computer of that department or agency that is exclusively for the use of the Government of the United States or, in the case of a computer not exclusively for such use, is used by or for the Government of the United States and such conduct affects that use by or for the Government of the United States;

(4) Knowingly and with intent to defraud, accesses a protected computer without authorization, or exceeds authorized access, and by means of such conduct furthers the intended fraud and obtains anything of value, unless the object of the fraud and the thing obtained consists only of the use of the computer and the value of such use is not more than $5,000 in any 1-year period;

(5) (a) Knowingly causes the transmission of a program, information, code, or command, and as a result of such conduct, intentionally causes damage without authorization, to a protected computer;

(b) Intentionally accesses a protected computer without authorization, and as a result of such conduct, recklessly causes damage; or

(c) Intentionally accesses a protected computer without authorization, and as a result of such conduct, causes damage;

(6) Knowingly and with intent to defraud traffics (as defined in section 1029) in any password or similar information through which a computer may be accessed without authorization, if--

(a) Such trafficking affects interstate or foreign commerce; or

(b) Such computer is used by or for the Government of the United States;

(7) With intent to extort from any person, firm, association, educational institution, financial institution, government entity, or other legal entity, any money or other thing of value,

transmits in interstate or foreign commerce any communication containing any threat to cause damage to a protected computer;

(a) Shall be punished as provided in subsection (c) of this section.

(b) Whoever attempts to commit an offense under subsection (a) of this section shall be punished as provided in subsection (c) of this section.

(c) The punishment for an offense under subsection (a) or (b) of this section is--

(1) (a) A fine under this title or imprisonment for not more than ten years, or both, in the case of an offense under subsection (a)(1) of this section which does not occur after a conviction for another offense under this section, or an attempt to commit an offense punishable under this subparagraph; and

(b) A fine under this title or imprisonment for not more than twenty years, or both, in the case of an offense under subsection (a)(1) of this section which occurs after a conviction for another offense under this section, oran attempt to commit an offense punishable under this subparagraph; and

(2) (a) A fine under this title or imprisonment for not more than one year, or both, in the case of an offense under subsection (a)(2), (a)(3), (a)(5)(C), or (a)(6) of this section which does not occur after a conviction for another offense under this section, or an attempt to commit an offense punishable under this subparagraph; and

(b) a fine under this title or imprisonment for not more than 5 years, or both, in the case of an offense under subsection (a)(2), if--

(i) The offense was committed for purposes of commercial advantage or private financial gain;

(ii) The offense was committed in furtherance of any criminal or tortious act in violation of the Constitution or laws of the United States or of any State; or

(iii) The value of the information obtained exceeds $5,000;

(c) A fine under this title or imprisonment for not more than ten years, or both, in the case of an offense under subsection (a)(2), (a)(3) or (a)(6) of this section which occurs after a conviction for another offense under this section, or an attempt to commit an offense punishable under this subparagraph; and

(3) (a) A fine under this title or imprisonment for not more than five years, or both, in the case of an offense under subsection (a)(4), (a)(5)(A), (a)(5)(B), or (a)(7) of this section which does not occur after a conviction for another offense under this section, or an attempt to commit an offense punishable under this subparagraph; and

(b) A fine under this title or imprisonment for not more than ten years, or both, in the case of an offense under subsection (a)(4), (a)(5)(A), (a)(5)(B), (a)(5)(C), or (a)(7)of this section which occurs after a conviction for another offense under this section, or an attempt to commit an offense punishable under this subparagraph; and

[former paragraph (4) stricken effective Oct. 11, 1996].

(d) The United States Secret Service shall, in addition to any other agency having such authority, have the authority to investigate offenses under subsections (a)(2)(A), (a)(2)(B), (a)(3), (a)(4), (a)(5), and (a)(6) of this section. Such authority of the United States Secret Service shall be exercised in accordance with an agreement which shall be entered into by the Secretary of the Treasury and the Attorney General.

(e) As used in this section--

(1) The term "computer" means an electronic, magnetic, optical, electrochemical, or other high speed data processing device performing logical, arithmetic, or storage functions, and includes any data storage facility or communications facility directly related to or operating in conjunction with such device, but such term does not include an automated typewriter or typesetter, a portable hand held calculator, or other similar device;

(2) The term "protected computer" means a computer--

(a) Exclusively for the use of a financial institution or the United States Government, or, in the case of a computer not exclusively for such use, used by or for a financial institution or the United States Government and the conduct constituting the offense affects that use by or for the financial institution or the Government; or

(b) Which is used in interstate or foreign commerce or communication;

(3) The term 'State" includes the District of Columbia, the Commonwealth of Puerto Rico, and any other commonwealth, possession or territory of the United States;

(4) The term "financial institution" means--

Anti Phishing Laws

U.S. SENATOR PATRICK LEAHY

New Leahy Bill Targets INTERNET "PHISHING" That Steals $2 b./yr. From Consumers

[Below are (1) the Senate Floor speech that Sen. Patrick Leahy delivered Friday in introducing his bill to explicitly target Internet "phishing", with new federal criminal penalties, and (2) a fact sheet on the bill. Leahy (D-Vt.), the ranking Democratic member of the Senate Judiciary Committee, is sometimes referred to as the "cyber senator" for his enthusiasm for and leadership on Internet issues. Internet phishing has grown to become a $2 billion a year fraud on consumers and on online commerce.]

Statement Of Senator Patrick Leahy
Introduction Of The "Anti-Phishing Act Of 2004"
Senate Floor / Congressional Record
Friday, July 9, 2004

Mr. President, today I am introducing a bill, the Anti-Phishing Act of 2004, which targets a large and growing class of crime that is spreading across the Internet.

Phishing is a rapidly growing class of identity theft scams on the Internet that is causing both short-term loses and long-term economic damage. In the short-term, these scams defraud individuals and financial institutions. Some estimates place the cost of phishing at over two billion dollars just over the last 12 months. Just imagine the concern we would all have about a series of bank robberies involving that much money. In the long run, phishing undermines the Internet itself. By making consumers uncertain about the integrity of the Internet's complex addressing system, phishing threatens to make us all less likely to use the Internet for secure transactions. If you can't trust where you are on the web, you are less likely to use it for commerce and communications.

Phishing is spelled "P-H-I-S-H-I-N-G". Those well-versed in popular culture may guess that it was named after the phenomenally popular Vermont band, Phish. But phishing over the Internet was in fact named from the sport of fishing, as an analogy for its technique of luring Internet prey with convincing email bait. The "F" is replaced by a "P-H" in keeping with a computer hacker tradition.

Phishing attacks usually start with E-mails that are, in Internet jargon, "Spoofed." That is, they are made to appear to be coming from some trusted financial institution or commercial entity. The spoofed E-mail usually asks the victim to go to a website to confirm or renew private account information. These E-mails offer a link that appears to take the victim to the website of the trusted institution. In fact the link takes the victim to a sham website that is visually identical to that of the trusted institution, but is in fact run by the criminal. When the victim takes the bait and sends their account information, the criminal uses it – sometimes within minutes – to transfer the victim's funds or to make purchases. Phishers are the new con artists of cyberspace.

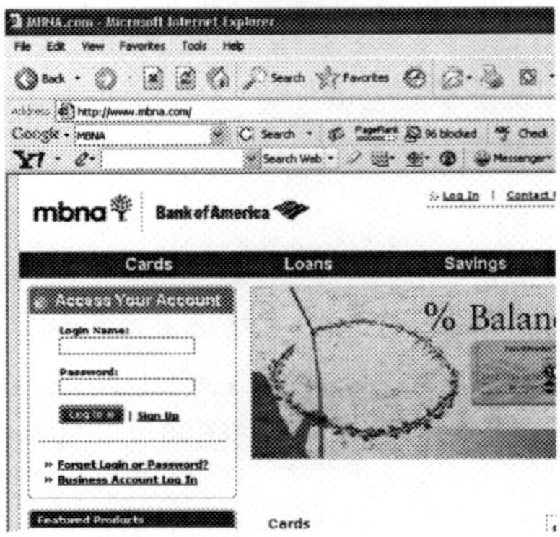

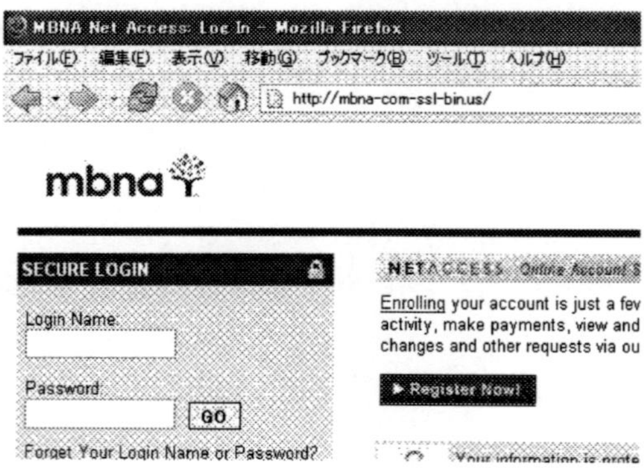

To give an idea of how easy it is to be fooled, we have reproduced some recent phishing charts, with the help of the Anti-Phishing Working Group. These are just two examples of a problem that affects countless companies.

The website on the right is an actual website of MBNA, a well-established financial institution and credit card issuer. On the left is a recently discovered phishing site that mimicked the MBNA site. As you can see, the two websites are practically identical. Both have the MBNA logo, and both have the same graphics, in the same layout. But if you end up going to the website on the left, when you enter your account information, you are giving it to an identity thief.

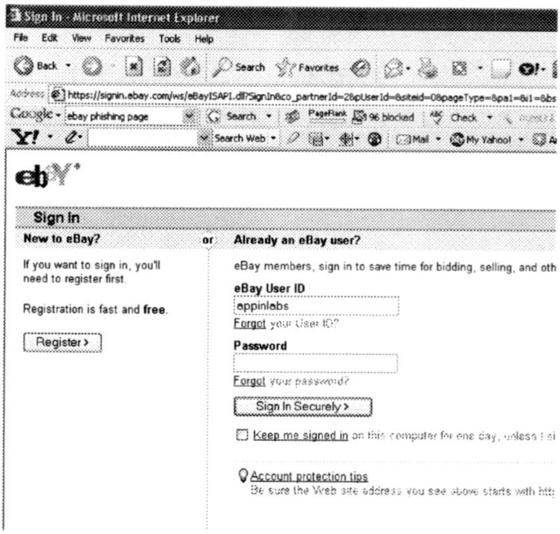

As another example, the next two websites both appear to be from eBay. Again, the one on the right is from the genuine website.

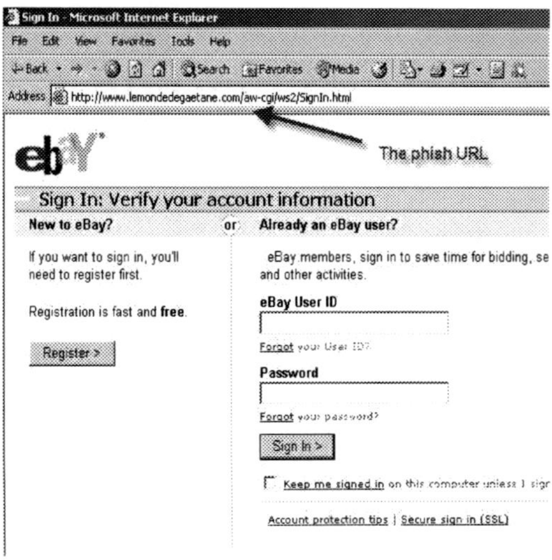

The one on the left is a fake website that is controlled by a Phisher. As you can see, if you end up at the website on the left, it would be next to impossible to know that you are not at the real eBay website. Informed Internet users can avoid this problem if they simply use their web browser to go to the website, instead of using a link sent to them in an email, but far too many people do not do this.

This is a growing problem. Phishing is on the rise. In recent months there has been an explosion of these types of attacks. As you can see from the next chart, these attacks are growing at an alarming rate. Roughly one million Americans already have been victims of phishing attacks.

And phishing attacks are increasingly sophisticated. Early phishing attacks were by novices, but there is evidence now that some attacks are backed by organized crime. And some attacks these days include spyware, which is software that is secretly installed on the victim's computer, which waits to capture account information when the victim even goes to legitimate websites.

Phishers also have become more sophisticated in how they cast their huge volumes of email bait on the Internet waters. Security experts recently discovered that vast networks of home computers are being hijacked by hackers using viruses, and then they are rented to Phishers – all without the knowledge of the owners of these home computers.

Some phishers can be prosecuted under wire fraud or identity theft statutes, but often these prosecutions take place only after someone has been defrauded. Moreover, the mere threat of phishing attacks undermines everyone's confidence in the Internet. When people cannot trust that websites are what they appear to be, they will not use the Internet for their secure transactions. So traditional wire fraud and identity theft statutes are not sufficient to respond to phishing.

The Anti-Phishing Act of 2004 protects the integrity of the Internet in two ways. First, it criminalizes the bait. It makes it illegal to knowingly send out spoofed email that links to sham websites, with the intention of committing a crime. Second, it criminalizes the sham websites that are the true scene of the crime.

It makes it illegal to knowingly create or procure a website that purports to be a legitimate online business, with the intent of collecting information for some criminal purpose.

There are important First Amendment concerns to be protected. The Anti-Phishing Act protects parodies and political speech from being prosecuted as Phishing. We have worked closely with various public interest organizations to ensure that the Anti-Phishing Act does not impinge on the important democratic role that the Internet plays.

To many Americans, phishing is a new word. It certainly is a new form of an old crime. It also is a serious crime, and we need to act aggressively to keep phishing from infecting the Internet and from eroding the public's trust in online commerce and communication. I look forward to working with others in the Senate in addressing this growing threat to the Internet, with effective and responsible action.

The Anti-Phishing Act of 2004
Fact Sheet

The Anti-Phishing Act of 2004, introduced in the U.S. Senate on July 9 by Sen. Patrick Leahy (D-Vt.), is intended to combat a rapidly growing Internet scam called "phishing". Phishers are con-artists in cyberspace. Phishing refers to a popular Internet scam in which the victim receives an email that appears to come from a trusted source such as a financial institution, and that asks for certain personal information. The email typically includes a hyperlink that appears to take the victim to the website of that financial institution, but which is actually a sham site. Any personal information entered is stolen and used – sometimes within minutes – for unlawful purposes such as transferring funds or purchasing goods.

Phishing is growing exponentially. During the last 12 months alone, the estimated losses have exceeded $2 billion, and the losses continue to mount. Moreover, current law does not adequately respond to this problem. Phishing does not always fit neatly into traditional wire fraud and identity theft statutes. Neither wire fraud nor identity theft statutes protect against one of the greatest harms caused by phishing: a diminished trust in the Internet's system of addressing and linking. Trust in this system is crucial to the Internet fulfilling its potential as a medium for all manner of secure communications.

The Anti-Phishing Act of 2004 would enter two new crimes into the U.S. Code. The first prohibits the creation or procurement of a website that represents itself to be that of a legitimate business, and that attempts to induce the victim to divulge personal information, with the intent to commit a crime of fraud or identity theft. The second prohibits the creation or procurement of an email that represents itself to be that of a legitimate business, and that attempts to induce the victim to divulge personal information, with the intent to commit a crime of fraud or identity theft.

In order to protect important First Amendment concerns, the Leahy bill carefully protects speech -- even speech that may be deceptive, such as the innocent parodying of commercial websites for political commentary. The bill protects such important speech by including the requirement that the actor must have the specific criminal purpose of committing a crime of fraud or identity theft.

# # # # #

9. Phishing/Case Study

"A heist!!!"
"I can't do it man, nope, I wont get myself involved in this"
"Oh c'mon pal, it's just a simple task, nothing will happen, trust us"
"Trust you!!! How could I if MY life is involved in this"

Breezy evening, terrace of a block in the huge campus of this university in southern part of India, Andie, Carrie, AJ and Joe are feeling the heat building in amongst these five shady silhouettes in the twilight as they pit themselves to bulldoze Viv. Their conversation under the dark blue sky was getting heavier and louder as none of these five boys seemed to be on their toes. They seemed like stomping each other verbally over something that may sound as astounding to a passerby as to themselves.

"No way, I would involve myself in this"

The conversation wasn't coming to any point and all of them just seemed to overcome each others' dilemma with more confusion over something that they all were feeling restless about but consciously were trying to convince Viv to join their bandwagon in their 'modus operandi'.

Youth, as they say, is intrigued by the unknown and that's what exactly happening here was for these engineering sophomores. They were just like any other easy going undergrads but they were just different in one aspect. As individuals they were just a part of a torrid system of uncanny monotony but when they teamed up, their individual abilities cracked open knew vistas of their creativity to venture into the unknown and rip open the doors of the unexpected.

Viv was an individual with a very thoughtful mind and his penchant to learn and learn whatever he does to the core made him different from rest of the pack, the other members being outrageously creative and introvertly submissive to the idea of the other side of the thin line. All these individuals hailed from very different demographies but their common thought process kept them driving as a team to build up new systems on new edges of virtuosity.

As a team, they fitted like a jigsaw to complete the puzzles that came in there way. There penchant for going behind the systems motivated them to explore new vistas. They gradually assimilated themselves to combine into a unassuming unit of disruptive strategies over virtual world.

Andie was known in his entire campus as the guy with the never ending resources for whatever he wanted. His ability to network with people and talk them out to reveal whatever they could was widely synonymous. He could work out with anyone anything he wanted and once in high school, Andie started working out new ways to exploit the loopholes of the existing system from airlines networks to corporate hierarchy. His eye for understanding the psychology on human interaction made him stand out of the crowd and this incident few years back he materialized embedded his name in the minds of his close associates as the ultimate craftsman of Social Engineering.

"To follow the path:
look to the master,
follow the master,
walk with the master,
see through the master,
become the master".

"Turn ... turn… turn" nice voice of a lady comes, "Welcome to Creative Offshore Services. Please dial the required extension… for technical services please press 10, for inquires press 20, for sales support press 600… for further assistant press 0 for operator". Andie grinned it seems good service corporation. Andie presses 600. Again a lady speaks out. "Welcome to Creative Offshore Services, How I can help you sir?" Andie with some anxiety but with smooth and confidant sound, "I am the Head of Technical Support at IT Set Corporation. Last day one of your support person came to fix my computer. He worked his job very well. Only your corporation is supposed to be having such excellent engineers". Miss Jacky at the other end of line feels some relief, as it is at last a pressure-releasing call since morning. It was end of the month and number of calls was high as usually and she was also worried about the dues to be paid at the week end. She speaks out, "Thank you Sir. How I can help you Sir?" Andie, "Actually I have a little problem here with my computer that Engineer gave me some tips to over come this, but unfortunately I forget the name of that gentleman" Andie is smiling but feeling a little bit sweating. Miss Jacky "Oh, Sir. This is not a good situation, as we don't know his name. This is somewhat unlucky Sir. Can I assign you another Service Engineer? Pleas give'm… Andie abruptly jumps in, "Thanks nice lady, but I feel he can help me better. He told me that he has just joined head office a few weeks ago. Do you know him?". Miss Jacky is feeling some moral pressure to help out such a nice person and not to lose a company customer. Suddenly some thing flashes in her mind, "Well Sir, we have quit a large number of Support Engineers but here I know few persons who joined the office few weeks ago" then she utters three names (Robert, Michel, John). Andie wrote down his required names and requested her for extensions, after writing down these extensions he thanked her for her nice work and told her that he will check these Engineers one by one.

"Turn… turn... turn" Recorded tape starts playing back but Andie was looking in hurry, he didn't bother to hear, he just dialed 20. "Good Morning, this is inquiries section". Andie stared, "I am the Head of Technical Support section, today I have some problems in my main office computer lab, I want to contact with your IT Manager for some assistant. What is his office number?". Inquires section checked a few lists of names and spoke out a number and name. Andie thanked him again. Andie felt great comfort to build such nice relations with the help desk people as it is always helping in future business.

It was midnight, no one was in building, as company to works since morning 9:00 to evening 5:00. "Turn... turn... turn", a phone rang up in one of IT manager's room. There is no one to receive the call. A person in a dark room is patiently holding a handset and listening the bells on the other side. Then a person speaks out, its Copperhead IT manager's office, and I am not available at this time. Please record your message" then recording system starts. He cuts off the line without uttering even a single word. He then dials out through the same sequence for some more time and listen the voice very carefully each time. At last he smiles a little with a twitch of his head.

"Turn... turn… turn" he is waiting anxiously until some one picks and speaks out. "This is support section, Michel with you Sir" A firm voice which is seemed to be always ordering uttered, "Mr. Michel, I am IT Admin Copperhead, and here we have some serious problem. Our servers are getting some data corruption and your files are also included in that corrupted data". Mr. Michel finds it a good time to impress his new senior, "Sir, how can I help you….?". "It's not a big matter to fix, thanks. Anyhow give me your login name and password to fix it. You can log in and log out after a few minutes to check normal work". Mr. Michel felt a little bit depressed and gave out his login details without any hesitation. The above conversations just appear normal telephony talks but it was not as simple as it was appearing. That was a dooms day for that company. Eventually that company get hacked and lost some money but a lot of reputation. Admins were still in fuss how the attacker came in initially. The company was using best software and hardware techniques to avoid such misfortune. Problem was not technical configurations in their case.

They were the victims of so under estimated or simply over looked art of cracking know as "Social Engineering". Social Engineering is a combination of art and science that is used to get some kind of information by the means of human resources with out breaking the systems itself. Mostly corporations are spending big bucks on technical and physical security like Firewalls, Intrusion Detection Systems (IDS), Intrusion Prevention Systems (IPS), biometrics and many other things. But mostly the administrators and management ignore the weakest point in security "Human beings". And the crackers are the persons how mostly pay their due attention to this aspect. By the way, how can we define voodoo art know as "Social Engineering"?

Because of different ways and natures of attacks involved in Social Engineering there are slightly different definitions but the definition that suits most criteria to our problem is as, "The art and Science of the psychological tricks to get the desired results from human beings and to make them comply accordingly for unauthorized operations is known as

Social Engineering (in contrast with computer security)". The goals of the Social Engineering are same as traditional hacking. But by Social Engineering hackers got these goals by implementing social skills and exploiting human tendencies. By Social Engineering crackers are not the mind controllers of the victim. Victim will not do the things out of his normal behavior. He will perform the usual acts but unconsciously he becomes the asset for cracker. Crackers are exploiting the nature of human beings. Most brilliant crackers of the day study the human psychology with same effort and attention as they learn new bugs in most secure operating systems. They will consider/study all the possibilities according to the nature of attack being performed. And they pay more attention in preparations for social engineering than to perform it like normal technical hacking. And every body knows that time taken in a hack is just a small fraction of the time to gather the proper information regarding the victim for real attack.

Andie is the master artiste of this aspect of Information Security paradigm and gels well with other teammates with similar capabilities to catapult the information they require out of the system. Carrie just knows where the best modes to monitor the resources of the system are. He knows the entire mechanics that goes into securing and cracking the system over personnel security. He is the best man to understand and spoof everything that involves technology for physical security or in other words he is the man of biometrics. Though biometrics often are touted as a way to restrict criminality, privacy advocates fear biometrics may be used to diminish personal liberties of law abiding citizens as well. Developments in a huge range of new technologies besides biometrics - digital video, infrared, x-ray, wireless, global positioning satellite systems, image scanning, voice recognition, DNA, and brain wave fingerprinting - provide government with new ways to "search" individuals and collect vast databases of information on law-abiding members of the public.

The best part comes when they always knew they had something in them, although being radically distinct from each other, which combined them to fit together to complete the jigsaw for something big. They always knew they would require each other at some or the other phase of time to wherever they go, whatever they do. And thus comes the commanding quality of Viv which truly distinguished him from the rest of the pack. He always had that knack of steering the ship to the shore and 'just in time' as their lingo goes. Viv was the man with ideas as well as resources, in short, he knew something about every thing and was the jack of all trades in true sense. And it was his original idea which actually took the shape of something he never predicted.

On this humid Sunday, the pack as they called themselves when 5 combined gathered at Viv's home just for regular chit chat when they started talking about their difficulty at school and the remedial measures. None of them were an above average student at school but were never looked down due to that distinct nature of theirs with their own niche to bank upon.

"It's getting really hard to sustain at school pals, I am clueless"
"Our grades are going down and down as usual, wish I could do something with these examination guys"
"Wish you could do something with these guys? What you gonna do, bribe them"
"I don't have that kinda money, none of us have, but we have something more precious"
"Oh c'mon man, don't say you will break open the exam network to alter the results"
"I am not saying that"
"Then?"
"I am doing that!!"

All of them were hinted by Andie over the turn of events due to this conversation started by Viv what they might be in if not now maybe some time later. And that's what exactly was happening although now with a different motive.

Over the years after the high school, Andie, Viv, AJ, Carrie and Joe developed unique skills to subconsciously complement each other in some or the other way. Andie reknwoned for his soft skills and hard hitting thoughts came to be known as the Social Engineer whence he kept on rolling his expertise to break open whatsoever he could come across till he could not be caught and nabbed and that has yet not happened. Viv was the artiste of planning and execution, the person who steered the team to the goal secreting what was needed from which person and in which magnitude. In short, he was the person of resource utilization and team management, without him being the focal point of the team; they loose sheen and subsequently fall apart like a bunch of loosely tied drumsticks. AJ is a mechanically technical guy, the kind of people who build the system from the inputs of others. Similar to an assembly line workforce, AJ could code anything under the sun in all the major languages and the warehouse of all the network security resources which subsequently will be needed as ammo to sustain and liven their dream. Carrie as they say is the authoritarian Cancer (his sunsign). He could plague any system with the world's best authentication plugins to plug out the information he required. Joe belonged to that rare breed of craftsmen who just could use simply any tool to work out something productive out of it. He could execute any network security task with aplomb combined with AJ's expertise to work out the details of the IP Cameras at the Stuggart Airport in Canada to the information security setup at a world class Bangalore Corporate's Campus.

And thus this day when they all stand together trying to save the falling apart due to the SMS all of them recieved that read

"URGNT M3TNG REQD, CME 2 APJ BLCK 8 5 SHRP"

from Andie which he rarely uses his cell phone for, they couldn't resist their reunion to form a brutal force on a tricky heist.

"Whatsup man, what's the matter"
"You won't believe your ears when I speak out what I have got for you people"
"You buying us Mercs"
"I am getting you resources for it"

At this juncture, Viv sensed something fishy as Andie doesn't talk anything he can't do and this sounded strange.

"Ok what we get here for is a plan, we will materialse and when we are done, we are driving away with our dreams"
"Speak clearly man, our patience is running away"
"Look, I came across these people who are rich and desperate to do anything to set their things rite at school"
'So???"
"So we will help them, we will use our expertise to access their school resources and set their things rite in lieu of which we would be making our dreams true"
"Hey hey hey, what all is this, what you talking about man"
'We will hack open the Central board of Education Server and will set their grades rite, what we required the most but couldn't do it that time"

Carrie added

"Hmmm it seemed like it will be a benevolent job too, we desperately needed to do that but couldn't so we realize how much they require it"
"Yeah pal, we just need to plan this heist well and everything will be a cakewalk for us"

And this was the flashpoint, when Viv couldn't stand this conversation any longer and retaliated with full denial. When finally the 5 of them thought of goin for the majority voting. However hard they tried but keeping them apart as individuals was the hardest thing they could do to themselves and finally Viv couldn't find any supporters for his cause. And half heartedly he gave into the honey trap.

Next day Andie explained to Vivek what all was the rough idea of what they would be doing for him to polish it. They would start with the apprentice of Andie, a victim of Social Engineering in the data warehouse of the computing facility of CBE. Raghu is a high profile techie with the computing facility and Andie came across him through the community gatherings of their native state. What now Viv's task with Raghu was to access the information of the Data Servers and at an appropriate time when no one else could know about the activities except Raghu going inside the facility. The Pack would be using the remote administration to monitor the time of hibernation for the servers and at the exact time span between the servers updation and hibernation, they would carry out the data transfer through physical as well as network tools.

Day 1 Saturday 2150 Hours

Carrie carries out the first test of the final plan when he uses a public GUI in the form of a search engine to spoof the IP cameras of the facility. He goes to the URL of the search engine and types the INURL command with the given IP Cameras address and bingo! He gets access to the cameras and can monitor any movements inside the facility even spoofing the screens at the reception allowing any intrusion activities at any hour. The perfect plan started with a bang and their motivation seemed at a real high.

Day 2 Sunday 0500 Hours

As Raghu had the late night shift, he stayed with his colleagues inside the facility itself when at the wee hours the shift was to be interchanged. All the colleagues left the facility at 0500 hours sharp when Raghu stayed back to wrap up the residual 'work'. The next shift was about to be taking place within 15 minutes but who knew these minutes are the years of solitude for these geeks to command the entire facility in their hands. As the IP cameras were already in the command of Carrie, the reception and the personnel security couldn't gauge what was going inside the facility within these 15 minutes. Raghu moves inside the computing facility and sends the dynamic IP of the systems with the required data to Viv when he monitors both AJ and Joe and telnets the two servers between the two cities miles away within seconds. The pack's installed setup of Pentium machines were tolerant to T1 data transfers and could sustain work of hours and hours without much performance deterioration. As soon as the servers gets connected, AJ uses the network scanner to find the open ports and to gain the administration password he uses his password cracker with the dictionary attack to compute the 5 digits password as informed by Raghu which the system kept updating every second hour. The password cracker starts computing the password when within minutes he couldn't still see any progress in the cracking. He uses an alternative to compute the password now with the Brute force attacks and AJ chooses 0 -9, ~ - & and A-Z, a-z as his options and 3 minutes...4

minutes their patience running away, 5 minutes...and they are done. So he logs on in the system as Admin and alters the XLS file with the given exam codes of those candidates. Joe backup the data and copies the file in order to maintain immediate assurity of the work. And thus they are done by the end of 12 minutes.

Raghu moves out of the facility with aplomb and the perfect plan has been executed without any hassles.

Day 3 Monday

The working day starts at the facility and Raghu comes at the morning shift when Akash stood there in the room of the systems with their colleagues. Akash looks at Raghu with indifference when he asks

"How is life goin?"
"As in?"

Raghu gets startled. Akash points at the anonymous IP logged in the system on Sunday Morning. Raghu gets a gripping chill running down his spine and stays calm. After constant grilling through the colleagues, Raghu still didn't spill any beans when Akash runs the traceroute program over the anonymous IP and it ends at the city and place known to Akash as well as Raghu. So Akash still asks Raghu if he knew anything as the IP was logged in the system exactly at the time when he took a time off during the Sunday morning. But he couldn't say anything. So Akash informs the local authorities to keep Raghu under vigil while he conducts the nabbing trail of the culprits and what they did with the systems.

Akash wanted to call the computer the IP Address was logged in but he knew it would extend the chase. So he preferred to land at the place with his teammates from 24 hours Information Security Response Team and books the itenary for the same.

Day 4 Tuesday

Andie is at an all time high as he couldn't believe what he executed with his mates actually came out this good. But the perfect plan was still inkling Viv of the lull before the storm. And he kept a low profile while Andie,

Joe and AJ carried on with the parties and planning of the money they got after altering the results of the Candidates in the Educational Board Server.

Suddenly, Andie gets a call in the middle of the Party from his college. Andie couldn't get a hint of what exactly was going to happen within such a short time and to all the involved.

"May I come in"

Andie gets inside the principal's room with the other 3 with cold feet and stands in front of him. While the gentlemen seated in front of the principal they still couldn't have clue about.

"How are your studies going?"
"Pretty good Sir"
"What have you people been doing lately part from your good studies?"
"Studying only Sir"
"May I confirm your home address please, all of yours"

And they confirmed the home address of each of the person including Viv and that was it. Akash stood up from the chair in front of the principal and matched the addresses of the IP with the place with what they confirmed. And handed them a dossier as well as notice slapping on them a Fine of Rs 2 Lac to be submitted within 20 days subject to which they would banned from using their PCs, Laptops etc for next 10 years and if they don't, an RI of 2 years for each of them.

appin
appinonline.com knowledge solutions
Discover technology, the right way !
Leaders In IT Security
& Ethical Hacking
www.appinlabs.com

10. Glossary

3-way Handshake

Machine A sends a packet with a SYN flag set to Machine B. B acknowledges A's SYN with a SYN/ACK. A acknowledges B's SYN/ACK with an ACK.

A

Access Control

Access Control ensures that resources are only granted to those users who are entitled to them.

Access Control List (ACL)

A mechanism that implements access control for a system resource by listing the identities of the system entities that are permitted to access the resource.

Access Control Service

A security service that provides protection of system resources against unauthorized access. The two basic mechanisms for implementing this service are ACLs and tickets.

Access Management Access

Management is the maintenance of access information which consists of four tasks: account administration, maintenance, monitoring, and revocation.

Access Matrix

An Access Matrix uses rows to represent subjects and columns to represent objects with privileges listed in each cell.

Account Harvesting

Account Harvesting is the process of collecting all the legitimate account names on a system.

ACK Piggybacking

ACK piggybacking is the practice of sending an ACK inside another packet going to the same destination.

Active Content

Program code embedded in the contents of a web page. When the page is accessed by a web browser, the embedded code is automatically downloaded and executed on the user's workstation. Ex. Java, ActiveX (MS).

Activity Monitors

Activity monitors aim to prevent virus infection by monitoring for malicious activity on a system, and blocking that activity when possible.

Address Resolution Protocol (ARP)

Address Resolution Protocol (ARP) is a protocol for mapping an Internet Protocol address to a physical machine address that is recognized in the local network. A table, usually called the ARP cache, is used to maintain a correlation between each MAC address and its corresponding IP Address. ARP provides the protocol rules for making this correlation and providing address conversion in both directions.

Advanced Encryption Standard (AES)

An encryption standard being developed by NIST. Intended to specify an unclassified, publicly-disclosed, symmetric encryption algorithm.

Algorithm

A finite set of step-by-step instructions for a problem-solving or computation procedure, especially one that can be implemented by a computer.

Applet

Java programs; an application program that uses the client's web browser to provide a user interface.

ARPANET

Advanced Research Projects Agency Network, a pioneer packet-switched network that was built in the early 1970s under contract to the US Government, led to the development of today's Internet, and was decommissioned in June 1990.

Asymmetric Cryptography

Public-key cryptography; A modern branch of cryptography in which the algorithms employ a pair of keys (a public key and a private key) and use a different component of the pair for different steps of the algorithm.

Asymmetric Warfare

Asymmetric warfare is the fact that a small investment, properly leveraged, can yield incredible results.

Auditing

Auditing is the information gathering and analysis of assets to ensure such things as policy compliance and security from vulnerabilities.

Authentication

Authentication is the process of confirming the correctness of the claimed identity.

Authenticity

Authenticity is the validity and conformance of the original information.

Authorization

Authorization is the approval, permission, or empowerment for someone or something to do something.

Autonomous System

One network or series of networks that are all under one administrative control. An autonomous system is also sometimes referred to as a routing domain. An autonomous system is assigned a globally unique number, sometimes called an Autonomous System Number (ASN).

Availability

Availability is the need to ensure that the business purpose of the system can be met and that it is accessible to those who need to use it.

B

Backdoor

A backdoor is a tool installed after a compromise to give an attacker easier access to the compromised system around any security mechanisms that are in place.

Bandwidth

Commonly used to mean the capacity of a communication channel to pass data through the channel in a given amount of time. Usually expressed in bits per second.

Banner

A banner is the information that is displayed to a remote user trying to connect to a service. This may include version information, system information, or a warning about authorized use.

Basic Authentication

Basic Authentication is the simplest web-based authentication scheme that works by sending the username and password with each request.

Bastion Host

A bastion host has been hardened in anticipation of vulnerabilities that have not been discovered yet.

BIND

BIND stands for Berkeley Internet Name Domain and is an implementation of DNS. DNS is used for domain name to IP Address resolution.

Biometrics

Biometrics use physical characteristics of the users to determine access.

Bit

The smallest unit of information storage; a contraction of the term "binary digit'; one of two symbols Ñ "0" (zero) and "1" (one) - that are used to represent binary numbers.

Block Cipher

A block cipher encrypts one block of data at a time.

Boot Record Infector

A boot record infector is a piece of malware that inserts malicious code into the boot sector of a disk.

Border Gateway Protocol (BGP)

An inter-autonomous system routing protocol. BGP is used to exchange routing information for the Internet and is the protocol used between Internet service providers (ISP).

Bridge

A product that connects a local area network (LAN) to another local area network that uses the same protocol (for example Ethernet or token ring).

British Standard 7799

A standard code of practice and provides guidance on how to secure an information system. It includes the management framework, objectives, and control requirements for information security management systems.

Broadcast

To simultaneously send the same message to multiple recipients. One host to all hosts on network.

Broadcast Address

An address used to broadcast a datagram to all hosts on a given network using UDP or ICMP protocol.

Browser

A client computer program that can retrieve and display information from servers on the World Wide Web.

Brute Force

A cryptanalysis technique or other kind of attack method involving an exhaustive procedure that tries all possibilities, one-by-one.

Buffer Overflow

A buffer overflow occurs when a program or process tries to store more data in a buffer (temporary data storage area) than it was intended to hold. Since buffers are created to contain a finite amount of data, the extra information - which has to go somewhere - can overflow into adjacent buffers, corrupting or overwriting the valid data held in them.

Business Continuity Plan (BCP)

A Business Continuity Plan is the plan for emergency response, backup operations, and post-disaster recovery steps that will ensure the availability of critical resources and facilitate the continuity of operations in an emergency situation.

Business Impact Analysis (BIA)

A Business Impact Analysis determines what levels of impact to a system are tolerable.

Byte

A fundamental unit of computer storage; the smallest addressable unit in a computer's architecture. Usually holds one character of information and usually means eight bits.

C

Cache

Pronounced cash, a special high-speed storage mechanism. It can be either a reserved section of main memory or an independent high-speed storage device. Two types of caching are commonly used in personal computers: memory caching and disk caching.

Cache Cramming

Cache Cramming is the technique of tricking a browser to run cached Java code from the local disk, instead of the internet zone, so it runs with less restrictive permissions.

Cache Poisoning

Malicious or misleading data from a remote name server is saved [cached] by another name server. Typically used with DNS cache poisoning attacks.

Cell

A cell is a unit of data transmitted over an ATM network.

Certificate-Based Authentication

Certificate-Based Authentication is the use of SSL and certificates to authenticate and encrypt HTTP traffic.

CGI

Common Gateway Interface. This mechanism is used by HTTP servers (web servers) to pass parameters to executable scripts in order to generate responses dynamically.

Chain of Custody

Chain of Custody is the important application of the Federal rules of evidence and its handling.

Challenge-Handshake Authentication Protocol (CHAP)

The Challenge-Handshake Authentication Protocol uses a challenge/response authentication mechanism where the response varies every challenge to prevent replay attacks.

Checksum

A value that is computed by a function that is dependent on the contents of a data object and is stored or transmitted together with the object, for the purpose of detecting changes in the data.

Cipher

A cryptographic algorithm for encryption and decryption.

Ciphertext

Ciphertext is the encrypted form of the message being sent.

Circuit Switched Network

A circuit switched network is where a single continuous physical circuit connected two endpoints where the route was immutable once set up.

Client

A system entity that requests and uses a service provided by another system entity, called a "server". In some cases, the server may itself be a client of some other server.

Collision

A collision occurs when multiple systems transmit simultaneously on the same wire.

Competitive Intelligence

Competitive Intelligence is espionage using legal, or at least not obviously illegal, means.

Computer Emergency Response Team (CERT)

An organization that studies computer and network INFOSEC in order to provide incident response services to victims of attacks, publish alerts concerning vulnerabilities and threats, and offer other information to help improve computer and network security.

Computer Network

A collection of host computers together with the sub-network or inter-network through which they can exchange data.

Confidentiality

Confidentiality is the need to ensure that information is disclosed only to those who are authorized to view it.

Configuration Management

Establish a known baseline condition and manage it.

Cookie

Data exchanged between an HTTP server and a browser (a client of the server) to store state information on the client side and retrieve it later for server use. An HTTP server, when sending data to a client, may send along a cookie, which the client retains after the HTTP connection closes. A server can use this mechanism to maintain persistent client-side state information for HTTP-based applications, retrieving the state information in later connections.

Corruption

A threat action that undesirably alters system operation by adversely modifying system functions or data.

Cost Benefit Analysis

A cost benefit analysis compares the cost of implementing countermeasures with the value of the reduced risk.

Countermeasure

Reactive methods used to prevent an exploit from successfully occurring once a threat has been detected. Intrusion Prevention Systems (IPS) commonly employs countermeasures to prevent intruders form gaining further access to a computer network. Other counter measures are patches, access control lists and malware filters.

Covert Channels

Covert Channels are the means by which information can be communicated between two parties in a covert fashion using normal system operations. For example by changing the amount of hard drive space that is available on a file server can be used to communicate information.

Cron

Cron is a UNIX application that runs jobs for users and administrators at scheduled times of the day.

Crossover Cable

A crossover cable reverses the pairs of cables at the other end and can be used to connect devices directly together.

Cryptanalysis

The mathematical science that deals with analysis of a cryptographic system in order to gain knowledge needed to break or circumvent the protection that the system is designed to provide. In other words, convert the cipher text to plaintext without knowing the key.

Cryptographic Algorithm or Hash

An algorithm that employs the science of cryptography, including encryption algorithms, cryptographic hash algorithms, digital signature algorithms, and key agreement algorithms.

Cryptography

Cryptography garbles a message in such a way that anyone who intercepts the message cannot understand it.

Cut-Through

Cut-Through is a method of switching where only the header of a packet is read before it is forwarded to its destination.

Cyclic Redundancy Check (CRC)

Sometimes called "cyclic redundancy code". A type of checksum algorithm that is not a cryptographic hash but is used to implement data integrity service where accidental changes to data are expected.

D

Daemon

A program which is often started at the time the system boots and runs continuously without intervention from any of the users on the system. The daemon program forwards the requests to other programs (or processes) as appropriate. The term daemon is a UNIX term, though many other operating systems provide support for daemons, though they're sometimes called other names. Windows, for example, refers to daemons and System Agents and services.

Data Aggregation

Data Aggregation is the ability to get a more complete picture of the information by analyzing several different types of records at once.

Data Custodian

A Data Custodian is the entity currently using or manipulating the data, and therefore, temporarily taking responsibility for the data.

Data Encryption Standard (DES)

A widely-used method of data encryption using a private (secret) key. There are 72,000,000,000,000,000 (72 quadrillion) or more possible encryption keys that can be used. For each given message, the key is chosen at random from among this enormous number of keys. Like other private key cryptographic methods, both the sender and the receiver must know and use the same private key.

Data Mining

Data Mining is a technique used to analyze existing information, usually with the intention of pursuing new avenues to pursue business.

Data Owner

A Data Owner is the entity having responsibility and authority for the data.

Data Warehousing

Data Warehousing is the consolidation of several previously independent databases into one location.

Datagram

Request for Comment 1594 says, "a self-contained, independent entity of data carrying sufficient information to be routed from the source to the destination computer without reliance on earlier exchanges between this source and destination computer and the transporting network". The term has been generally replaced by the term packet. Datagrams or packets are the message units that the Internet Protocol deals with and that the Internet transports. A datagram or packet needs to be self-contained without reliance on earlier exchanges because there is no connection of fixed duration between the two communicating points as there is, for example, in most voice telephone conversations. (This kind of protocol is referred to as connectionless).

Day Zero

The "Day Zero" or "Zero Day" is the day a new vulnerability is made know. In some cases, a "zero day" exploit is referred to an exploit for which no patch is available yet. ("day one"-> day at which the patch is made available).

Decapsulation

Decapsulation is the process of stripping off one layer's headers and passing the rest of the packet up to the next higher layer on the protocol stack.

Decryption

Decryption is the process of transforming an encrypted message into its original plaintext.

Defacement

Defacement is the method of modifying the content of a website in such a way that it becomes "vandalized" or embarrassing to the website owner.

Defense In-Depth

Defense In-Depth is the approach of using multiple layers of security to guard against failure of a single security component.

Demilitarized Zone (DMZ)

In computer security, in general a demilitarized zone (DMZ) or perimeter network is a network area (a subnetwork) that sits between an organization's internal network and an external network, usually the Internet. DMZ's help to enable the layered security model in that they provide subnetwork segmentation based on security requirements or policy. DMZ's provide either a transit mechanism from a secure source to an insecure destination or from an insecure source to a more secure destination. In some cases, a screened subnet which is used for servers' accessible form the outside is referred to as a DMZ.

Denial of Service

The prevention of authorized access to a system resource or the delaying of system operations and functions.

Dictionary Attack

An attack that tries all of the phrases or words in a dictionary, trying to crack a password or key. A dictionary attack uses a predefined list of words compared to a brute force attack that tries all possible combinations.

Diffie-Hellman

A key agreement algorithm published in 1976 by Whitfield Diffie and Martin Hellman. Diffie-Hellman does key establishment, not encryption. However, the key that it produces may be used for encryption, for further key management operations, or for any other cryptography.

Digest Authentication

Digest Authentication allows a web client to compute MD5 hashes of the password to prove it has the password.

Digital Certificate

A digital certificate is an electronic "credit card" that establishes your credentials when doing business or other transactions on the Web. It is issued by a certification authority. It contains your name, a serial number, expiration dates, a copy of the certificate holder's public key (used for encrypting messages and digital signatures), and the digital signature of the certificate-issuing authority so that a recipient can verify that the certificate is real.

Digital Envelope

A digital envelope is an encrypted message with the encrypted session key.

Digital Signature

A digital signature is a hash of a message that uniquely identifies the sender of the message and proves the message hasn't changed since transmission.

Digital Signature Algorithm (DSA)

An asymmetric cryptographic algorithm that produces a digital signature in the form of a pair of large numbers. The signature is computed using rules and parameters such that the identity of the signer and the integrity of the signed data can be verified.

Digital Signature Standard (DSS)

The US Government standard that specifies the Digital Signature Algorithm (DSA), which involves asymmetric cryptography.

Disassembly

The process of taking a binary program and deriving the source code from it.

Disaster Recovery Plan (DRP)

A Disaster Recovery Plan is the process of recovery of IT systems in the event of a disruption or disaster.

Discretionary Access Control (DAC)

Discretionary Access Control consists of something the user can manage, such as a document password.

Disruption

A circumstance or event that interrupts or prevents the correct operation of system services and functions.

Distance Vector

Distance vectors measure the cost of routes to determine the best route to all known networks.

Distributed Scans

Distributed Scans are scans that use multiple source addresses to gather information.

Domain

A sphere of knowledge, or a collection of facts about some program entities or a number of network points or addresses, identified by a name. On the Internet, a domain consists of a set of network addresses. In the Internet's domain name system, a domain is a name with which name server records are associated that describe sub-domains or host. In Windows NT and Windows 2000, a domain is a set of network resources (applications, printers, and so forth) for a group of users. The user need only to log in to the domain to gain access to the resources, which may be located on a number of different servers in the network.

Domain Hijacking

Domain hijacking is an attack by which an attacker takes over a domain by first blocking access to the domain's DNS server and then putting his own server up in its place.

Domain Name

A domain name locates an organization or other entity on the Internet. For example, the domain name "www.sans.org" locates an Internet address for "sans.org" at Internet point 199.0.0.2 and a particular host server named 'www". The "org" part of the domain name reflects the purpose of the organization or entity (in this example, "organization') and is called the top-level domain name. The "sans" part of the domain name defines the organization or entity and together with the top-level is called the second-level domain name.

Domain Name System (DNS)

The domain name system (DNS) is the way that Internet domain names are located and translated into Internet Protocol addresses. A domain name is a meaningful and easy-to-remember "handle" for an Internet address.

Due Care

Due care ensures that a minimal level of protection is in place in accordance with the best practice in the industry.

Due Diligence

Due diligence is the requirement that organizations must develop and deploy a protection plan to prevent fraud, abuse, and additional deploy a means to detect them if they occur.

DumpSec

DumpSec is a security tool that dumps a variety of information about a system's users, file system, registry, permissions, password policy, and services.

Dumpster Diving

Dumpster Diving is obtaining passwords and corporate directories by searching through discarded media.

Dynamic Link Library

A collection of small programs, any of which can be called when needed by a larger program that is running in the computer. The small program that let's the larger program communicate with a specific device such as a printer or scanner is often packaged as a DLL program (usually referred to as a DLL file).

Dynamic Routing Protocol

Allows network devices to learn routes. Ex. RIP, EIGRP Dynamic routing occurs when routers talk to adjacent routers, informing each other of what networks each router is currently connected to. The routers must communicate using a routing protocol, of which there are many to choose from. The process on the router that is running the routing protocol, communicating with its neighbor routers, is usually called a routing daemon. The routing daemon updates the kernel's routing table with information it receives from neighbor routers.

E

Eavesdropping

Eavesdropping is simply listening to a private conversation which may reveal information which can provide access to a facility or network.

Echo Reply

An echo reply is the response a machine that has received an echo request sends over ICMP.

Echo Request

An echo request is an ICMP message sent to a machine to determine if it is online and how long traffic takes to get to it.

Egress Filtering

Filtering outbound traffic.

Emanations Analysis

Gaining direct knowledge of communicated data by monitoring and resolving a signal that is emitted by a system and that contains the data but is not intended to communicate the data.

Encapsulation

The inclusion of one data structure within another structure so that the first data structure is hidden for the time being.

Encryption

Cryptographic transformation of data (called "plaintext") into a form (called "cipher text") that conceals the data's original meaning to prevent it from being known or used.

Ephemeral Port

Also called a transient port or a temporary port. Usually is on the client side. It is set up when a client application wants to connect to a server and is destroyed when the client application terminates. It has a number chosen at random that is greater than 1023.

Escrow Passwords

Escrow Passwords are passwords that are written down and stored in a secure location (like a safe) that are used by emergency personnel when privileged personnel are unavailable.

Ethernet

The most widely-installed LAN technology. Specified in a standard, IEEE 802.3, an Ethernet LAN typically uses coaxial cable or special grades of twisted pair wires. Devices are connected to the cable and compete for access using a CSMA/CD protocol.

Event

An event is an observable occurrence in a system or network.

Exponential Backoff Algorithm

An exponential backoff algorithm is used to adjust TCP timeout values on the fly so that network devices don't continue to timeout sending data over saturated links.

Exposure

A threat action whereby sensitive data is directly released to an unauthorized entity.

Extended ACLs (Cisco)

Extended ACLs are a more powerful form of Standard ACLs on Cisco routers. They can make filtering decisions based on IP addresses (source or destination), Ports (source or destination), protocols, and whether a session is established.

Extensible Authentication Protocol (EAP)

A framework that supports multiple, optional authentication mechanisms for PPP, including clear-text passwords, challenge-response, and arbitrary dialog sequences.

Exterior Gateway Protocol (EGP)

A protocol which distributes routing information to the routers which connect autonomous systems.

F

False Rejects

False Rejects are when an authentication system fails to recognize a valid user.

Fast File System

The first major revision to the UNIX file system, providing faster read access and faster (delayed, asynchronous) write access through a disk cache and better file system layout on disk. It uses inodes (pointers) and data blocks.

Fault Line Attacks

Fault Line Attacks use weaknesses between interfaces of systems to exploit gaps in coverage.

File Transfer Protocol (FTP)

A TCP/IP protocol specifying the transfer of text or binary files across the network.

Filter

A filter is used to specify which packets will or will not be used. It can be used in sniffers to determine which packets get displayed, or by firewalls to determine which packets get blocked.

Filtering Router

An inter-network router that selectively prevents the passage of data packets according to a security policy. A filtering router may be used as a firewall or part of a firewall. A router usually receives a packet from a network and decides where to forward it on a second network. A filtering router does the same, but first decides whether the packet should be forwarded at all, according to some security policy. The policy is implemented by rules (packet filters) loaded into the router.

Finger

A protocol to lookup user information on a given host. A UNIX program that takes an E-mail address as input and returns information about the user who owns that e-mail address. On some systems, finger only reports whether the user is currently logged on. Other systems return additional information, such as the user's full name, address, and telephone number. Of course, the user must first enter this information into the system. Many e-mail programs now have a finger utility built into them.

Fingerprinting

Sending strange packets to a system in order to gauge how it responds to determine the operating system.

Firewall

A logical or physical discontinuity in a network to prevent unauthorized access to data or resources.

Flooding

An attack that attempts to cause a failure in (especially, in the security of) a computer system or other data processing entity by providing more input than the entity can process properly.

Forest

A forest is a set of Active Directory domains that replicate their databases with each other.

Fork Bomb

A Fork Bomb works by using the fork() call to create a new process which is a copy of the original. By doing this repeatedly, all available processes on the machine can be taken up.

Form-Based Authentication

Form-Based Authentication uses forms on a webpage to ask a user to input username and password information.

Forward Lookup

Forward lookup uses an Internet domain name to find an IP address

Forward Proxy

Forward Proxies are designed to be the server through which all requests are made.

Fragment Offset

The fragment offset field tells the sender where a particular fragment falls in relation to other fragments in the original larger packet.

Fragment Overlap Attack

A TCP/IP Fragmentation Attack that is possible because IP allows packets to be broken down into fragments for more efficient transport across various media. The TCP packet (and its header) are carried in the IP packet. In this attack the second fragment contains incorrect offset. When packet is reconstructed, the port number will be overwritten.

Fragmentation

The process of storing a data file in several "chunks" or fragments rather than in a single contiguous sequence of bits in one place on the storage medium.

Frames

Data that is transmitted between network points as a unit complete with addressing and necessary protocol control information. A frame is usually transmitted serial bit by bit and contains a header field and a trailer field that "frame" the data. (Some control frames contain no data).

Full Duplex

A type of duplex communications channel which carries data in both directions at once. Refers to the transmission of data in two directions simultaneously. Communications in which both sender and receiver can send at the same time.

Fully-Qualified Domain Name

A Fully-Qualified Domain Name is a server name with a hostname followed by the full domain name.

Fuzzing

The use of special regression testing tools to generate out-of-spec input for an application in order to find security vulnerabilities. Also see "regression testing".

G

Gateway

A network point that acts as an entrance to another network.

Gethostbyaddr

The gethostbyaddr DNS query is when the address of a machine is known and the name is needed.

Gethostbyname

The gethostbyname DNS quest is when the name of a machine is known and the address is needed.

GNU

GNU is a UNIX-like operating system that comes with source code that can be copied, modified, and redistributed. The GNU project was started in 1983 by Richard Stallman and others, who formed the Free Software Foundation.

Gnutella

An Internet file sharing utility. Gnutella acts as a server for sharing files while simultaneously acting as a client that searches for and downloads files from other users.

H

Hardening

Hardening is the process of identifying and fixing vulnerabilities on a system.

Hash Function

An algorithm that computes a value based on a data object thereby mapping the data object to a smaller data object.

Hash Functions

(Cryptographic) hash functions are used to generate a one way "check sum" for a larger text, which is not trivially reversed. The result of this hash function can be used to validate if a larger file has been altered, without having to compare the larger files to each other. Frequently used hash functions are MD5 and SHA1.

Header

A header is the extra information in a packet that is needed for the protocol stack to process the packet.

Hijack Attack

A form of active wiretapping in which the attacker seizes control of a previously established communication association.

Honey Client

see Honeymonkey.

Honey pot

Programs that simulate one or more network services that you designate on your computer's ports. An attacker assumes you're running vulnerable services that can be used to break into the machine. A honey pot can be used to log access attempts to those ports including the attacker's keystrokes. This could give you advanced warning of a more concerted attack.

Honeymonkey

Automated system simulating a user browsing websites. The system is typically configured to detect web sites which exploit vulnerabilities in the browser. Also known as Honey Client.

Hops

A hop is each exchange with a gateway a packet takes on its way to the destination.

Host

Any computer that has full two-way access to other computers on the Internet. Or a computer with a web server that serves the pages for one or more Web sites.

Host-Based ID

Host-based intrusion detection systems use information from the operating system audit records to watch all operations occurring on the host that the intrusion detection software has been installed upon. These operations are then compared with a pre-defined security policy. This analysis of the audit trail imposes potentially significant overhead requirements on the system because of the increased amount of processing power which must be utilized by the intrusion detection system. Depending on the size of the audit trail and the processing ability of the system, the review of audit data could result in the loss of a real-time analysis capability.

HTTP Proxy

An HTTP Proxy is a server that acts as a middleman in the communication between HTTP clients and servers.

HTTPS

When used in the first part of a URL (the part that precedes the colon and specifies an access scheme or protocol), this term specifies the use of HTTP enhanced by a security mechanism, which is usually SSL.

Hub

A hub is a network device that operates by repeating data that it receives on one port to all the other ports. As a result, data transmitted by one host is retransmitted to all other hosts on the hub.

Hybrid Attack

A Hybrid Attack builds on the dictionary attack method by adding numerals and symbols to dictionary words.

Hybrid Encryption

An application of cryptography that combines two or more encryption algorithms, particularly a combination of symmetric and asymmetric encryption.

Hyperlink

In hypertext or hypermedia, an information object (such as a word, a phrase, or an image; usually highlighted by color or underscoring) that points (indicates how to connect) to related information that is located elsewhere and can be retrieved by activating the link.

Hypertext Markup Language (HTML)

The set of markup symbols or codes inserted in a file intended for display on a World Wide Web browser page.

Hypertext Transfer Protocol (HTTP)

The protocol in the Internet Protocol (IP) family used to transport hypertext documents across an internet.

I

Identity

Identity is whom someone or what something is, for example, the name by which something is known.

Incident

An incident as an adverse network event in an information system or network or the threat of the occurrence of such an event.

Incident Handling

Incident Handling is an action plan for dealing with intrusions, cyber-theft, denial of service, fire, floods, and other security-related events. It is comprised of a six step process: Preparation, Identification, Containment, Eradication, Recovery, and Lessons Learned.

Incremental Backups

Incremental backups only backup the files that have been modified since the last backup. If dump levels are used, incremental backups only backup files changed since last backup of a lower dump level.

Inetd (xinetd)

Inetd (or Internet Daemon) is an application that controls smaller internet services like telnet, ftp, and POP.

Inference Attack

Inference Attacks rely on the user to make logical connections between seemingly unrelated pieces of information.

Information Warfare

Information Warfare is the competition between offensive and defensive players over information resources.

Ingress Filtering

Ingress Filtering is filtering inbound traffic.

Input Validation Attacks

Input Validations Attacks are where an attacker intentionally sends unusual input in the hopes of confusing an application.

Integrity

Integrity is the need to ensure that information has not been changed accidentally or deliberately, and that it is accurate and complete.

Integrity Star Property

In Integrity Star Property a user cannot read data of a lower integrity level then their own.

Internet

A term to describe connecting multiple separate networks together.

Internet Control Message Protocol (ICMP)

An Internet Standard protocol that is used to report error conditions during IP datagram processing and to exchange other information concerning the state of the IP network.

Internet Engineering Task Force (IETF)

The body that defines standard Internet operating protocols such as TCP/IP. The IETF is supervised by the Internet Society Internet Architecture Board (IAB). IETF members are drawn from the Internet Society's individual and organization membership.

Internet Message Access Protocol (IMAP)

A protocol that defines how a client should fetch mail from and return mail to a mail server. IMAP is intended as a replacement for or extension to the Post Office Protocol (POP). It is defined in RFC 1203 (v3) and RFC 2060 (v4).

Internet Protocol (IP)

The method or protocol by which data is sent from one computer to another on the Internet.

Internet Protocol Security (IPsec)

A developing standard for security at the network or packet processing layer of network communication.

Internet Standard

A specification, approved by the IESG and published as an RFC, that is stable and well-understood, is technically competent, has multiple, independent, and interoperable implementations with substantial operational experience, enjoys significant public support, and is recognizably useful in some or all parts of the Internet.

Interrupt

An Interrupt is a signal that informs the OS that something has occurred.

Intranet

A computer network, especially one based on Internet technology, that an organization uses for its own internal, and usually private, purposes and that is closed to outsiders.

Intrusion Detection

A security management system for computers and networks. An IDS gathers and analyzes information from various areas within a computer or a network to identify possible security breaches, which include both intrusions (attacks from outside the organization) and misuse (attacks from within the organization).

IP Address

A computer's inter-network address that is assigned for use by the Internet Protocol and other protocols. An IP version 4 address is written as a series of four 8-bit numbers separated by periods.

IP Flood

A denial of service attack that sends a host more echo request ("ping") packets than the protocol implementation can handle.

IP Forwarding

IP forwarding is an Operating System option that allows a host to act as a router. A system that has more than 1 network interface card must have IP forwarding turned on in order for the system to be able to act as a router.

IP Spoofing

The technique of supplying a false IP address.

ISO

International Organization for Standardization, a voluntary, non-treaty, non-government organization, established in 1947, with voting members that are designated standards bodies of participating nations and non-voting observer organizations.

Issue-Specific Policy

An Issue-Specific Policy is intended to address specific needs within an organization, such as a password policy.

ITU-T

International Telecommunications Union, Telecommunication Standardization Sector (formerly "CCITT"), a United Nations treaty organization that is composed mainly of postal, telephone, and telegraph authorities of the member countries and that publishes standards called "Recommendations".

J

Jitter

Jitter or Noise is the modification of fields in a database while preserving the aggregate characteristics of that make the database useful in the first place.

Jump Bag

A Jump Bag is a container that has all the items necessary to respond to an incident inside to help mitigate the effects of delayed reactions.

K

Kerberos

A system developed at the Massachusetts Institute of Technology that depends on passwords and symmetric cryptography (DES) to implement ticket-based, peer entity authentication service and access control service distributed in a client-server network environment.

Kernel

The essential center of a computer operating system, the core that provides basic services for all other parts of the operating system. A synonym is nucleus. A kernel can be contrasted with a shell, the outermost part of an operating system that interacts with user commands. Kernel and shell are terms used more frequently in UNIX and some other operating systems than in IBM mainframe systems.

L

Lattice Techniques

Lattice Techniques use security designations to determine access to information.

Layer 2 Forwarding Protocol (L2F)

An Internet protocol (originally developed by Cisco Corporation) that uses tunneling of PPP over IP to create a virtual extension of a dial-up link across a network, initiated by the dial-up server and transparent to the dial-up user.

Layer 2 Tunneling Protocol (L2TP)

An extension of the Point-to-Point Tunneling Protocol used by an Internet service provider to enable the operation of a virtual private network over the Internet.

Least Privilege

Least Privilege is the principle of allowing users or applications the least amount of permissions necessary to perform their intended function.

Legion

Software to detect unprotected shares.

Lightweight Directory Access Protocol (LDAP)

A software protocol for enabling anyone to locate organizations, individuals, and other resources such as files and devices in a network, whether on the public Internet or on a corporate Intranet.

Link State

With link state, routes maintain information about all routers and router-to-router links within a geographic area, and creates a table of best routes with that information.

List Based Access Control

List Based Access Control associates a list of users and their privileges with each object.

Loadable Kernel Modules (LKM)

Loadable Kernel Modules allow for the adding of additional functionality directly into the kernel while the system is running.

Log Clipping

Log clipping is the selective removal of log entries from a system log to hide a compromise.

Logic Gate

A logic gate is an elementary building block of a digital circuit. Most logic gates have two inputs and one output. As digital circuits can only understand binary, inputs and outputs can assume only one of two states, 0 or 1.

Loopback Address

The loopback address (127.0.0.1) is a pseudo IP address that always refer back to the local host and are never sent out onto a network.

M

MAC Address

A physical address; a numeric value that uniquely identifies that network device from every other device on the planet.

Malicious Code

Software (e.g., Trojan horse) that appears to perform a useful or desirable function, but actually gains unauthorized access to system resources or tricks a user into executing other malicious logic.

Malware

A generic term for a number of different types of malicious code.

Mandatory Access Control (MAC)

Mandatory Access Control controls is where the system controls access to resources based on classification levels assigned to both the objects and the users. These controls cannot be changed by anyone.

Masquerade Attack

A type of attack in which one system entity illegitimately poses as (assumes the identity of) another entity.

MD5

A one way cryptographic hash function. Also see "hash functions" and "sha1"

Measures of Effectiveness (MOE)

Measures of Effectiveness is a probability model based on engineering concepts that allows one to approximate the impact a give action will have on an environment. In Information warfare it is the ability to attack or defend within an Internet environment.

Monoculture

Monoculture is the case where a large number of users run the same software, and are vulnerable to the same attacks.

Morris Worm

A worm program written by Robert T. Morris, Jr. that flooded the ARPANET in November, 1988, causing problems for thousands of hosts.

Multi-Cast

Broadcasting from one host to a given set of hosts.

Multi-Homed

You are "multi-homed" if your network is directly connected to two or more ISP's.

Multiplexing

To combine multiple signals from possibly disparate sources, in order to transmit them over a single path.

N

NAT

Network Address Translation. It is used to share one or a small number of publically routable IP addresses among a larger number of hosts. The hosts are assigned private IP addresses, which are then "translated" into one of the publicaly routed IP addresses. Typically home or small business networks use NAT to share a single DLS or Cable modem IP address. However, in some cases NAT is used for servers as an additional layer of protection.

National Institute of Standards and Technology (NIST)

National Institute of Standards and Technology, a unit of the US Commerce Department. Formerly known as the National Bureau of Standards, NIST promotes and maintains measurement standards. It also has active programs for encouraging and assisting industry and science to develop and use these standards.

Natural Disaster

Any "act of God" (e.g., fire, flood, earthquake, lightning, or wind) that disables a system component.

Netmask

32-bit number indicating the range of IP addresses residing on a single IP network/subnet/supernet. This specification displays network masks as hexadecimal numbers. For example, the network mask for a class C IP network is displayed as 0xffffff00. Such a mask is often displayed elsewhere in the literature as 255.255.255.0.

Network Address Translation

The translation of an Internet Protocol address used within one network to a different IP address known within another network. One network is designated the inside network and the other is the outside.

Network Mapping

To compile an electronic inventory of the systems and the services on your network.

Network Taps

Network taps are hardware devices that hook directly onto the network cable and send a copy of the traffic that passes through it to one or more other networked devices.

Network-Based IDS

A network-based IDS system monitors the traffic on its network segment as a data source. This is generally accomplished by placing the network interface card in promiscuous mode to capture all network traffic that crosses its network segment. Network traffic on other segments and traffic on other means of communication (like phone lines) can't be monitored. Network-based IDS involves looking at the packets on the network as they pass by some sensor. The sensor can only see the packets that happen to be carried on the network segment it's attached to. Packets are considered to be of interest if they match signature. Network-based intrusion detection passively monitors network activity for indications of attacks. Network monitoring offers several advantages over traditional host-based intrusion detection systems. Because many intrusions occur over networks at some point, and because networks are increasingly becoming the targets of attack, these techniques are an excellent method of detecting many attacks which may be missed by host-based intrusion detection mechanisms.

Non-Printable Character

A character that doesn't have a corresponding character letter to its corresponding ASCII code. Examples would be the Linefeed, which is ASCII character code 10 decimal, the Carriage Return, which is 13 decimal, or the bell sound, which is decimal 7. On a PC, you can often add non-printable characters by holding down the Alt key, and typing in the decimal value (i.e., Alt-007 gets you a bell). There are other character encoding schemes, but ASCII is the most prevalent.

Non-Repudiation

Non-repudiation is the ability for a system to prove that a specific user and only that specific user sent a message and that it hasn't been modified.

Null Session

Known as Anonymous Logon, it is a way of letting an anonymous user retrieve information such as user names and shares over the network or connect without authentication. It is used by applications such as explorer.exe to enumerate shares on remote servers.

O

Octet

A sequence of eight bits. An octet is an eight-bit byte.

One-Way Encryption

Irreversible transformation of plaintext to cipher text, such that the plaintext cannot be recovered from the cipher text by other than exhaustive procedures even if the cryptographic key is known.

One-Way Function

A (mathematical) function, f, which is easy to compute the output based on a given input. However given only the output value it is impossible (except for a brute force attack) to figure out what the input value is.

Open Shortest Path First (OSPF)

Open Shortest Path First is a link state routing algorithm used in interior gateway routing. Routers maintain a database of all routers in the autonomous system with links between the routers, link costs, and link states (up and down).

OSI

OSI (Open Systems Interconnection) is a standard description or "reference model" for how messages should be transmitted between any two points in a telecommunication network. Its purpose is to guide product implementers so that their products will consistently work with other products. The reference model defines seven layers of functions that take place at each end of a communication. Although OSI is not always strictly adhered to in terms of keeping related functions together in a well-defined layer, many if not most products involved in telecommunication make an attempt to describe themselves in relation to the OSI model. It is also valuable as a single reference view of communication that furnishes everyone a common ground for education and discussion.

OSI layers

The main idea in OSI is that the process of communication between two end points in a telecommunication network can be divided into layers, with each layer adding its own set of special, related functions. Each communicating user or program is at a computer equipped with these seven layers of function. So, in a given message between users, there will be a flow of data through each layer at one end down through the layers in that computer and, at the other end, when the message arrives, another flow of data up through the layers in the receiving computer and ultimately to the end user or program. The actual programming and hardware that furnishes these seven layers of function is usually a combination of the computer operating system, applications (such as your Web browser), TCP/IP or alternative transport and network protocols, and the software and hardware that enable you to put a signal on one of the lines attached to your computer. OSI divides telecommunication into seven layers. The layers are in two groups. The upper four layers are used whenever a message passes from or to a user. The lower three layers (up to the network layer) are used when any message passes through the host computer or router. Messages intended for this computer pass to the upper layers. Messages destined for some other host are not passed up to the upper layers but are forwarded to another host. The seven layers are: Layer 7: The application layer...This is the layer at which communication partners are identified, quality of service is identified, user authentication and privacy are considered, and any constraints on data syntax are identified. (This layer is not the application itself, although some applications may perform application layer functions.) Layer 6: The presentation layer...This is a layer, usually part of an operating system, that converts incoming and outgoing data from one presentation format to another (for example, from a text stream into a popup window with the newly arrived text). Sometimes called the syntax layer. Layer 5: The session layer...This layer sets up, coordinates, and terminates conversations, exchanges, and dialogs between the applications at each end. It deals with session and connection coordination. Layer 4: The transport layer...This layer manages the end-to-end control (for example, determining whether all packets have arrived) and error-checking. It ensures complete data transfer. Layer 3: The network layer...This layer handles the routing of the data (sending it in the right direction to the right destination on outgoing transmissions and receiving incoming transmissions at the packet level). The network layer does routing and forwarding. Layer 2: The data-link layer...This layer provides synchronization for the physical level and does bit-stuffing for strings of 1's in excess of 5. It furnishes transmission protocol knowledge and management. Layer 1: The physical layer...This layer conveys the bit stream through the network at the electrical and mechanical level. It provides the hardware means of sending and receiving data on a carrier.

Overload

Hindrance of system operation by placing excess burden on the performance capabilities of a system component.

P

Packet

A piece of a message transmitted over a packet-switching network. One of the key features of a packet is that it contains the destination address in addition to the data. In IP networks, packets are often called datagrams.

Packet Switched Network

A packet switched network is where individual packets each follow their own paths through the network from one endpoint to another.

Partitions

Major divisions of the total physical hard disk space.

Password Authentication Protocol (PAP)

Password Authentication Protocol is a simple, weak authentication mechanism where a user enters the password and it is then sent across the network, usually in the clear.

Password Cracking

Password cracking is the process of attempting to guess passwords, given the password file information.

Password Sniffing

Passive wiretapping, usually on a local area network, to gain knowledge of passwords.

Patch

A patch is a small update released by a software manufacturer to fix bugs in existing programs.

Patching

Patching is the process of updating software to a different version.

Payload

Payload is the actual application data a packet contains.

Penetration

Gaining unauthorized logical access to sensitive data by circumventing a system's protections.

Penetration Testing

Penetration testing is used to test the external perimeter security of a network or facility.

Permutation

Permutation keeps the same letters but changes the position within a text to scramble the message.

Personal Firewalls

Personal firewalls are those firewalls that are installed and run on individual PCs.

Pharming

This is a more sophisticated form of MITM attack. A user's session is redirected to a masquerading website. This can be achieved by corrupting a DNS server on the Internet and pointing a URL to the masquerading website's IP. Almost all users use a URL like www.worldbank.com instead of the real IP (192.86.99.140) of the website. Changing the pointers on a DNS server, the URL can be redirected to send traffic to the IP of the pseudo website. At the pseudo website, transactions can be mimicked and information like login credentials can be gathered. With this the attacker can access the real www.worldbank.com site and conduct transactions using the credentials of a valid user on that website.

Phishing

The use of E-mails that appear to originate from a trusted source to trick a user into entering valid credentials at a fake website. Typically the E-mail and the web site looks like they are part of a bank the user is doing business with.

Ping of Death

An attack that sends an improperly large ICMP echo request packet (a "ping") with the intent of overflowing the input buffers of the destination machine and causing it to crash.

Ping Scan

A ping scan looks for machines that are responding to ICMP Echo Requests.

Ping Sweep

An attack that sends ICMP echo requests ("pings") to a range of IP addresses, with the goal of finding hosts that can be probed for vulnerabilities.

Plaintext

Ordinary readable text before being encrypted into ciphertext or after being decrypted.

Point-to-Point Protocol (PPP)

A protocol for communication between two computers using a serial interface, typically a personal computer connected by phone line to a server. It packages your computer's TCP/IP packets and forwards them to the server where they can actually be put on the Internet.

Point-to-Point Tunneling Protocol (PPTP)

A protocol (set of communication rules) that allows corporations to extend their own corporate network through private "tunnels" over the public Internet.

Poison Reverse

Split horizon with poisoned reverse (more simply, poison reverse) does include such routes in updates, but sets their metrics to infinity. In effect, advertising the fact that there routes are not reachable.

Polyinstantiation

Polyinstantiation is the ability of a database to maintain multiple records with the same key. It is used to prevent inference attacks.

Polymorphism

Polymorphism is the process by which malicious software changes its underlying code to avoid detection.

Port

A port is nothing more than an integer that uniquely identifies an endpoint of a communication stream. Only one process per machine can listen on the same port number.

Port Scan

A port scan is a series of messages sent by someone attempting to break into a computer to learn which computer network services, each associated with a "well-known" port number, the computer provides. Port scanning, a favorite approach of computer cracker, gives the assailant an idea where to probe for weaknesses. Essentially, a port scan consists of sending a message to each port, one at a time. The kind of response received indicates whether the port is used and can therefore be probed for weakness.

Possession

Possession is the holding, control, and ability to use information.

Post Office Protocol, Version 3 (POP3)

An Internet Standard protocol by which a client workstation can dynamically access a mailbox on a server host to retrieve mail messages that the server has received and is holding for the client.

Practical Extraction and Reporting Language (Perl)

A script programming language that is similar in syntax to the C language and that includes a number of popular UNIX facilities such as sed, awk, and tr.

Preamble

A preamble is a signal used in network communications to synchronize the transmission timing between two or more systems. Proper timing ensures that all systems are interpreting the start of the information transfer correctly. A preamble defines a specific series of transmission pulses that is understood by communicating systems to mean "someone is about to transmit data". This ensures that systems receiving the information correctly interpret when the data transmission starts. The actual pulses used as a preamble vary depending on the network communication technology in use.

Pretty Good Privacy (PGP)TM

Trademark of Network Associates, Inc., referring to a computer program (and related protocols) that uses cryptography to provide data security for electronic mail and other applications on the Internet.

Private Addressing

IANA has set aside three address ranges for use by private or non-Internet connected networks. This is referred to as Private Address Space and is defined in RFC 1918. The reserved address blocks are: 10.0.0.0 to 10.255.255.255 (10/8 prefix) 172.16.0.0 to 172.31.255.255 (172.16/12 prefix) 192.168.0.0 to 192.168.255.255 (192.168/16 prefix)

Program Infector

A program infector is a piece of malware that attaches itself to existing program files.

Program Policy

A program policy is a high-level policy that sets the overall tone of an organization's security approach.

Promiscuous Mode

When a machine reads all packets off the network, regardless of who they are addressed to. This is used by network administrators to diagnose network problems, but also by unsavory characters who are trying to eavesdrop on network traffic (which might contain passwords or other information).

Proprietary Information

Proprietary information is that information unique to a company and its ability to compete, such as customer lists, technical data, product costs, and trade secrets.

Protocol

A formal specification for communicating; an IP address the special set of rules that end points in a telecommunication connection use when they communicate. Protocols exist at several levels in a telecommunication connection.

Protocol Stacks (OSI)

A set of network protocol layers that work together.

Proxy Server

A server that acts as an intermediary between a workstation user and the Internet so that the enterprise can ensure security, administrative control, and caching service. A proxy server is associated with or part of a gateway server that separates the enterprise network from the outside network and a firewall server that protects the enterprise network from outside intrusion.

Public Key

The publicly-disclosed component of a pair of cryptographic keys used for asymmetric cryptography.

Public Key Encryption

The popular synonym for "asymmetric cryptography".

Public Key Infrastructure (PKI)

A PKI (public key infrastructure) enables users of a basically unsecured public network such as the Internet to securely and privately exchange data and money through the use of a public and a private cryptographic key pair that is obtained and shared through a trusted authority. The public key infrastructure provides for a digital certificate that can identify an individual or an organization and directory services that can store and, when necessary, revoke the certificates.

Public-Key Forward Secrecy (PFS)

For a key agreement protocol based on asymmetric cryptography, the property that ensures that a session key derived from a set of long-term public and private keys will not be compromised if one of the private keys is compromised in the future.

Q

QAZ

A network worm.

R

Race Condition

A race condition exploits the small window of time between a security control being applied and when the service is used.

Radiation Monitoring

Radiation monitoring is the process of receiving images, data, or audio from an unprotected source by listening to radiation signals.

Reconnaissance

Reconnaissance is the phase of an attack where an attackers finds new systems, maps out networks, and probes for specific, exploitable vulnerabilities.

Reflexive ACLs (Cisco)

Reflexive ACLs for Cisco routers are a step towards making the router act like a stateful firewall. The router will make filtering decisions based on whether connections are a part of established traffic or not.

Registry

The Registry in Windows operating systems in the central set of settings and information required to run the Windows computer.

Regression Analysis

The use of scripted tests which are used to test software for all possible input is should expect. Typically developers will create a set of regression tests that are executed before a new version of a software is released. Also see "fuzzing".

Request for Comment (RFC)

A series of notes about the Internet, started in 1969 (when the Internet was the ARPANET). An Internet Document can be submitted to the IETF by anyone, but the IETF decides if the document becomes an RFC. Eventually, if it gains enough interest, it may evolve into an Internet standard.

Resource Exhaustion

Resource exhaustion attacks involve tying up finite resources on a system, making them unavailable to others.

Response

A response is information sent that is responding to some stimulus.

Reverse Address Resolution Protocol (RARP)

RARP (Reverse Address Resolution Protocol) is a protocol by which a physical machine in a local area network can request to learn its IP address from a gateway server's Address Resolution Protocol table or cache. A network administrator creates a table in a local area network's gateway router that maps the physical machine (or Media Access Control - MAC address) addresses to corresponding Internet Protocol addresses. When a new machine is set up, its RARP client program requests from the RARP server on the router to be sent its IP address. Assuming that an entry has been set up in the router table, the RARP server will return the IP address to the machine which can store it for future use.

Reverse Engineering

Acquiring sensitive data by disassembling and analyzing the design of a system component.

Reverse Lookup

Find out the hostname that corresponds to a particular IP address. Reverse lookup uses an IP (Internet Protocol) address to find a domain name.

Reverse Proxy

Reverse proxies take public HTTP requests and pass them to back-end webservers to send the content to it, so the proxy can then send the content to the end-user.

Risk

Risk is the product of the level of threat with the level of vulnerability. It establishes the likelihood of a successful attack.

Risk Assessment

A Risk Assessment is the process by which risks are identified and the impact of those risks determined.

Risk Averse

Avoiding risk even if this leads to the loss of oportunity. For example, using a (more expensive) phone call Vs sending an E-mail in order to avoid risks associated with E-mail may be considered "Risk Averse".

Rivest-Shamir-Adleman (RSA)

An algorithm for asymmetric cryptography, invented in 1977 by Ron Rivest, Adi Shamir, and Leonard Adleman.

Role Based Access Control

Role based access control assigns users to roles based on their organizational functions and determines authorization based on those roles.

Root

Root is the name of the administrator account in UNIX systems.

Rootkit

A collection of tools (programs) that a hacker uses to mask intrusion and obtain administrator-level access to a computer or computer network.

Router

Routers interconnect logical networks by forwarding information to other networks based upon IP addresses.

Routing Information Protocol (RIP)

Routing Information Protocol is a distance vector protocol used for interior gateway routing which uses hop count as the sole metric of a path's cost.

Routing Loop

A routing loop is where two or more poorly configured routers repeatedly exchange the same packet over and over.

RPC Scans

RPC scans determine which RPC services are running on a machine.

Rule Set Based Access Control (RSBAC)

Rule Set Based Access Control targets actions based on rules for entities operating on objects.

S

S/Key

A security mechanism that uses a cryptographic hash function to generate a sequence of 64-bit, one-time passwords for remote user login. The client generates a one-time password by applying the MD4 cryptographic hash function multiple times to the user's secret key. For each successive authentication of the user, the number of hash applications is reduced by one.

Safety

Safety is the need to ensure that the people involved with the company, including employees, customers, and visitors, are protected from harm.

Scavenging

Searching through data residue in a system to gain unauthorized knowledge of sensitive data.

Secure Electronic Transactions (SET)

Secure Electronic Transactions is a protocol developed for credit card transactions in which all parties (customers, merchant, and bank) are authenticated using digital signatures, encryption protects the message and provides integrity, and provides end-to-end security for credit card transactions online.

Secure Shell (SSH)

A program to log into another computer over a network, to execute commands in a remote machine, and to move files from one machine to another.

Secure Sockets Layer (SSL)

A protocol developed by Netscape for transmitting private documents via the Internet. SSL works by using a public key to encrypt data that's transferred over the SSL connection.

Security Policy

A set of rules and practices that specify or regulate how a system or organization provides security services to protect sensitive and critical system resources.

Segment

Segment is another name for TCP packets.

Sensitive Information

Sensitive information, as defined by the federal government, is any unclassified information that, if compromised, could adversely affect the national interest or conduct of federal initiatives.

Separation of Duties

Separation of duties is the principle of splitting privileges among multiple individuals or systems.

Server

A system entity that provides a service in response to requests from other system entities called clients.

Session

A session is a virtual connection between two hosts by which network traffic is passed.

Session Hijacking

Take over a session that someone else has established.

Session Key

In the context of symmetric encryption, a key that is temporary or is used for a relatively short period of time. Usually, a session key is used for a defined period of communication between two computers, such as for the duration of a single connection or transaction set, or the key is used in an application that protects relatively large amounts of data and, therefore, needs to be re-keyed frequently.

SHA1

A one way cryptographic hash function. Also see "MD5"

Shadow Password Files

A system file in which encryption user password are stored so that they aren't available to people who try to break into the system.

Share

A share is a resource made public on a machine, such as a directory (file share) or printer (printer share).

Shell

A UNIX term for the interactive user interface with an operating system. The shell is the layer of programming that understands and executes the commands a user enters. In some systems, the shell is called a command interpreter. A shell usually implies an interface with a command syntax (think of the DOS operating system and its "C:>" prompts and user commands such as "dir" and "edit").

Signals Analysis

Gaining indirect knowledge of communicated data by monitoring and analyzing a signal that is emitted by a system and that contains the data but is not intended to communicate the data.

Signature

A Signature is a distinct pattern in network traffic that can be identified to a specific tool or exploit.

Simple Integrity Property

In Simple Integrity Property a user cannot write data to a higher integrity level than their own.

Simple Network Management Protocol (SNMP)

The protocol governing network management and the monitoring of network devices and their functions. A set of protocols for managing complex networks.

Simple Security Property

In Simple Security Property a user cannot read data of a higher classification than their own.

Smartcard

A smartcard is an electronic badge that includes a magnetic strip or chip that can record and replay a set key.

Smurf

The Smurf attack works by spoofing the target address and sending a ping to the broadcast address for a remote network, which results in a large amount of ping replies being sent to the target.

Sniffer

A sniffer is a tool that monitors network traffic as it received in a network interface.

Sniffing

A synonym for "passive wiretapping".

Social Engineering

A euphemism for non-technical or low-technology means - such as lies, impersonation, tricks, bribes, blackmail, and threats - used to attack information systems.

Socket

The socket tells a host's IP stack where to plug in a data stream so that it connects to the right application.

Socket Pair

A way to uniquely specify a connection, i.e., source IP address, source port, destination IP address, destination port.

SOCKS

A protocol that a proxy server can use to accept requests from client users in a company's network so that it can forward them across the Internet. SOCKS uses sockets to represent and keep track of individual connections. The client side of SOCKS is built into certain Web browsers and the server side can be added to a proxy server.

Software

Computer programs (which are stored in and executed by computer hardware) and associated data (which also is stored in the hardware) that may be dynamically written or modified during execution.

Source Port

The port that a host uses to connect to a server. It is usually a number greater than or equal to 1024. It is randomly generated and is different each time a connection is made.

Spam

Electronic junk mail or junk newsgroup postings.

Spanning Port

Configures the switch to behave like a hub for a specific port.

Split Horizon

Split horizon is a algorithm for avoiding problems caused by including routes in updates sent to the gateway from which they were learned.

Split Key

A cryptographic key that is divided into two or more separate data items that individually convey no knowledge of the whole key that results from combining the items.

Spoof

Attempt by an unauthorized entity to gain access to a system by posing as an authorized user.

SQL Injection

SQL injection is a type of input validation attack specific to database-driven applications where SQL code is inserted into application queries to manipulate the database.

Stack Mashing

Stack mashing is the technique of using a buffer overflow to trick a computer into executing arbitrary code.

Standard ACLs (Cisco)

Standard ACLs on Cisco routers make packet filtering decisions based on Source IP address only.

Star Property

In Star Property, a user cannot write data to a lower classification level without logging in at that lower classification level.

State Machine

A system that moves through a series of progressive conditions.

Stateful Inspection

Also referred to as dynamic packet filtering. Stateful inspection is a firewall architecture that works at the network layer. Unlike static packet filtering, which examines a packet based on the information in its header, stateful inspection examines not just the header information but also the contents of the packet up through the application layer in order to determine more about the packet than just information about its source and destination.

Static Host Tables

Static host tables are text files that contain hostname and address mapping.

Static Routing

Static routing means that routing table entries contain information that does not change.

Stealthing

Stealthing is a term that refers to approaches used by malicious code to conceal its presence on the infected system.

Steganalysis

Steganalysis is the process of detecting and defeating the use of steganography.

Steganography

Methods of hiding the existence of a message or other data. This is different than cryptography, which hides the meaning of a message but does not hide the message itself. An example of a steganographic method is "invisible" ink.

Stimulus

Stimulus is network traffic that initiates a connection or solicits a response.

Store-and-Forward

Store-and-Forward is a method of switching where the entire packet is read by a switch to determine if it is intact before forwarding it.

Straight-Through Cable

A straight-through cable is where the pins on one side of the connector are wired to the same pins on the other end. It is used for interconnecting nodes on the network.

Stream Cipher

A stream cipher works by encryption a message a single bit, byte, or computer word at a time.

Strong Star Property

In Strong Star Property, a user cannot write data to higher or lower classifications levels than their own.

Sub Network

A separately identifiable part of a larger network that typically represents a certain limited number of host computers, the hosts in a building or geographic area, or the hosts on an individual local area network.

Subnet Mask

A subnet mask (or number) is used to determine the number of bits used for the subnet and host portions of the address. The mask is a 32-bit value that uses one-bits for the network and subnet portions and zero-bits for the host portion.

Switch

A switch is a networking device that keeps track of MAC addresses attached to each of its ports so that data is only transmitted on the ports that are the intended recipient of the data.

Switched Network

A communications network, such as the public switched telephone network, in which any user may be connected to any other user through the use of message, circuit, or packet switching and control devices. Any network providing switched communications service.

Symbolic Links

Special files which point at another file.

Symmetric Cryptography

A branch of cryptography involving algorithms that use the same key for two different steps of the algorithm (such as encryption and decryption, or signature creation and signature verification). Symmetric cryptography is sometimes called "secret-key cryptography" (versus public-key cryptography) because the entities that share the key.

Symmetric Key

A cryptographic key that is used in a symmetric cryptographic algorithm.

SYN Flood

A denial of service attack that sends a host more TCP SYN packets (request to synchronize sequence numbers, used when opening a connection) than the protocol implementation can handle.

Synchronization

Synchronization is the signal made up of a distinctive pattern of bits that network hardware looks for to signal that start of a frame.

Syslog

Syslog is the system logging facility for UNIX systems.

System Security Officer (SSO)

A person responsible for enforcement or administration of the security policy that applies to the system.

System-Specific Policy

A System-specific policy is a policy written for a specific system or device.

T

T1, T3

A digital circuit using TDM (Time-Division Multiplexing).

Tamper

To deliberately alter a system's logic, data, or control information to cause the system to perform unauthorized functions or services.

TCP Fingerprinting

TCP fingerprinting is the user of odd packet header combinations to determine a remote operating system.

TCP Full Open Scan

TCP Full Open scans check each port by performing a full three-way handshake on each port to determine if it was open.

TCP Half Open Scan

TCP Half Open scans work by performing the first half of a three-way handshake to determine if a port is open.

TCP Wrapper

A software package which can be used to restrict access to certain network services based on the source of the connection; a simple tool to monitor and control incoming network traffic.

TCP/IP

A synonym for "Internet Protocol Suite;" in which the Transmission Control Protocol and the Internet Protocol are important parts. TCP/IP is the basic communication language or protocol of the Internet. It can also be used as a communications protocol in a private network (either an Intranet or an Extranet).

TCPDump

TCPDump is a freeware protocol analyzer for UNIX that can monitor network traffic on a wire.

TELNET

A TCP-based, application-layer, Internet Standard protocol for remote login from one host to another.

Threat

A potential for violation of security, which exists when there is a circumstance, capability, action, or event that could breach security and cause harm.

Threat Assessment

A threat assessment is the identification of types of threats that an organization might be exposed to.

Threat Model

A threat model is used to describe a given threat and the harm it could to do a system if it has a vulnerability.

Threat Vector

The method a threat uses to get to the target.

Time to Live

A value in an Internet Protocol packet that tells a network router whether or not the packet has been in the network too long and should be discarded.

Tiny Fragment Attack

With many IP implementations it is possible to impose an unusually small fragment size on outgoing packets. If the fragment size is made small enough to force some of a TCP packet's TCP header fields into the second fragment, filter rules that specify patterns for those fields will not match. If the filtering implementation does not enforce a minimum fragment size, a disallowed packet might be passed because it didn't hit a match in the filter. STD 5, RFC 791 states: Every Internet module must be able to forward a datagram of 68 octets without further fragmentation. This is because an Internet header may be up to 60 octets, and the minimum fragment is 8 octets.

Token Ring

A token ring network is a local area network in which all computers are connected in a ring or star topology and a binary digit or token-passing scheme is used in order to prevent the collision of data between two computers that want to send messages at the same time.

Token-Based Access Control

Token based access control associates a list of objects and their privileges with each user. (The opposite of list based.)

Token-Based Devices

A token-based device is triggered by the time of day, so every minute the password changes, requiring the user to have the token with them when they log in.

Topology

The geometric arrangement of a computer system. Common topologies include a bus, star, and ring. The specific physical, i.e., real, or logical, i.e., virtual, arrangement of the elements of a network. Note 1: Two networks have the same topology if the connection configuration is the same, although the networks may differ in physical interconnections, distances between nodes, transmission rates, and/or signal types. Note 2: The common types of network topology are illustrated

Traceroute (tracert.exe)

Traceroute is a tool the maps the route a packet takes from the local machine to a remote destination.

Transmission Control Protocol (TCP)

A set of rules (protocol) used along with the Internet Protocol to send data in the form of message units between computers over the Internet. While IP takes care of handling the actual delivery of the data, TCP takes care of keeping track of the individual units of data (called packets) that a message is divided into for efficient routing through the Internet. Whereas the IP protocol deals only with packets, TCP enables two hosts to establish a connection and exchange streams of data. TCP guarantees delivery of data and also guarantees that packets will be delivered in the same order in which they were sent.

Transport Layer Security (TLS)

A protocol that ensures privacy between communicating applications and their users on the Internet. When a server and client communicate, TLS ensures that no third party may eavesdrop or tamper with any message. TLS is the successor to the Secure Sockets Layer.

Triple DES

A block cipher, based on DES, that transforms each 64-bit plaintext block by applying the Data Encryption Algorithm three successive times, using either two or three different keys, for an effective key length of 112 or 168 bits.

Triple-Wrapped

S/MIME usage: data that has been signed with a digital signature, and then encrypted, and then signed again.

Trojan Horse

A computer program that appears to have a useful function, but also has a hidden and potentially malicious function that evades security mechanisms, sometimes by exploiting legitimate authorizations of a system entity that invokes the program.

Trunking

Trunking is connecting switched together so that they can share VLAN information between them.

Trust

Trust determine which permissions and what actions other systems or users can perform on remote machines.

Trusted Ports

Trusted ports are ports below number 1024 usually allowed to be opened by the root user.

Tunnel

A communication channel created in a computer network by encapsulating a communication protocol's data packets in (on top of) a second protocol that normally would be carried above, or at the same layer as, the first one. Most often, a tunnel is a logical point-to-point link - i.e., an OSI layer 2 connection - created by encapsulating the layer 2 protocol in a transport protocol (such as TCP), in a network or inter-network layer protocol (such as IP), or in another link layer protocol. Tunneling can move data between computers that use a protocol not supported by the network connecting them.

U

UDP Scan

UDP scans perform scans to determine which UDP ports are open.

Unicast

Broadcasting from host to host.

Uniform Resource Identifier (URI)

The generic term for all types of names and addresses that refer to objects on the World Wide Web.

Uniform Resource Locator (URL)

The global address of documents and other resources on the World Wide Web. The first part of the address indicates what protocol to use, and the second part specifies the IP address or the domain name where the resource is located. For example, http://www.pcwebopedia.com/index.html .

Unix

A popular multi-user, multitasking operating system developed at Bell Labs in the early 1970s. Created by just a handful of programmers, Unix was designed to be a small, flexible system used exclusively by programmers.

Unprotected Share

In Windows terminology, a "share" is a mechanism that allows a user to connect to file systems and printers on other systems. An "unprotected share" is one that allows anyone to connect to it.

User

A person, organization entity, or automated process that accesses a system, whether authorized to do so or not.

User Contingency Plan

User contingency plan is the alternative methods of continuing business operations if IT systems are unavailable.

User Datagram Protocol (UDP)

A communications protocol that, like TCP, runs on top of IP networks. Unlike TCP/IP, UDP/IP provides very few error recovery services, offering instead a direct way to send and receive datagrams over an IP network. It's used primarily for broadcasting messages over a network. UDP uses the Internet Protocol to get a datagram from one computer to another but does not divide a message into packets (datagrams) and reassemble it at the other end. Specifically, UDP doesn't provide sequencing of the packets that the data arrives in.

V

Virtual Private Network (VPN)

A restricted-use, logical (i.e., artificial or simulated) computer network that is constructed from the system resources of a relatively public, physical (i.e., real) network (such as the Internet), often by using encryption (located at hosts or gateways), and often by tunneling links of the virtual network across the real network. For example, if a corporation has LANs at several different sites, each connected to the Internet by a firewall, the corporation could create a VPN by (a) using encrypted tunnels to connect from firewall to firewall across the Internet and (b) not allowing any other traffic through the firewalls. A VPN is generally less expensive to build and operate than a dedicated real network, because the virtual network shares the cost of system resources with other users of the real network.

Virus

A hidden, self-replicating section of computer software, usually malicious logic, that propagates by infecting - i.e., inserting a copy of itself into and becoming part of - another program. A virus cannot run by itself; it requires that its host program be run to make the virus active.

Vulnerability

A flaw or weakness in a system's design, implementation, or operation and management that could be exploited to violate the system's security policy.

W

War Chalking

War chalking is marking areas, usually on sidewalks with chalk, that receive wireless signals that can be accessed.

War Dialer

A computer program that automatically dials a series of telephone numbers to find lines connected to computer systems, and catalogs those numbers so that a cracker can try to break into the systems.

War Dialing

War dialing is a simple means of trying to identify modems in a telephone exchange that may be susceptible to compromise in an attempt to circumvent perimeter security.

War Driving

War driving is the process of traveling around looking for wireless access point signals that can be used to get network access.

Web of Trust

A web of trust is the trust that naturally evolves as a user starts to trust other's signatures, and the signatures that they trust.

Web Server

A software process that runs on a host computer connected to the Internet to respond to HTTP requests for documents from client web browsers.

WHOIS

An IP for finding information about resources on networks.

Windowing

A windowing system is a system for sharing a computer's graphical display presentation resources among multiple applications at the same time. In a computer that has a graphical user interface (GUI), you may want to use a number of applications at the same time (this is called task). Using a separate window for each application, you can interact with each application and go from one application to another without having to reinitiate it. Having different information or activities in multiple windows may also make it easier for you to do your work. A windowing system uses a window manager to keep track of where each window is located on the display screen and its size and status. A windowing system doesn't just manage the windows but also other forms of graphical user interface entities.

Windump

Windump is a freeware tool for Windows that is a protocol analyzer that can monitor network traffic on a wire.

Wired Equivalent Privacy (WEP)

A security protocol for wireless local area networks defined in the standard IEEE 802.11b.

Wireless Application Protocol

A specification for a set of communication protocols to standardize the way that wireless devices, such as cellular telephones and radio transceivers, can be used for Internet access, including E-mail, the World Wide Web, newsgroups, and Internet Relay Chat.

Wiretapping

Monitoring and recording data that is flowing between two points in a communication system.

World Wide Web ("the Web", WWW, W3)

The global, hypermedia-based collection of information and services that is available on Internet servers and is accessed by browsers using Hypertext Transfer Protocol and other information retrieval mechanisms.

Worm

A computer program that can run independently, can propagate a complete working version of itself onto other hosts on a network, and may consume computer resources destructively.

Wrap

To use cryptography to provide data confidentiality service for a data object.

Z

Zone

Transfer A zone transfer is when a DNS server performs a complete dump of the database for a domain and sends the information from the primary DNS server to the secondary DNS servers.

Source: www.sans.org

Lightning Source UK Ltd.
Milton Keynes UK
02 March 2011

168511UK00001B/271/A

9 781905 986002